Mastering
Government
Securities

Mastering Government Securities

A step-by-step guide to the products, applications and markets

STEPHEN MAHONY

PITMAN PUBLISHING

market editions

PITMAN PUBLISHING
128 Long Acre, London WC2E 9AN
Tel: +44 (0)171 447 2000
Fax: +44 (0)171 240 5771

A Division of Pearson Professional Limited

First published in Great Britain 1996

© Pearson Professional Limited 1996

ISBN 0 273 62416 4

British Library Cataloguing in Publication Data
A CIP catalogue record for this book can be obtained from the British Library.

10 9 8 7 6 5 4 3 2 1

Typeset by Pantek Arts, Maidstone, Kent
Printed and bound in Great Britain by Bell & Bain Ltd, Glasgow

The Publishers' policy is to use paper manufactured from sustainable forests.

The Author

Stephen Mahony was born in Ireland and educated at Ampleforth and Oxford University. From 1977 to 1991 he was a banker, during which time he worked for Citibank and Swiss Bank Corporation, and specialised in capital markets and derivatives. Since 1991 he has worked as a consultant and writer on financial subjects. His other publications include works on securities markets, swaps, options and borrowing techniques. He lives in Somerset, England, with his wife and two children.

CONTENTS

Acknowledgments

I am grateful for the help of the following individuals: Patrick J. Brown at ISMA, Andrew Brownlee, Nathalie Devilaine at MATIF in Paris, Deborah Fowler at the Bank of England, Graeme Grady at the European Office of the Chicago Board of Trade in London, Sam van Holthe, John Howell, Sallie A. Keith at the Bureau of the Public Debt in Washington, Richard Metcalfe at *Futures and Options World* in London, Ruth Maria Müller at the Deutsche Börse in Frankfurt, Andy Nybo at the Public Securities Association in New York, Susan Tether at Salomon Brothers in London, and Nick Wiseman at Research Department of *The Economist* in London.

Richard Stagg and Amelia Lakin at Pitman Publishing were all the good things that publishers are supposed to be.

■ ■ ■

"This book is concerned with one part of government borrowing: the public issue of domestic securities which are direct obligations of the state and with the derivatives based on those securities."

INTRODUCTION

"I used to think that if there was reincarnation, I wanted to come back as the President or the Pope. But now I want to be the bond market: you can intimidate everyone."

James Carville, election adviser to President Clinton, expressed a popular point of view. It is the idea that national sovereignty is being eroded by large speculative capital flows in and out of domestic markets. This process, which is the result of the liberalization and globalization of capital markets in the last twenty years, can affect the daily lives of everyone. A government hoping to fund a budget deficit must satisfy foreign investors in order to provide its own citizens with the services they require.

The second intimidating aspect of the bond market is its size; the 13 largest borrowing countries were expected to borrow more than US$1,500 billion in 1996. The total debt of these countries is increasing rapidly both absolutely and in relation to GDP.

Governments borrow in many different ways. The differences lie not only in how they borrow, loan or security, short or long term, public or private, domestic or international, but also in the choice of borrowing entity. This book is concerned with one part of government borrowing: the public issue of domestic securities which are direct obligations of the state and with the derivatives based on those securities.

The book is divided into two sections which deal with the theory and the practice of government securities. The first part explains the principles which lie behind the instruments, the arithmetic which values them and the derivatives which are based on them. Turning then from theory to practice the second part surveys the largest markets, describing the various instruments, the different ways in which they are issued and traded, and the directions in which they are developing. In both sections practical examples are used so that the reader can master both the theory and the practice of markets.

This introduction is a tour of the horizon considering some of the fundamental questions which lie behind much of what follows.

IS DEBT WRONG?

Charles Dickens's Mr Micawber summarized a simple view of the matter. "Annual income twenty pounds, annual expenditure twenty pounds ought and six, result misery." However, governments are not in the same position as Mr Micawber. Governments cannot go to a debtors' prison. But there is another, more important difference. An individual can obtain extra resources by borrowing, but a government borrowing domestically does not increase the resources of the country. Domestic borrowing by governments simply transfers resources within an economy.

> "The starting-point is the question: 'Should governments borrow at all?'"

Government borrowing is said to be bad because it is more likely than taxation to crowd out productive private investment. Above all reduced public spending is preferable to borrowing or taxation. This criticism supposes that all government borrowing is wasteful or for non-productive purposes. This need not, and often is not, true. The use to which borrowed money is put and the alternative uses which it replaces determine whether domestic government borrowing is a burden on future generations. Further, public spending achieves certain unique benefits which may not be quantifiable. The UK's national debt has in the past exceeded 200 percent of gross domestic product (GDP). Was this irresponsible? Perhaps in theory, but not in 1945.

The argument that government borrowing need not burden future generations has a flaw. It assumes no foreign borrowing. The liberalization of capital flows results in transfers of resources between countries. Debt so incurred is a burden on future generations in a way that domestic borrowing need not be. Resources will have to be transferred out of the country in the future to repay it. There are some markets where foreign investors hold 30 percent or more of the securities in issue. These transfers are therefore significant.

TOO MUCH DEBT?

Thomas Jefferson argued, on moral and religious grounds, that national debt ought to be no more than could be repaid during one generation which he calculated to be about nineteen years. Two hundred years later we might extend the definition of a generation by a few years but our national imprudence has increased faster than our longevity

The evidence is that governments have taken advantage of their new freedom in the manner of an alcoholic let loose in a bonded warehouse. Since 1974 total net public sector debt in the Organization for Economic Cooperation and Development (OECD) countries has risen from 15 percent to over 40 percent of GDP. The countries on the greatest binges have managed over 100 percent of GDP.

The scale of this debt has political consequences. Few members of the European Union can meet the 60 percent of GDP limit on public borrowing or the 3 percent of GDP limit on the public deficit required by the Maastricht Treaty as a qualifying condition for monetary union. Only Luxembourg can meet both. If future pension liabilities were added in the picture would be even more bleak.

The interest burden may be substantial. The OECD estimated that in 1995 Italy's net interest payments were equivalent to 10 percent of GDP. Greece was in an even worse position with net interest equivalent to 13 percent of GDP.

Jefferson complained that some people, including Hamilton, seemed to think that a large national debt was a sign of vigour and prosperity. "Plus ça change." In 1996 it was expected that the 13 OECD countries in the J. P. Morgan Global Government Bond Index would issue more than US$1,500 billion of debt.

A further ominous aspect of the global market in government debt is the refinancing burden. About US$1,000 billion was expected to be borrowed in 1996 just to refinance maturing debt. In some countries this refinancing is itself a significant percentage of GDP. In Italy, for example, the debt to be refinanced in 1996 exceeds 10 percent of GDP. This is a measure of a country's vulnerability in the face of turbulent markets.

SOVEREIGN POWER?

The economic power of governments has rested on the ability to tax, the ability to borrow and the ability to print money. Liberal and global capital markets effectively limit all three powers. High tax rates drive away investment, profligate borrowing drives away investors and printing money leads to a currency crisis.

This may be healthy in that it rewards 'virtuous' governments and punishes the others. On the other hand this view supposes that markets are good economic judges. Clearly in the short term markets can display all the wisdom of an irrational casino. In the long term markets may be rational but the timing and strength of market moves are erratic. This is an unpredictable discipline at best.

IS LIBERALIZATION GOOD?

Opening a domestic capital market to the world does have obvious immediate benefits. A larger pool of investors will make it easier for the government to sell debt and to reduce the cost of that debt. Large scale borrowing in one country no longer need crowd out domestic corporate borrowers.

> "States no longer commit themselves to full employment; they do not believe it to be possible. Instead they crave price stability and the approval of the global bond markets for their fiscal rectitude."

A further benefit of liberalization may be that reciprocal changes by other governments will allow your financial institutions to diversify abroad and grow profitably. Alternatively, if you are not so confident, the arrival of sophisticated foreign firms in your domestic market may serve to sharpen and modernize your own sleepy banking system.

However the long-term result may not be so comfortable. Foreign investors can quickly come to dominate the 'float' in a bond market because domestic institutions are often long-term holders not traders of debt. Governments quickly find that they no longer control interest rates quite as once they did.

Critics point to the possible social costs of pursuing virtuous but deflationary policies in order to satisfy volatile foreign investors. Will Hutton in *The State We're In*, a popular 1995 analysis of Britain critical of free-market economics, lamented that: "States no longer commit themselves to full employment; they do not believe it to be possible. Instead they crave price stability and the approval of the global bond markets for their fiscal rectitude."

HOW GLOBAL?

Globalization has not really progressed very far. Look at two observable facts. First, real interest rates vary from country to country largely because of exchange rate expectations. Currencies are a cause of market segmentation. Second, countries with high savings ratios tend also to be countries with high rates of investment. Most money stays at home. It is estimated that only 10 percent of the assets of the world's 500 largest institutional portfolios are invested in foreign securities. Nonetheless the amount of money which can be switched from one market to another almost instantly has increased greatly. At the margin it is this which determines security prices.

WHAT CAN BE GOVERNED?

In a world without exchange controls governments must choose between having an exchange rate policy or a monetary policy. They cannot have both. With a fixed exchange rate governments lose monetary control. In a European monetary union some would say that the participants will have neither.

Polemics apart, governments can still control short-term interest rates and thereby influence economic activity and inflation. This is not as easy as it was when credit or interest rate ceilings were common instruments of policy. What governments and central banks can no longer do is to control long-term interest rates.

> "In a world without exchange controls governments must choose between having an exchange rate policy or a monetary policy. They cannot have both."

TOO MANY TRADERS ?

The growth of the debt markets and the structural reforms introduced in many countries have increased the volume of trading in government securities. Prominent among traders have been what are termed 'speculators' in the popular press. It is widely thought that speculators disrupt the markets in which they are active, making large profits and contributing nothing to economic well-being.

Many of these so-called speculators are in fact arbitrageurs. These traders try not to take price risk but instead try to exploit price anomalies between financial instruments. By so doing they eliminate the price differences and thus make markets more efficient.

It is clear, however, that traders and governments do not have identical interests. Consider their attitude to volatility. Traders tend to profit from volatile markets and from changes in volatility. Governments, on the other hand, tend to suffer if market fluctuations disrupt the orderly financing of the state deficit.

ARE CRISES CONTAGIOUS ?

Shortly after the December 1994 Mexican peso crisis, the chairman of the US Federal Reserve, Alan Greenspan, commented to Congress that:

> "although the speed of transmission of positive economic events has been an important plus for the world in recent years, it is becoming increasingly obvious – and Mexico is the first major case – that significant mistakes in macroeconomic policy also reverberate around the world at a prodigious pace." (*Federal Reserve Bulletin*, March 1995).

The Federal Reserve's account of the crisis has an illuminating comment on the way in which crisis in one market may spread to others.

> "When the crisis erupted, investors panicked, not only investors in the Mexican stock market and in Mexico's debt instruments but also investors in similar instruments issued by borrowers in other countries, especially countries in the same part of the world or perceived to be in similar circumstances. These contagion sales of assets were induced by a least two forces. First, as perceived risks rose and expected returns fell, individual investors wanted to disinvest. Second, institutional holders such as mutual funds, faced with actual or threatened redemptions, liquidated their holdings not only of Mexican paper but also of the paper of other countries, especially if they could do so while limiting their capital losses." (*Federal Reserve Bulletin*, March 1996).

The author of this study commented that "The behavior of financial markets during the Mexican crisis has more in common with their behavior during the European monetary crises of 1992 and 1993 and the bond market collapse in 1994 than many observers may be willing to contemplate or acknowledge." The international capital markets panic repeatedly. Members of a future European Monetary Union might find that a crisis in, say, Italy caused panic sales of the euro-denominated securities of other countries, leading to a widespread disruption of markets and of government funding.

INSTRUMENTS OF THE DEVIL ?

A further superstition is that derivatives based on government securities compound the evil of speculators. Specifically derivatives are said to make markets more volatile. The facts do not support this idea.

While trading volumes have risen quickly, there has not been a comparable rise in volatility. In fact OECD figures suggest that for the world's bond markets as a whole volatility peaked in the period between 1980 and 1985 and has since fallen back to the same level as observed in 1970 to 1979 before derivatives were widely traded.

CONCLUSION

It is futile to protest that the weather ought to be better. So, too, with international capital flows. The workings of the international capital markets may have uncomfortable consequences, but the process of liberalization is almost certainly not reversible. The reader of this book will at least understand what is happening.

Part One

■ ■ ■

"Government securities are obligations of the state in respect of borrowed money. They are generally transferable securities with a defined rate of interest and maturity date."

What are Government Securities?

INTRODUCTION

This chapter deals with:

- the size and growth rates of the major markets
- competition between borrowers
- the most important securities in those markets
- the key features of government securities
  legal obligations of the state
  transferability
  definition by price, coupon and maturity
  structural variations
- repos
- risk
- methods of issue
- regulation.

SIZE AND GROWTH

The relative size of the major government bond markets may be summarized as shown in Table 1.1.

Size of major government bond markets

Table 1.1

Country	Forecast new borrowing 1996 in US$ bn
USA	601
Japan	366
Italy	182
France	100
Germany	85
UK	40
Spain	37
Canada	32
Belgium	28
Netherlands	25
Sweden	19
Denmark	18
Australia	7

Source: J.P. Morgan

These are rapidly growing markets as Table 1.2 shows. Net public debt is expressed as a percentage of GDP.

Growth of major government bond markets

Table 1.2

Country	Net public debt/GDP %		
	1975	1985	1995
Belgium	48.9	112.5	128.4
Italy	53.2	79.9	109.2
Canada	7.3	34.7	66.2
USA	27.3	33.0	51.5
Spain	3.5	27.5	50.1
Germany	1.0	20.8	49.0
UK	42.8	30.6	38.8
France	−1.0	10.8	35.0
Sweden	−28.8	14.3	26.8
Japan	−3.0	25.9	11.1

Source: OECD

This debt matters for more than just economic reasons. Consider the position of the European Union. The Maastricht Treaty required member countries to achieve certain economic targets as part of the timetable set out for monetary union. In the context of this book the two important targets relate to public debts and public deficits. As of 1995 only the small state of Luxembourg had achieved both of them as Table 1.3 shows.

The Maastricht Treaty also sets targets for inflation and bond yields at not more than 1.5 percent above the average of the three countries with the lowest inflation in the EU.

Table 1.3

Achievement of EU economic targets

Country	Public deficit as % of GDP	Public debt as % of GDP	Consumer inflation	10-year govt. bond yield %
Maastricht target	3.0	60.0	2.9	8.03
Germany	3.6	59.0	1.8	5.93
France	5.6	51.6	1.8	6.41
Italy	7.4	124.8	5.4	10.44
UK	5.1	52.5	2.8	7.57
Spain	5.9	64.5	4.7	9.71
Netherlands	3.6	78.4	1.9	5.93
Belgium	4.7	135.7	1.5	6.36
Sweden	6.8	80.0	2.9	8.43
Austria	5.5	68.0	2.3	6.19
Denmark	2.0	74.2	2.1	7.13
Finland	5.0	63.2	1.0	7.31
Portugal	5.6	70.1	4.2	9.58
Greece	9.3	113.2	9.3	na
Ireland	2.1	85.9	2.5	7.34
Luxembourg	(0.4)	6.3	1.9	na

Source: Salomon Brothers
Note: 10-year government bond yields as at 29 January 1996

COMPETITION BETWEEN BORROWERS

Domestic securities markets are becoming international markets, or perhaps parts of one international debt market. The issuers of all debt, including government debt are in competition with each other for investors' money. Two key features are necessary for a country to compete; transparent issuance procedures and robust market-making arrangements. The reforms which are described in the chapters devoted to each country in the second part of this book are best thought of as responses to this competition. It will be seen that some countries have responded more quickly and effectively than others.

THE MAIN INSTRUMENTS

Many readers will be familiar with at least the names of the chief securities issued in each country. The most important securities in the largest markets, which form the focus of this book, are shown in Table 1.4.

More important securities in largest markets

Table 1.4

USA	Short term	Treasury Bills (T-bills)
	Long term	Treasury Notes Treasury Bonds
Germany	Long term	Finanzierungs-Schätze Bundesschatzanweisungen Bundesobligationen (Bobls) Bundesanleihen (Bunds)
France	Short term	Bons du Trésor a taux fixe et intérêt précompté (BTF)
	Long term	Bons du Trésor a taux fixe et intérêt annuel (BTAN) Obligations assimilables du Trésor (OAT)
Japan	Short term	Treasury bills Financing bills
	Long term	Bonds (JGB)
UK	Short term	Treasury bills
	Long term	Bonds (Gilts)

HOW DO YOU DEFINE GOVERNMENT SECURITIES?

> **Government securities** *are obligations of the state in respect of borrowed money. They are generally transferable securities with a defined rate of interest and maturity date.*

Obligations of the state

Government securities are claims on the state. Gilts in the UK, for example, are issued by the Bank of England but are "a charge on the National Loans Fund, with recourse to the Consolidated Fund of the United Kingdom."

In many cases government securities are the subject of specific legal statutes.

In the USA the Secretary of the Treasury is authorized under Chapter 31 of Title 31, United States Code, to issue Treasury Securities and to prescribe terms and conditions for their issuance and sale (31 U.S.C. § 3121). The Secretary may issue bonds under 31 U.S.C. § 3102, notes under 31 U.S.C. § 3103 and bills under 31 U.S.C. § 3104.

Japanese Government Bonds (JGBs) are issued under three different laws. Construction Bonds are issued under Article 4 of the Public Finance Law. Deficit Financing Bonds are issued under a specific law for each fiscal year where there is a deficit that cannot be financed with Construction Bonds. Refinancing Bonds are issued under Article 5 of the Law Concerning Special Account of Government Bonds Consolidation Fund.

Agency and other semi-state borrowers

In many domestic bond markets government agencies or semi-state bodies are large issuers of securities. In the USA, for example, government agencies and government sponsored enterprises issue substantial amounts of debt. These issuers are not the primary focus of this book.

Transferability

Increasingly the transfer of ownership is by a book entry on a central register rather than by physical delivery of a document. Transferability allows a security to be traded. Thus a price setting mechanism is created which allows investors to value or realize their investments and establishes a market level at which further securities may be issued.

Trading

Government securities may be traded before issue, at issue or after issue.

Definition | **Grey market trading or when-issued trading** is *the trading which takes place after a new issue of securities has been announced but before it has taken place. It is permitted in many markets.*

> **Primary market trading** *is the trading which takes place as soon as the securities have been issued until the first settlement date for the new issue.*
>
> **Secondary market trading** *is the trading which takes place once a new security has been issued and paid for.*

Definition

Price, coupon & maturity

These are the three key elements in any government security which determine its value.

> The **price of a security** *is set at issue. Subsequently it fluctuates as the securities are traded. Sometimes the price at issue will be the nominal value of the security but it may be issued at a discount to nominal value, or more rarely at a premium.*
>
> The **coupon** *is the periodic interest payment to which the holder is entitled. This is an interest rate applied to the nominal value of the security.*

Definition

Certain securities carry no right to periodic interest but are sold at a discount to their face value. The investor therefore receives a return on his investment at maturity.

> **Maturity** *is the time to redemption when the security is exchanged for its nominal value.*

Definition

The key distinction is between short-dated securities with maturities typically between one and twelve months such as Treasury Bills, and longer dated securities with maturities up to thirty years or more such as Treasury Notes or Bonds.

Definition **Accrued interest** *is interest which has accumulated since the last coupon payment but which has not yet been paid.*

Some security prices are quoted to include this and some are quoted excluding accrued interest. In the latter case the purchaser will pay the price quoted plus the accrued interest.

In diagramatic form a non-interest-bearing government security of any maturity may be represented as shown in Figure 1.1.

Fig 1.1

Non-interest-bearing security

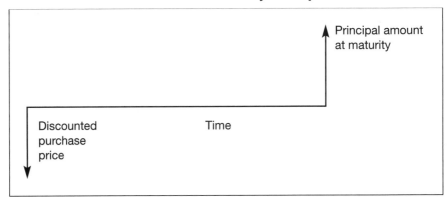

Fig 1.2

In diagramatic form a fixed-interest-bearing government security may be represented as shown in Figure 1.2.

Fixed-rate, interest-bearing security

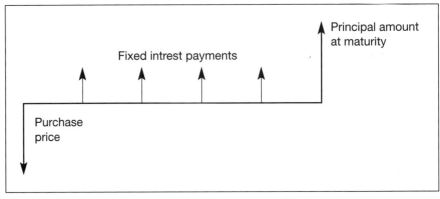

VARIATIONS OF STRUCTURE

Not all securities are as described above. The variations can be gathered into three sorts:

● variations in purchase
● variations in interest
● variations in redemption.

Partly-paid securities

The main variations in purchase relate to the method of issue. This will be dealt with later in the chapter. One other variation relates to part-payment. On issue the investor may not be required to pay all the consideration at once but in two or more stages over a specified period of time. A fixed-rate, partly-paid bond with one interest payment due before the final purchase payment might be shown as in Figure 1.3.

Partly-paid, fixed-interest bond

Fig 1.3

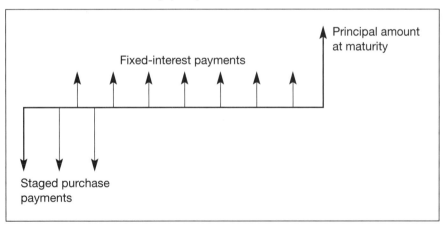

Principal amount at maturity

Fixed-interest payments

Staged purchase payments

Interest is paid only on that part of the total price which has been actually paid. The advantage for the issuer is that such a structure secures funds at a fixed cost on certain future dates which may be set to match known funding needs. For the investor a partly-paid bond is a more leveraged bond in its partly-paid state than a conventional bond and may be attractive to speculators. For investors also there may be an advantage in having secured a known return on funds to be invested on certain specified future dates.

Variable-rate securities

Besides fixed-rate bonds, governments issue variable-rate securities. The rate of interest may be set for each period in relation to inter-bank rates or to the yield on certain short-dated instruments such as treasury bills. In diagramatic form a variable rate instrument may be shown as in Figure 1.4.

Fig 1.4

Variable-rate bond

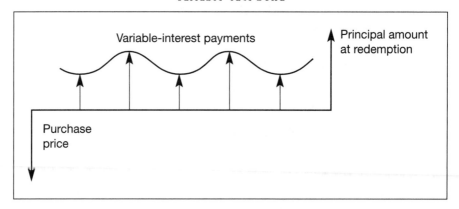

The advantage for the issuer is that he is not committed to a fixed rate of interest which may become relatively expensive in the future. Variable-rate government securities carry very little market risk for the investor. The instrument should trade close to par at least on each interest reset date when the coupon is set at or near current market levels.

Index-linked securities

Index-linked securities may have payments of interest, principal or both tied to an index. Usually this is an index of inflation and the bonds carry an interest rate set at a margin above the index.

In diagramatic form an index-linked bond in a period of continuing steady inflation might be as shown in Figure 1.5.

Index-linked securities

Fig 1.5

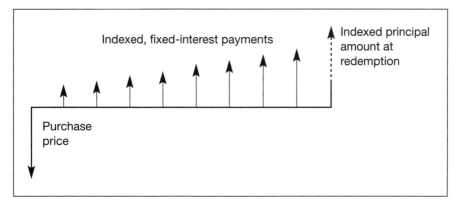

If a government believes that it will control inflation this basis of borrowing is cheap because the investor assumes less risk than in the case of a fixed-rate bond. The investor will accept a lower coupon related to his real yield requirement rather than, as in the case of a fixed-rate bond, a coupon related to his nominal yield requirement. There may, too, be institutions such as insurance companies with long-term liabilities which can be matched with index-linked securities.

A possible disadvantage arises if the index used, often a retail price index, does not have a direct relevance to the investor's needs. In the UK the retail price index (RPI) includes the prices of some 600 items including muesli, aerobics classes and funerals. This index is the basis for the UK's index-linked government bonds.

Foreign currency

In Europe particularly, governments have issued domestic debt denominated in foreign currency, notably ECU. Italian CTE, special ECU-denominated French OATs and BTANs, and UK ECU-denominated Treasury bills are all examples. Countries which have experienced difficulty in issuing enough debt in their own currencies have also issued foreign currency domestic debt. Greece, for example, has issued bonds with repayment values linked to the ECU, US$ and £.

Zero-coupon

A **zero-coupon security** *carries no coupon but is sold at a discount to its face value so that the investor receives income only at maturity equivalent to the amount of the discount.*

Zero-coupon or deep discount securities are usually created as a result of the "stripping" of conventional fixed-rate securities. This is a process by which the coupons are detached and sold separately leaving the bond, shorn of its right to receive interest, to trade at a discount to its face value. Such stripped bonds are created by securities firms and are not yet issued by governments.

The amount of stripped bonds is quite large in some markets. In the US market at 31 December 1995 the nominal value of stripped debt was US$221.6 billion. France also has a well-developed market in stripped securities. The UK announced the intention to permit stripping in 1997.

Governments allow their securities to be stripped because it increases market efficiency. This is largely for arithmetical reasons (explained in Chapter 2) relating to the inadequacies of yield-to-maturity as a measure for comparing different fixed-interest securities. For investors a zero-coupon instrument offers a yield which is certain because no assumptions are necessary about the rate at which interest payments received are reinvested. This subject, too, is discussed in Chapter 2.

Convertible bonds

Convertible bonds *contain an embedded option which gives the holder the right but not the obligation to exchange his convertible bond for another bond with different terms.*

In diagramatic form a convertible bond would be as shown in Figure 1.6.

Convertible bond

Fig 1.6

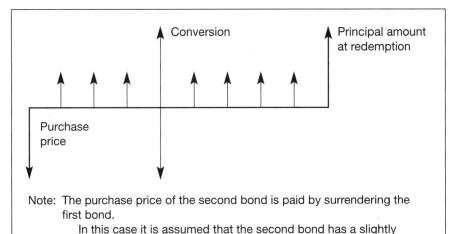

Note: The purchase price of the second bond is paid by surrendering the first bond.
   In this case it is assumed that the second bond has a slightly lower coupon than the first bond.

The issuer of such a bond must calculate that in return for granting the embedded option he is required to pay less interest on the first bond. The investor may value the option because such options are not easily obtainable or because the conversion feature offers a leverage not otherwise available to him. For example, there are investors who are not allowed to buy pure options but who are not prohibited from buying embedded options.

Puts and calls

A **put** is an option which gives an investor the right but not the obligation to require the issuer to redeem a security at a specified price at specified times prior to its specified maturity date.

A **call**, which is the opposite of a put, is an option which gives the issuer of a security the right but not the obligation to redeem the security prior to its specified maturity date.

Some government debt issues carry options, exerciseable either by the issuer or the holder, to cause a bond to be redeemed prior to its specified maturity date. In diagramatic form a bond with a put option could be described as shown in Figure 1.7.

Fig 1.7

Bond with a put

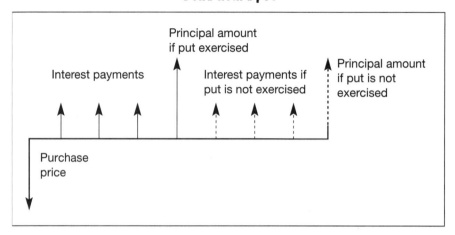

The advantages of such bonds are similar to those described for convertible bonds.

Perpetual bonds

Some bonds have been issued with no redemption date. These are equivalent to annuities and therefore trade well below their nominal value. In diagramatic form they may be shown as shown in Figure 1.8.

Many such issues are very old and carry coupons which are low so that while in theory they may be redeemed by the government such a prospect is unlikely. For example the UK undated gilt (government bond) known as Consols 2.5 percent was trading at about 30 percent of its nominal value in March 1996. The one form of security which has not been issued is a Zero-coupon perpetual bond!

Fig 1.8

Perpetual bond

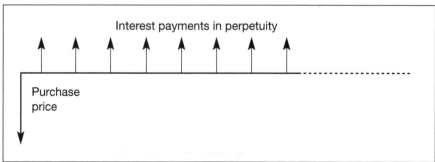

REPOS

A vital part of most markets in government securities is the repo market.

> A **repo** is a transaction in which one party sells securities to another and at the same time undertakes as part of the same transaction to repurchase identical securities on a specified date at a specified price.

Definition

Essentially a repo is a collateralized short-term loan. The owner of securities can use the repo market to help finance his portfolio. Short positions in securities may be covered by reverse repos where the party effectively borrows the securities. Repos are described in more detail in Chapter 4.

RISK

Risk in financial markets may be analyzed under five headings:

- credit risk
- operational risk
- liquidity risk
- market risk
- aggregating risk.

Credit risk

The significance of being domestic government debt is that the security is of the highest credit quality. This is not quite so comforting as it may seem. First, a government can always print more money. This policy usually fuels inflation. High inflation may reduce the value of a domestic investor's holding of government bonds. The consequent depreciation of the currency may further reduce the value of an overseas investor's holding when expressed in his own currency. Thus credit risk is still a factor.

Operational risk

This risk arises from payment or settlement errors. In many countries transactions in government securities are through government-run systems which ensure payment against delivery. The risk characteristics of these systems are for the most part very low. Trading in derivatives, however, is often settled through clearing houses with a higher level of settlement risk. Each clearing house has different procedures and resources.

Liquidity risk

This is the risk that a firm is unable to fund or to realize illiquid assets. Government securities generally have the most liquid market of any in that currency. The existence of an active repo market is an important factor enhancing liquidity.

Market risk

An investor in government securities faces price risk. We will see that coupon and maturity are key factors. But quality of markets is also crucial. Whatever the mathematics suggest, the value of a security is the price at which it may be sold. In the largest markets conditions are usually orderly. This is not always so in other markets.

Market risk can be thought of as absolute risk or as relative risk. Absolute market risk is an estimate of potential loss arising from changes in prices or volatility. This is sometimes called Value at Risk (VAR). Relative market risk measures the potential risk that a portfolio will underperform a specific benchmark. As such it is of great concern to investment managers.

Aggregating risk

It is a constant need of financial institutions to measure the risks to which they are exposed. Some of these risks may be partly offsetting. Therefore it is necessary to use data series to calculate volatilities of prices and correlations between prices.

One such service is J.P. Morgan's RiskMetrics™ which offers three datasets of volatility and correlation estimates on over 400 instruments, including the government bonds of 16 countries. These datasets are updated daily and distributed on the Internet (http://www.jpmorgan.com). Subsets of the data are on Reuters (RKMS-Z), Telerate (17379-17385) and Bloomberg (RMMX Go).

Using RiskMetrics™ VAR methodologies users can estimate with a predefined confidence interval how much they could lose from holding a position over a set time period. This time period might be one day for a typical trading operation or might be a month or longer for portfolio management. Essentially the different VAR methodologies use historical returns to forecast volatilities and correlations which are then used to estimate market risk.

HOW ARE GOVERNMENT SECURITIES ISSUED?

Fixed syndicates

In many countries the business of issuing and distributing government securities was a comfortable cartel. Fixed underwriting syndicates often worked on fixed amounts and commissions.

This system had some merits. The government was sure to sell the debt it required, an orderly market was maintained and long-term ownership was encouraged. Domestic institutions such as insurance companies and pension funds were "encouraged", often by law, to buy government securities.

Today civil servants obliged to finance large and growing deficits in volatile market conditions must sometimes look back at the past with envy.

Competition for capital

As domestic markets have opened up most countries are engaged in a competition to attract foreign investment. Two key elements which enable a country to compete are transparent issuing procedures and robust trading arrangements.

Transparency

The first objective is achieved by many OECD countries through the issue of government securities by auction. The issuing authorities often establish a calendar with explicit statements of their intentions. Information about the level of bids received, and the prices and volumes of bonds sold, are widely and instantly publicized.

Liquidity

> **"Highly volatile trading may excite traders but it frightens responsible public servants with deficits to finance. Hence the existence in some countries of restrictions on sale and repurchase agreements ('repos') or on 'shorting' the market."**

The second requirement of an attractive market is a core of market-makers, committed to making two-way prices in a minimum size at all times. Such market-making is not always profitable and requires a commitment of capital. These market-makers are sometimes compensated by being designated primary dealers and given special rights related to the issue of securities and access to preferential financing from the central bank.

The interests of traders and governments do not always coincide. Highly volatile trading may excite traders but it frightens responsible public servants with deficits to finance. Hence the existence in some countries of restrictions on sale and repurchase agreements ("repos") or on "shorting" the market.

Markets differ

The picture is a varied one. In some countries the old and sometimes very large syndicates continue to distribute securities. They may operate in parallel with an auction system which has assumed the price-setting function previously achieved by negotiation. In others the auction system and the primary dealers function alone. Table 1.5 summarizes the position of the main markets.

Position of the main markets

Table 1.5

Country	Designation	Number*
USA	Primary dealers	38
France	Specialistes en Valeurs du Trésor	20
Germany	Members of the Federal Bond Consortium (not primary dealers)	95
Japan	Syndicate (not primary dealers)	826
UK	Gilt-edged market-makers (GEMMs)	18

Note: * as at 1st March 1996

THE MAIN ISSUING METHODS

Securities may be issued in numerous ways. Three of the most significant are

- auction
- tap
- negotiated issue by syndicate.

Auctions

There are four types of auction.

Multiple-price, sealed bid auction

This is often called an English auction, except in England, where it is called an American auction. Bids are made before a deadline. Each is known only to the bidder and the auctioneer. Each contains a price and a quantity. The auctioneer ranks the bids received and makes awards starting at the highest price bid until the auction is covered.

Winning is losing because the highest bid carries the greatest risk of loss.

Uniform-price, sealed bid auction

The auctioneer receives sealed bids and ranks them as above but makes awards at a single price chosen to cover the auction.

The effect of this is to reduce the risk of a bidder owning bonds above the market consensus price. This method is therefore less penalizing to inexpert or badly informed bidders.

Descending-price, open outcry auction

This is called a Dutch auction because it was once used to auction flowers in the Netherlands.

Bidders meet in one room or electronically. The auctioneer calls out prices in a descending sequence. Bids are accepted until the auction is covered. In effect this is very similar to the first technique described above.

Ascending-price, open outcry auction

The auctioneer calls out an ascending sequence of prices. The volume of bids at each price is announced. The price is raised until the volume of bids is less than the size of the auction. The auctioneer then knows that the previous price was the market-clearing price. Awards are made to all those who bid at the highest price and partial awards are made to those who made lower bids at the market-clearing price

Non-competitive bids

Many governments are anxious to encourage investors who may be long-term holders of the securities. For this reason non-competitive bids are often allowed. These may be limited by size but are sure to be satisfied at or just above the average price at which competitive bids are accepted.

Tap issues

A tap issue is one where the government announces the interest rate and maturity of the issue, and often the price also, and invites subscriptions. A tap may be open for a few days or for much longer periods of time. An issue may be auctioned and subsequently be the subject of a tap offering. This is often because in some markets selling bonds under a tap mechanism allows a larger amount of a single issue to be sold than would be possible at a single offering. This in turn tends to improve the liquidity of the issue in the secondary market.

Distribution by syndicate

Negotiated issuance through a syndicate is less usual than in the past though still a significant part of the Japanese and, to a lesser extent, German markets. The pricing, amount and timing of each issue are agreed by negotiation between the government and the syndicate.

Who uses these methods?

Some countries use multiple price or yield auctions to sell all marketable securities. These include Australia, France and New Zealand. Some governments use this method for some but not all sales. These include Belgium, Canada, Italy and Japan.

Sealed bid, uniform-price auctions are also employed for some issues by Denmark, Italy, and Switzerland. The UK's minimum price tender method is a modified form of uniform price auction.

Tap issues of marketable securities are used by Australia, Denmark, Germany, the Netherlands and the UK.

Germany and Japan employ underwriting syndicates to sell a proportion of issues which are auctioned.

REGULATION

Supervision

There is no uniform way in which the major markets are regulated. Perhaps the most complicated is the US regulatory system.

The Treasury, the Justice Department, the Federal Reserve, the Securities and Exchange Commission and the self-regulatory organizations (SROs) have various responsibilities. Brokers and dealers in the secondary market are regulated under the Government Securities Act of 1986. Broker-dealers also are regulated by the Securities Exchange Act of 1934 and banks are subject to the banking laws.

Elsewhere there is some diversity. In Canada, Germany and Switzerland there is prudential regulation of the depository institutions by central government and provincial or state supervision of trading in securities. In Australia and New Zealand, on the other hand, while there is central regulation of banks there is no specific regulation of the government securities market.

Tax

The fear that domestic investors may avoid paying income tax lies behind many of the laws relating to the taxation of interest on government securities.

Withholding tax, a deduction from interest payments at source, was until recently levied by Italy. More usual is the system of the Bank of England where interest is paid gross "so long as it is shown that the stock is in the beneficial ownership of persons who are neither domiciled nor ordinarily resident in the United Kingdom."

"The fear that domestic investors may avoid paying income tax lies behind many of the laws relating to the taxation of interest on government securities."

■ ■ ■

"Performance measurement is a notoriously difficult subject."

2

Why buy Government Securities?

INTRODUCTION

This chapter considers the investment process. It begins with the institutional investment process, asset allocation, and comparative returns. Then considering international bond investment specifically it highlights the importance of currency changes in investment returns. Next we look at performance measurement and the construction of bond indices against which portfolios are assessed. Historical data are presented to show exactly the significance of currency and duration choices in past returns. Last the chapter deals with national differences in pension fund and mutual fund investment, highlighting the various regulations prevailing in different countries.

THE INSTITUTIONAL INVESTMENT PROCESS

Asset allocation

In most firms of investment managers a "top down" macroeconomic analysis leads to views on currencies and markets which form the basis for the general asset allocation policy. The policy will set out percentage ranges for each asset class for different types of portfolios. Often there will be a currency overlay This will reflect the opinions of the currency strategists. It may lead to some or all of the foreign investments being hedged back into the base currency of the portfolio or sometimes into a third currency.

Equities and bonds require a different decision-making process. On the equity side stock selection is usually delegated to individual fund managers who may add considerable value by skillful stock picking. However, bond fund managers are in a different position. Considerations of credit and liquidity generally confine bond fund managers to government and supranational issuers in most markets. One of the consequences of this difference is that bond funds are cheaper to run because they are less labor intensive.

The range of assets

Now consider what the analysts have to choose between. The range is very wide. Table 2.1 takes a long view from an American perspective

American investments 1976–95: average annual return and standard deviation of the annual returns

Table 2.1

Asset	Annual rate of return %	Standard deviation of annual returns %
Venture capital	20.8	25.1
Small company equities	19.6	19.9
Standard & Poor's 500	14.6	13.7
Non-US equities	14.4	21.6
Long-term government bonds	10.5	13.6
Emerging markets	10.3	27.9
Commercial property	8.1	7.0
Treasury bills	7.3	3.0
Gold	5.2	32.6

Source: *The Economist*, quoting Morgan Stanley

and shows average annual nominal returns over a twenty-year period. Average inflation in the period was 5.2 percent. Both equities and bonds achieved significant real returns. However, commentators did not expect nominal returns in the period 1996–2000 to match those shown in the table.

Table 2.1 shows that volatility and return are correlated but not very precisely. Gold, for example, had the lowest average return of the asset classes in the table but also the highest volatility.

In the UK a similar relationship between returns on equities and on government bonds has been see. In the five years to the end of 1995 UK equities returned an annual average of 16.7 percent compared with an annual average return on gilts of 13.7 percent.

In some years the choice between equity and bond markets is very significant for the performance of a portfolio; 1995 was not such a year. The FT/S&P Actuaries World Index rose 20.5 percent in sterling terms. The J.P. Morgan Global Government Bond Index rose 20.1 percent in sterling (though only 19.3 percent in US$ terms).

Over the very long term, however, equities have earned higher returns. In the UK, for example, accumulated real returns in the 20 years to 1994 were 6.49 percent per annum on long-term fixed income stocks but 13.73 percent per annum for ordinary shares.

Fig 2.1

Accumulated real returns in the UK

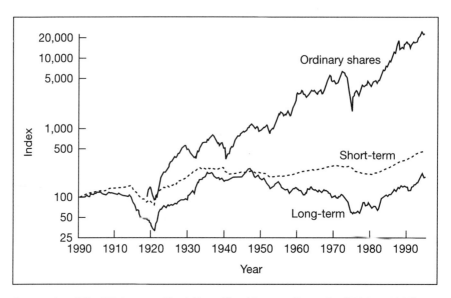

Accumulated Real Return on Short-Term Fixed Interest Deposits (1900 to 1994)
Accumulated Real Return on Long-Term Fixed Interest Stocks (1900 to 1994)
Accumulated Real Return on Ordinary Shares (1919 to 1994)

Source: Watson Wyatt

The importance of currencies

Much bond investment is currency driven. This is a sensitive subject. Pension fund trustees are much happier talking about the prospects for real interest rates in a market than about currency speculation. In practice bond investors are active hedgers, putting a currency overlay on top of their bond selections. In the case of funds managed for a UK institution this might be simply a hedge back to sterling with the choice of security giving a yield advantage over the relevant gilt benchmark. In other cases there will be a great variety of cross hedges as managers select the bond markets and currencies they like.

Adding value in bond fund management

The head of fixed income fund management at one UK house described the value added at each stage of the process as follows:

Choosing the market	45%
Choosing the currency	35%
Choosing the duration	10%
Everything else	10%

Other fund managers would put more emphasis on currencies where the volatility is greater than in bond markets. For example Table 2.2 compares bond market and currency volatility for seven countries in the period 1990–94.

Bond market and currency volatility for seven countries, 1990–94   `Table 2.2`

Country	Volatility of bond yields	Volatility of exchange rates
USA	0.23	1.5
Japan	0.38	2.4
Germany	0.22	0.9
France	0.31	0.7
Italy	0.46	1.9
UK	0.36	2.0
Canada	0.31	1.1

Source: OECD, Economics Department Working Papers, No 154, 1995
Note: Volatility is measured as the standard deviation of monthly changes in percent

PERFORMANCE MEASUREMENT

As with other asset classes the most usual way to measure performance is against a benchmark index based on comparable securities.

Performance measurement is a notoriously difficult subject. The key areas of difficulty lie in duration and credit quality. It is often hard to find an index which has the same duration as that required by the trustees. Most bond indices are based on government bonds and do not include corporate or mortgage-backed debt which may be higher yielding. It is not difficult for a fund manager to beat such an index.

"A partner at a firm of consulting actuaries in London was quoted as advising trustees to be 'twice as skeptical when choosing a bond fund manager as an equity fund manager.'"

In general equity fund managers find it hard to outperform the equity indices against which they are measured. Bond fund investment managers are luckier. Because of the way in which bond indices are constructed, bond fund managers may outperform the indices for extended periods of time.

For example, in the five years to 1993 the WM universe of overseas bond portfolios outperformed the J.P. Morgan World Index (excluding the UK) by an average of 1.70 percent per annum. The equivalent equity funds underperformed the FT/S&P World Index (excluding the UK) by 0.60 percent per annum.

The reason for much of this outperformance is not that bond fund managers are cleverer but that their benchmark indices are narrowly constructed to include the government bonds of, say, fourteen countries. Fund managers may earn higher yields by investing in corporate bonds, asset-backed debt, or emerging market debt. They may also stray from the duration or currency composition of the indices. Currency choices are often crucial. In 1994, for example, the majority of fund managers were surprised by the strength of the yen and underperformed their index by a large margin, at least in the first half of that year.

For the future, however, it is thought that as international bond holdings grow it will become harder to exploit inefficiencies and that will make beating the indices less likely.

One general function of indices is that they do effectively govern the composition of portfolios and provide an anchor restraining managers from taking exotic positions. It may be that more managers are worried about underperformance than are confident of using their judgement to outperform. It is instructive, therefore, to see how an index is put together.

BOND INDICES

What constitutes a good index? Salomon Brothers identify six factors which they consider are not necessarily an exhaustive list.

Key features

A good index

Comprehensiveness
An index should include all the opportunities that are realistically available to market participants under normal market conditions. It should not be subject to opinions about which securities to include on a particular day.

Replicability
The total returns reported for an index should be replicable by market participants. Information about the composition of an index and its historical returns must be readily available.

Stability
An index should not change composition very often and changes should be well understood and predictable. Investors should not

be forced to execute a significant number of transactions just to keep pace.

Barriers to entry

The markets or market segments included in an index should not have significant barriers to entry.

Expenses

It is normal for investment activity to result in expenses relating to withholding tax, safekeeping and transactions. These expenses should be predictable and not excessive.

Objective selection criteria

There should be a clear set of rules governing the inclusion of securities in an index.

Return calculations

Typically total returns are calculated assuming that each security is bought at the beginning of the period and sold at the end of it. Normally bid-side valuations are used. An issue's total rate of return is the percentage change in its total value over the measurement period. Total returns are market capitalization weighted using the security's beginning-of-period market value. The components of total return are:

- price change
- principal payments
- coupon payments
- accrued interest
- reinvestment income
- currency movements (where applicable).

Example of a bond index

The Salomon Brothers World Government Bond Index (WGBI) covers sixteen government bond markets. A market's eligible issues must total at least US$20 billion, DM30 billion and ¥2.5 trillion for three consecutive months for the market to be considered eligible for inclusion. Once a market meets these criteria it is added to the WGBI at the end of the following quarter.

Salomon Brothers also publishes a series of indices called the Additional Market Indices (AMI) which include markets not (yet) eligible for inclusion in the WGBI. The countries in each category in July 1996 are shown in Table 2.3.

Table 2.3

Countries in WGBI and AMI categories, early 1996

WGBI		AMI
Australia	Italy	Ireland
Austria	Japan	New Zealand
Belgium	Netherlands	Norway
Canada	Spain	Portugal
Denmark	Sweden	
Finland	Switzerland	
France	UK	
Germany	USA	

The design criteria of the two indices may be summarized as shown in Table 2.4.

Table 2.4

WGBI categories and criteria

Category	Criteria
Stated coupon	Fixed rate
Minimum maturity	One year
Weighting	Market capitalization updated once a month
Minimum amount outstanding	Varies by market as follows:

Australia: A$250m   Netherlands: Dfl500m
Austria: Sch3bn   New Zealand: NZ$100m
Belgium: Bfr15bn   Norway: Nok5bn
Canada: C$250m   Portugal: Esc50bn
Denmark: Dkr1,500m   Spain: Pta100bn
Finland: Fim1,500m   Sweden: Skr200m
France: Ffr10bn   Switzerland: Sfr200m
Germany: DM500m   UK: £250m
Ireland: IR£200m   USA: US$1bn public
Italy: Lit500m   amount outstanding
Japan: ¥200m

Generally the index does not include discount bonds, index-linked bonds, variable-rate bonds, private placements and retail-directed bonds.

Index weighting and duration

The weightings in Table 2.5 illustrate a benchmark against which a bond portfolio manager may be measured. For this reason many portfolios will be structured to match these weightings and durations quite closely.

WGBI at February 1996

Table 2.5

	Market weight	Modified duration
Australia	1.01	4.13
Austria	0.86	4.16
Belgium	2.58	4.67
Canada	3.05	4.99
Denmark	1.70	4.24
Finland	0.39	4.07
France	7.47	5.01
Germany	10.28	4.10
Italy	6.39	3.34
Japan	19.49	5.63
Netherlands	3.43	5.00
Spain	2.44	3.71
Sweden	1.67	4.27
Switzerland	0.45	5.42
UK	5.48	5.64
USA	33.28	4.80
WGBI	100.0	4.81

Source: Salomon Brothers, International Market Indexes, July 1996

Current returns

While return information is published daily in various newspapers it is also available on Reuters SOLS-T, SOLY-Z, and Bloomberg SBI<GO>, SALO<GO>.

HISTORIC RETURNS

Would a US-based investor have increased return over a long period by diversifying into the major government bond markets outside the USA?

One answer can be had from looking at the WGBI in the ten-year period up to 31 December 1994. The WGBI excluding US-Treasuries returned an annualized 15.04 percent in the period measured in US$ terms. The Salomon Brothers Broad Investment-Grade Index (BIG) which represents the major sectors of the USA domestic fixed-income market, returned 10.03 percent in the same period. So the superficial answer is that diversification abroad really did produce superior returns.

However, when this same measure (WGBI ex US-Treasuries over ten years) is examined on a currency hedged basis the return falls to an annualized 7.57percent, just half the unhedged return. This was because of the fall in value of the US$ against the major currencies. This fall was equivalent to an annualized 7.35 percent against the Deutschemark and 9.70 percent against the Japanese yen.

Table 2.6 summarizes from an American point of view the returns of the different markets, hedged or not. It also shows the volatility or annualized standard deviations of monthly returns.

Table 2.6

USA market returns, hedged or not

Market sector	Annualized return %	Annualized risk %
WGBI (unhedged)	12.34	7.26
WGBI (unhedged,excluding US)	15.04	11.56
WGBI (hedged)	8.68	4.08
WGBI (hedged, excluding US)	7.57	3.87
BIG	10.03	4.96
Treasuries	9.63	5.26
Corporates	10.80	5.50
Mortgages	10.45	4.76

Source: Salomon Brothers, Global Index, Ten-Year Review, January 1995

The data confirm that in this period investors received higher returns for higher risk.

Which country was best?

From an American perspective the countries with currencies which appreciated against the US$ performed best in the ten year period (see Table 2.7). Reflecting the relative importance of currency and the volatility of currencies, the range of average returns was much narrower for hedged returns (2.58percent) than for unhedged returns (8.06percent).

Range of average returns, 1985–94

Table 2.7

1985–94 Country	Average hedged return	Average unhedged return
USA	8.97	8.97
Japan	8.30	16.81
Canada	8.03	9.71
France	7.10	16.93
Germany	7.06	14.89
UK	6.48	14.22
Italy	6.39	15.21

Source: Salomon Brothers

Did longer duration pay?

Table 2.8 overleaf shows that long-term bonds (7–10 years) outperformed short-term bonds (1–3 years) in all countries. In many cases this was because the period saw declining interest rates as shown in the last column of the table.

Table 2.8

Performance of long-term and short-term bonds, 1985–94

1985–94 Country	Average return difference 7–10 vs 1–3 yrs	Average yield difference 7–10 vs 1–3 yrs	Yield change Jan 85–Dec 94
USA	2.51%	1.11%	–3.70%
Japan	1.63	0.55	–2.17
Canada	1.36	0.41	–2.48
France	1.67	0.23	–3.54
Germany	0.06	0.56	0.46
UK	1.45	0.24	–2.56

Source: Salomon Brothers

NATIONAL VARIATIONS

The institutional investment landscape varies from country to country. Insurance companies are large players in most markets. Pension funds are significant only in some markets.

Pension funds

For example, in the United Kingdom (UK) pension fund assets total about US$700bn. This is equal to only 15 percent of USA pension funds. In a European context, however, UK pension funds represent about 60 percent of all EC-funded pension assets. The Netherlands with US$225bn in funded pension assets has a further 20 percent of the EC total. Outside the EC, Switzerland is the most significant European country with US$150bn of pension funds.

Size is not the only difference. Investment policies and legislative provisions also differ. To take a UK example again, UK pension funds are notably international in their investment policies with typically 25 to 30 percent in overseas investments. By contrast there are legal limits to foreign investment by pension funds in many European countries. In the Netherlands the Government Employee pension fund (ABP), the largest fund in Europe, has a 5 percent overseas limit. German pension funds can invest no more than 5 percent abroad, Danish funds no more than 15 percent and Swiss funds no more than 30 percent.

UK pension funds invest more heavily in equities than European funds with typically three-quarters of assets in equities. By contrast German pension funds are forbidden to invest more than 30 percent in equities and rarely reach that level. Swiss funds typically have 10 to 15 percent invested in equities though having a 50 percent limit.

The significance of this for the bond markets is that UK funds had been quite small investors in fixed income securities of all sorts until the 1990s. Holdings by UK pension funds of UK government gilts, for instance, doubled between the beginning of 1992 and the end of 1995. Even so such holdings totalled only some 6 percent of portfolios at the end of the period.

Dutch funds, in contrast, have typically invested more than half their portfolios in fixed income securities and the majority of this is usually in Dutch government bonds. In some countries, therefore, it is clear that pension funds have been encouraged, informally or by law, to buy government bonds in order to help the government finance itself.

Mutual funds

A similar pattern of national differences may be observed among mutual funds also. UK mutual funds are significantly more invested in equities than in any other major country. Roughly 95 percent of British mutual fund assets are in equities compared to about one-third in USA funds and roughly 10 percent in German funds. British funds have typically had 3 percent of assets in bonds compared to three-quarters of all assets in German funds.

■ ■ ■

"The internal rate of return is the rate which if used to discount all future payments to present value produces a sum of present values equal to the price of the bond, It is the discount rate implied by the price of the bond."

3

How do you Value and Compare Bonds?

INTRODUCTION

This chapter sets out the analytical framework for valuing and comparing fixed-income bonds. It begins with the concepts of the time value of money, discount rates, internal rates of return and yield to maturity. Next there is a detailed discussion of interest calculations, accrued interest and compounding. Last, the chapter deals with duration.

YIELD CALCULATIONS

Example

1. Cash flows

DM100,000 nominal value of a five-year fixed-rate bond with an 5 percent annual coupon held until maturity will generate the cash flows shown in Table 3.1.

Table 3.1

Cash flows

At issue	DM (100,000)
Year 1	5,000
Year 2	5,000
Year 3	5,000
Year 4	5,000
Year 5	105,000

These cash flows are predictable. Discounted cash flow techniques may be used to calculate the return on the investment or to establish a value for the holding.

In the case of a fixed-rate bond price is the only uncertainty. A floating-rate instrument which has its coupon reset periodically involves two uncertainties (price and coupon). However, the price of a floating-rate instrument is usually less volatile than that of a fixed-interest security. This is because the resetting of the coupon reduces the interest rate risk of the instrument.

2. Time value of money

A sum of money today is worth more than the certainty of the same sum tomorrow. This is the concept of the time value of money.

The formula used to calculate the present value of a future cash sum is:

$$PV = FV/(1+i)^n$$

where   FV is the future cash sum,
i is the periodic interest rate, and
n is the number of periods.

To calculate the value of DM100,000 to be received in two years time when the appropriate discount rate is 5 percent we apply the formula as follows:

Example

$$DM100,000/(1+0.05)^2$$

which is   DM100,000/1.1025

or   DM90,702.95.

We can also look at the process in reverse. If the present value of a known future cash flow is given we can calculate the implied discount rate. The formula is:

$$((FV/PV)^{1/n})-1$$

where   FV is the future cash flow,
PV is the present value, and
n is the number of periods.

Suppose that $100,000 in three years time is said to have a present value of $81,060.28. We can apply the formula as follows:

Example

$$((100,000/81,060.28)^{1/3})-1$$

or $(1.23365)^{0.33333}-1$

which equals   0.0725 or 7.25%

So the implied discount rate is 7.25%

3. Internal rate of return

The internal rate of return is the rate which if used to discount all future payments to present value produces a sum of present values equal to the price of the bond. It is the discount rate implied by the price of the bond.

It can also be described as the rate at which all future payments are reinvested until the final maturity date so as to produce a lump sum which if discounted back to present value at the same rate produces a value equal to the price of the bond. Mathematically this is the same as the first definition.

Example

Let us take the example of a $100,000 five-year 8 percent bond with annual coupons trading at par (100 percent of nominal value) The IRR is 8.00 percent and the calculation (on either definition) would be as follows:

	$ Cash flow	$ Present value	$ Future value
Year 1	8,000	7,407.41	10,883.91
Year 2	8,000	6,858.71	10,077.70
Year 3	8,000	6,350.66	9,331.20
Year 4	8,000	5,880.24	8,640.00
Year 5	108,000	73,502.98	108,000.00
Sum of values		100,000.00	146,932.81

$146,932.81 discounted back over five years at 8 percent produces a present value of $100,000.

The price of the bond at an IRR of 8.00 percent is 100.00. In reality the IRR is calculated by a reiterative process (using a calculator unless you are very unlucky).

When the price is deducted from the net present value we have a value of zero as we expected from (3) above.

4. Yield to maturity

In the above examples the running yield of the bond, expressed as the coupon divided by the purchase price, was the same as the IRR. In fact this is rare. Most bonds will not be bought or sold at exactly 100 percent of their nominal value. Yield to maturity is the same calculation as that for the internal rate of return.

Example

We would like to buy a five-year bond with an IRR or yield to maturity of 8.5 percent. We are offered the same bond as described in (5) above. How much would we pay for it?

	$ Cash flow	$ Present value at 8.5%
Year 1	8,000	7,373.27
Year 2	8,000	6,795.64
Year 3	8,000	6,263.26
Year 4	8,000	5,772.59
Year 5	108,000	71,824.91
Sum of present values		98,029.67

So we would be prepared to pay 98.03 for the bond.

The second definition of IRR above in (3) highlights the reinvestment risk which this calculation may encourage us to overlook. Only with an instrument which returns only a single payment to the investor (eg a zero coupon bond) is there no reinvestment risk. Otherwise the yield to maturity will be achieved in fact only if it is possible to reinvest each of the coupon payments at the same yield until the maturity date.

5. The term structure of interest rates

So far we have valued all the payments arising from a bond at a single rate. However, the correct discount rate is, in theory, a weighted blend of rates, each being the appropriate rate of return for a single period of time. To choose the correct discount rate we must use the appropriate zero coupon rate for each cash flow. This zero coupon rate is the yield of an instrument making only one payment to the investor on a particular date.

Thus in the case of the bond at (1) above the discount rate would be derived from five rates being the zero coupon rates for one, two, three, four and five years. How are these rates to be calculated?

We have already used the formula for the present value of a future payment above. It was

$$PV = FV/(1+i)^n$$

The present value of a series of cash flows (CF_1, CF_2, CF_3, etc.) each discounted at its own appropriate rate (i_1, i_2, i_3, etc.) over a number of years (t_1, t_2, t_3, etc.) can therefore be expressed as

$$PV = \frac{CF_1}{(1+i_1)^{t1}} + \frac{CF_2}{(1+i_2)^{t2}} + \frac{CF_3}{(1+i_3)^{t3}} + \frac{CF_4}{(1+i_4)^{t4}} + \frac{CF_n}{(1+i_n)^{tn}}$$

How do we establish i_1, i_2, i_3 and so on?

Example

This is best answered with an example. Suppose that there are two annual coupon bonds, both paying interest at 8 percent, one with one year to maturity, the other with two years to maturity. The price of the first bond is 101 and the price of the second bond is 99.

The yield to maturity of the first bond which will make only one more payment is calculated, as we saw above, as

$$((FV/PV)^{1/n})-1$$

which in this case is

$$((108/101)^{1/1})-1$$

or $\qquad (1.06931)-1$

which equals $\qquad 6.93\%.$

Now, turning to the second bond, we can use this rate as appropriate rate to value the first coupon payment as follows using

$$PV = FV/(1+i)^n$$

which gives $\qquad 8/(1+0.0693)^1 = 7.4815.$

We knew the price of the second bond was 99 and now know that 7.4815 of that is attributable to the first coupon. So the value of the last payment (108) in two years time must be $99 - 7.4815$ which is 91.5185. Using the implied discount rate formula we can calculate the implied rate as

$$((FV/PV)^{1/n})-1$$

which in this case is $\qquad ((108/91.5185)^{1/2})-1$

or $\qquad (1.18009)^{1/2}-1$

which equals $\qquad 8.63\%.$

So, if we return to the formula which we set out earlier and apply it to this example:

$$PV = \frac{CF_1}{(1+i_1)^{t1}} + \frac{CF_2}{(1+i_2)^{t2}}$$

becomes
$$PV = \frac{8}{(1+1+0.0693)^1} + \frac{108}{(1+0.0863)^2}$$

or
$$PV = 7.48 + 91.52$$

which as we would expect = 99.

This method of calculating the zero coupon yield curve from the price of conventional bonds could be continued for each subsequent date in the same manner.

In practice this is made both easier and harder in the real world. In some markets it is made easier because there is a liquid market in stripped zero coupon government bonds. The prices at which these trade can be used to establish quickly a zero-coupon term interest rate structure. However, in many markets there is no such short cut and the choice of which conventional bonds to use for the calculation process is difficult. The difficulty lies in the tax treatment of bonds. If in a particular country interest income is taxable but capital gains are tax free, then it is likely that low coupon issues will be more favored than high coupon issues of the same maturity by investors subject to tax. Such factors distort the prices of bonds and may also distort the term structure calculation.

6. Use of the term structure

Once we have calculated the two zero coupon rates we can also calculate the forward rate which would be offered now for a one-year investment starting in one year's time. To prevent arbitrage this must be the forward rate ($_1f_2$) which satisfies the following equation:

$$(1+i_1) \times (1+_1f_2) = (1+i_2)^2$$

In this example the calculation would be

$$(1+0.0693) \times (1+_1f_2) = (1+0,0863)^2$$

which gives $_1f_2$ equal to 10.357%.

The significance of this figure is that this is the extra return available for extending an investment horizon from one to two years.

One may generalize and show the relationship of the coupon bond yield curve to the forward yield curve in diagramatic form. If the coupon bond curve is normal or positive then the forward rate curve will be above it (Figure 3.1). Conversely with an inverse or negative yield curve, the forward rate curve will be below the coupon bond yield curve (Figure 3.2).

Fig 3.1

Normal yield curve and the forward curve

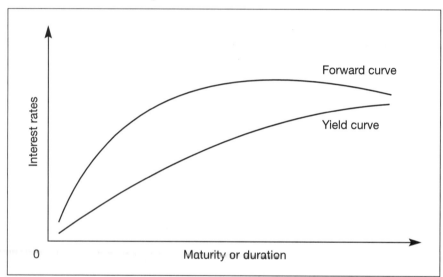

Fig 3.2

Inverted yield curve and the forward curve

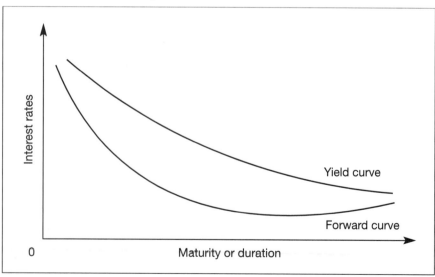

7. Broken periods

All our calculations until now have been in terms of whole interest periods. In real life this will not always be the case.

We know the amounts and dates of future cash flows for a given fixed income security. The only additional knowledge we need is how to calculate their present value on any given date.

We will do this on a bond basis though, as is explained below, there are various calculation conventions used in different markets. All we have to do is to substitute for n (the number of periods) a fraction calculated as $d/360$ where d is the number of days from the valuation date until the future cash flow. Because we are using a bond valuation date we are working with a 360-day year and months of 30 days. The same principle may be applied to other calculation bases.

We can recast the formulae learned above as follows:

Formula	Whole periods	Broken periods
Present value	$FV/(1+i)^n$	$FV/(1+i)^{(d/360)}$
Implied discount rate	$((FV/PV)^{1/n})-1$	$((FV/PV)^{1/(d/360)})-1$

Let us suppose that the 8 percent bond issue described in previous examples pays interest on 30 June in each year and that it matures on 30 June 2001. Today's date is 31 January 1997. What is the bond's value at a yield to maturity of 8 percent?

Example

We can calculate the present value and the future value of each cash flow. It will be seen that, naturally, the future values have not changed. All the present values have changed however.

	Days	$ Cash flow	$ Present value	$ Future value
30 June 1997	150	8,000	7,741.94	10,883.91
30 June 1998	510	8,000	7,168.46	10,077.70
30 June 1999	870	8,000	6,637.46	9,331.20
30 June 2000	1,230	8,000	6,145.80	8,640.00
30 June 2001	1,590	108,000	76,822.47	108,000.00
Sum of values			104,516.13	146,932.81

The present value of $146,932.81 at 8 percent is $104,516.13.

Why is the sum of the present values not $100,000? After all this is an 8 percent coupon bond which we are valuing at 8 percent. The answer lies in the accrued interest. On this date (31 January 1997) the accrued interest totals $4,666.66 (calculated as $100,000 × 8% × 210/360 days) which is due on 30 June 1997. The present value of this accrued interest on 31 January 1997 is $4,516.13 (calculated as $4,666.66/((1.08)(150/360)))

8. Accrued interest

A bond investor may buy or sell a bond within a coupon period. How is the price to be calculated?

> "A bond investor may buy or sell a bond within a coupon period. How is the price to be calculated?"

In most bond markets prices are quoted "clean", that is to say excluding accrued interest. Thus, in (7) above the clean price of the bond would be $104,516.13 less $4,666.66 or $99,849.47. The accrued interest is paid in addition to the clean price.

Table 3.2 sets out the conventions in the main markets.

MARKET CONVENTIONS

Payment frequency

United States Treasuries pay interest semi-annually. So do the government securities of Canada, Ireland, Italy(some), Japan, New Zealand and the UK. The debt of most other countries pays an annual coupon.

In markets where interest is paid semi-annually the quoted yield is the semi-annual yield. That is a six-monthly rate of 3 percent will be quoted as a yield of 6 percent (2 × 3 percent). The equivalent annual yield is calculated by compounding. In this case the calculation is 1.03^2 which is 1.0609 or 6.09 percent. However, by market convention this would be quoted as 6 percent (twice the semi-annual yield) rather than 6.09 percent.

The annual yield of a bond is always higher than its semi-annual equivalent even though the actual return is the same. This difference increases as rates increase. We have seen that a semi-annual yield of 6 percent is equal to an annual yield of 6.09 percent. A semi-annual yield of 12 percent is equal to an annual yield of 12.36 percent.

Conventions in major markets

Table 3.2

Country	Payment	Accrual
USA	Semi-annual	Actual/actual
France	Annual	Actual/actual
Germany	Annual	30/360
Italy	Semi-annual	30/360
Japan	Semi-annual	Actual/365
UK	Semi-annual	Actual/365

Day counts

There are two parts to this. The accrual day count (the top half of the fraction) and the year basis (the bottom half of the fraction).

> **Accrual day counts** *are described as being:* **"actual"**, *which means the actual number of days elapsed in a year of 365 days or (366 days in a leap year); or* **"30"**, *which means that a year is divided into 12 months of 30 days and completed months count as 30 days whatever their actual length. The year basis can be 360 days, 365 days or actual days.*

Definition

Table 3.2 summarizes the conventions in the major markets.

There are refinements in each market which will be dealt with in the relevant chapters.

Compounding

It is important to note the difference between a nominal rate and its effective yield if compounded or paid more frequently.

To illustrate the effect Table 3.3 shows the annual equivalent of certain nominal rates at different payment frequencies:

"It is important to note the difference between a nominal rate and its effective yield if compounded or paid more frequently."

Table 3.3 — **Annual equivalent of nominal rates at different payment frequencies**

Nominal rate %	6.00	8.00	10.00	12.00
Annual	6.00	8.00	10.00	12.00
Semi-annual	6.09	8.16	10.25	12.36
Quarterly	6.14	8.24	10.38	12.55
Monthly	6.17	8.30	10.47	12.68

The formula for this calculation (with the interest rates expressed in decimals) is:

$$A = ((1+(i/n))^n - 1$$

where　　　　A is the equivalent annual interest rate,

i is the nominal interest rate, and

n is the number of compounding periods.

Example　A nominal rate of 10 percent is paid monthly. What is the equivalent annual rate? The formula would give:

$$A = ((1+(0.10/12)^{12} - 1$$

which is　　　　$1.008333３^{12} - 1$

or　　　　0.104713

ie 10.4713%.

The calculation may be needed in the opposite direction also. The formula to calculate an equivalent periodic interest rate from an annually paid equivalent is as follows:

$$i = ((^n\sqrt{(1+A)}) - 1) \times n$$

where　　　　A is the annual interest rate,

i is the equivalent nominal rate, and

n is the number of compounding periods

(interest rates are expressed in decimals).

An annual rate of 10.25 percent is paid by a bond. What is the semi-annual equivalent? The formula would give:

$$i = ((2\sqrt{(1+ 0.1025)}) -1) \times 2$$

which is $\quad\quad (1.05 -1) \times 2$

or $\quad\quad\quad\quad 0.1000$

$\quad\quad\quad\quad\quad$ ie 10.00%.

Continuous compounding

The compounding effect is not infinite. Suppose we had a 10 percent bond which paid interest in very small amounts continuously over a year. If we apply the formula discussed above

$$A = ((1+(i/n))^n - 1$$

we have $\quad\quad A = ((1+.10/\infty))^\infty - 1$

"The compounding effect is not infinite."

This is not infinite. In fact it can be demonstrated that this annual equivalent rate can be calculated as

$$A = e^i - 1$$

In this case $\quad\quad A = e^{0.10} - 1$

which is $\quad\quad\quad 1.10517 - 1$

or $\quad\quad\quad\quad\quad 10.517\%.$

That is to say that 10 percent compounded continuously is equivalent to an annual rate of 10.517 percent.

DURATION AND CONVEXITY

Price behavior of bonds

Bonds are often referred to by their maturity. As a measure of risk maturity is not completely adequate. We know that a longer maturity bond will change more in

"As a measure of risk maturity is not completely adequate."

price than a shorter maturity bond for a given change in interest rates. But neither do bonds of identical maturity always move in price identically.

Let us compare the price behavior of two bonds, each with ten years remaining life but with coupons of 5 percent and 12 percent.

Let us assume that each was issued at prevailing market levels but that shortly afterwards interest rates rose by 1 percent. If in each case

10-year, 5 percent coupon bond will yield 6 percent at a price of 92.64

10-year, 12 percent coupon bond will yield 13 percent at a price of 94.57

we calculate the new market prices of each bond we would find that:

Definition

Duration *is the present value weighted time to maturity of the cash flows of a fixed interest security. It is calculated by calculating the present value of each cash flow, weighting the present value by maturity and dividing the resulting number by the principal amount of the security.*

Example

The reason for this finding is that the more volatile bond is the bond with the longer duration.

Imagine, as before, a five-year bond with an 8 percent coupon in an 8 percent yield environment.

	$ Cash flow	$ Present value @ 8%	$ Weighted value
Year 1	8,000	7,407.41	7,407.41
Year 2	8,000	6,858.71	13,717.42
Year 3	8,000	6,350.66	19,051.98
Year 4	8,000	5,880.24	23,520.96
Year 5	108,000	73,502.98	367,514.90
Total			431,212.67
Duration			4.312 years

If we were to calculate the duration of the two bonds described at the beginning of this section, assuming a nominal amount of $100,000 of each, our workings would look as follows:

(i) Ten-year 5 percent coupon bond in a 6 percent interest rate environment:

	$ Cash flow	$ Present value @ 6%	$ Weighted value
Year 1	5,000	4,716.98	4,716.98
Year 2	5,000	4,449.98	8,899.96
Year 3	5,000	4,198.10	12,594.29
Year 4	5,000	3,960.47	15,841.87
Year 5	5,000	3,736.29	18,681.45
Year 6	5,000	3,524.80	21,148.82
Year 7	5,000	3,325.29	23,277.00
Year 8	5,000	3,137.06	25,096.49
Year 9	5,000	2,959.49	26,635.43
Year 10	105,000	58,631.45	586,314.52
			743,206.81
			7.432 years

(ii) 10-year 12 percent coupon bond in a 13 percent interest rate environment:

	$ Cash Flow	$ Present Value @ 13%	$ Weighted Value
Year 1	12,000	10,619.47	10,619.47
Year 2	12,000	9,397.76	18,795.52
Year 3	12,000	8,316.60	24,949.81
Year 4	12,000	7,359.82	29,439.30
Year 5	12,000	6,513.12	32,565.50
Year 6	12,000	5,763.82	34,582.93
Year 7	12,000	5,100.73	35,705.09
Year 8	12,000	4,513.92	36,111.35
Year 9	12,000	3,994.62	35,951.56
Year 10	112,000	32,993.89	329,938.95
			588.659.48
			5.887 years

Note that there is in fact more than 1.5 years difference in duration between the two bonds of the same maturity.

Two interesting things may be noted about duration. First, for coupon-paying bonds duration does not decrease smoothly our the life of the bond. Duration jumps at each coupon payment date. Second, duration does not always increase as maturity increases. This is true, for example, in the case of long-dated low coupon bonds where the yield to maturity is higher than the coupon. Table 3.4 sets out the duration for different lives to maturity of a 5 percent annual coupon bond trading at a discount to yield 10 percent to redemption.

Table 3.4

Duration for different lives to maturity, 5 percent annual coupon bond trading at discount to yield 10 percent redemptlon

Life to maturity	Price to yield 10%	Duration in years
10 years	69.277	7.661
20 years	57.432	10.741
30 years	52.865	11.433
40 years	51.105	11.389
50 years	50.426	11.236
100 years	50.004	11.006

Source: International Securities Makret Association Ltd (ISMA)

Formulae for duration

For a bond with a fixed coupon g payable h times per annum, with a normal first coupon payment, which is redeemable on one coupon date, duration (D) can be calculated as

$$f1/h + (g \times vf^1)/(P \times h^2) \times \{v + {}^2v2 + \ldots {}^{(n-1)}v(n-1)\} + C/(P \times h) \times (n-1)v^{(n+f1-1)}$$

where g = annual coupon rate %
h = number of coupon payments per year
n = number of coupon payments to redemption
P = gross price of bond (including accrued interest)
C = redemption price
fl = fraction of period from value date to first coupon date
v = discounting factor. For example, if the yield compounded h times per annum is y then v = 1/(1+y/h)

For example, take a four-year bond with a 9 percent annual coupon trading at par. In order to calculate the duration we must first calculate the discounting factor v as follows

$$v = 1/1.09 = 0.91743$$

We can now apply the formula as follows:

$$D = 1 + 9v/100 \times \{v + 2v^2 + 3v^3\} + 100/100 \times 3v^4$$

which gives us a duration of 3.531 years.

The formula set out above can be modified so as to calculate the duration of a perpetual security. The formula reduces to

$$D = f1/h + 1/y$$

where the terms are as given above.

For example, we would like to calculate the duration of a perpetual security which pays 8 percent interest semi-annually on 15 January and 15 July. On 15 April it has a redemption yield of 10.00 percent compounded semi-annually and f1 has a value of 0.5. The duration is given as

Example

$$DFF = 0.5/2 + 1/0.1$$

$$= 10.25 \text{ years.}$$

The author is indebted to Patrick J. Brown of International Securities Market Association Ltd (ISMA) for several of the examples in this and the next section which are taken from his excellent book *Formmulae for Yield and other Calculations* published by ISMA.

The effect of coupon on duration

The payment of principal in the higher coupon issue is less important than in the other. The duration of a 100-year 12 percent bond at par is about 9.33 years and, taken to an extreme, a perpetual annuity has a duration of about 10.5 years.

On the other hand a zero coupon bond has a duration equal to its maturity. In between these two extremes a bond trading at a discount can behave oddly with the duration of a very low coupon bond decreasing with a very long maturity. This is because the payment of principal becomes almost insignificant at, say, 50 years but is very significant at 15 years.

A graph of duration versus maturity will differ for bonds at par, at a premium or at a discount.

The effect of yields on duration

As will be readily apparent from the two examples calculated above, when yields rise the further distant cash flows are most reduced in value and duration is thereby shortened. Conversely as interest rates fall the further cash flows gain in present value and duration lengthens.

Uses of duration

The concept of duration has various uses for the trader or portfolio manager. A trader may use duration to determine hedge ratios. A portfolio manager might use it to compare bonds or to measure risk in a portfolio of assets and liabilities.

Modifications to duration

Duration was first expressed by Frederick Macaulay in 1938 and is sometimes called Macaulay Duration to distinguish it from Modified Duration. Modified Duration is expressed as Macaulay Duration divided by the periodic yield and provides a measure of percentage price volatility. The larger the modified duration the greater the price volatility for a specified yield change.

The formula for modified duration (MD) is

$$MD = dP/dy \times 1/P$$

where P = gross price of bond (including accrued interest)
     dP = small change in price
     dy = small change in yield compounded with the frequency of the coupon payment.

The relationship between duration (D) and modified duration (MD) can be expressed as

$$MD = D \times v$$

where v = discounting factor. For example, if the yield compounded
    h times per annum is y then
    $v = 1/(1+y/h)$

h = number of coupon payments per year.

In the case of a 9 percent annual coupon bond trading at par with **Example**
four years remaining life, which we considered above, the duration
was calculated to be 3.531 years.
  The modified duration would be given as

$$MD = 3.531/(1 + 0.09) = 3.239$$

Applying the first equation for modified duration given above we
see that if the yield on this bond were to drop by 0.1 percent to
8.9 percent the price should increase by 0.324 to 100.3245 percent
  It will thus be clear that of the two forms of duration the former
tends to be used for immunization, the latter for measuring volatility.

Convexity

Modified duration shows how the price of security will change for a
small change in yield. It does not work well for large changes. This is
because the relationship between price and yield is not a straight line
when drawn on a graph, but takes the form of a curve. This curve,
which varies from bond to bond, is called convexity. It can be a desir-
able property for fixed income investors because it may allow a
security or portfolio to rise in value in response to a fall in rates faster
than it will fall in value for a corresponding rise in interest rates.
  Convexity (CX) can be approximated using the following formula:

$$CX = 10^6 \times (P_1 + P_2 - 2P)/P$$

where P = gross price of the bond at the current yield
      P_1 = gross price of the bond if the yield were to increase by
           0.1%
      P_2 = gross price of the bond if the yield were to decrease by
           0.1%.

Take the case of a 10-year 10 percent annual coupon bond trading at **Example**
par. In this case

P_1 = 99.388174, a yield of 10.1%
P_1 = 100.617105, a yield of 9.9%

Therefore we can calculate convexity to be

$$\begin{aligned} CX &= 10^6 \times (99.388174 + 100.617105 - 200)/100 \\ &= 10^4 \times 0.005279 \\ &= 53. \end{aligned}$$

In this case we can see that the bond loses in price less than it gains in price for a change of the same size in yield in either direction. A rise in yields of 0.1 percent causes a 0.611826 fall in price while a fall in yields of 0.1 percent causes a 0.617105 gain in price.

■ ■ ■

"The word 'repo' is an abbreviation of repurchase and is used to denote a sale and repurchase agreement. A repo is a sale of securities for cash with a simultaneous commitment to repurchase them on a specified future date."

The Repo Market

INTRODUCTION

> **"The repo market is simply a collateralized money market in which borrowers of cash lend liquid marketable securities as collateral against the loan."**

It is often said that the repo market is a vital part of the market in government securities. For example, the clearing organization Euroclear has been quoted as estimating that half of its settlement activity in major government bonds is attributable to repo trading.

It is difficult to separate out repos based on government bonds from other repo business. The US domestic repo market has been estimated at about US$1,000 billion Estimates of the size of the international market are inevitably imprecise but the non-US dollar repo market is thought to exceed US$300 billion outstanding.

This chapter explains what a repo is and what function repos perform.

WHAT IS A REPO?

Definition *The word 'repo' is an abbreviation of repurchase and is used to denote a sale and repurchase agreement. A repo is a sale of securities for cash with a simultaneous commitment to repurchase them on a specified future date.*

The repo market is simply a collateralized money market in which borrowers of cash lend liquid marketable securities as collateral against the loan.

In a repo the seller usually delivers securities on a delivery-versus-payment basis and receives cash from the buyer. The money is lent for the period of the transaction at an agreed rate, the "repo rate", which is usually fixed for the term of the deal.

When a counterparty lends collateral and borrows cash they are said to repo the collateral. When a counterparty borrows the collateral and lends cash they are said to engage in a "reverse repo."

VARIATIONS

Though the term repo describes one type of transaction it is also used loosely to include two other similar sorts of transaction. So there are three separate transaction structures covered by the term:

- sell and buy back
- repurchase agreement (repo)
- collateralized lending.

Sell and buy-back

This is the simplest form. An outright sale of a security is accompanied by an outright repurchase of the same security for value at a more distant date. This is sometimes called a "buy-sell."

The sale invoice price will include accrued coupon interest to the sale date and the buy-back price will include accrued coupon interest to the buy-back date. The clean price of the buy-back (that is excluding interest accrued) will be set at such a level as to represent an interest cost. The cost of borrowing cash by the sale and buy-back transaction lies in this price adjustment.

> "An outright sale of a security is accompanied by an outright repurchase of the same security for value at a more distant date."

Sell/buy-back

Fig 4.1

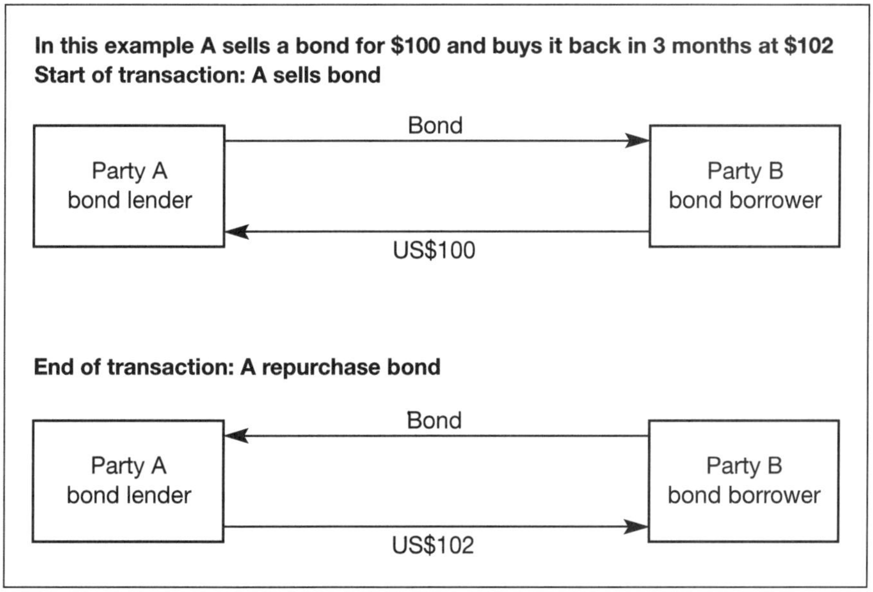

In this example A sells a bond for $100 and buys it back in 3 months at $102

Start of transaction: A sells bond

Bond →

| Party A bond lender | | Party B bond borrower |

← US$100

End of transaction: A repurchase bond

← Bond

| Party A bond lender | | Party B bond borrower |

US$102 →

The documentation between the two counterparties is simply the confirmations of the two securities transactions. Sale and buy-back transactions can sometimes be used by institutions which are not allowed to lend or borrow securities but which are allowed to buy and sell them.

An important difference between sale and buy-back transactions and the two other types described below is in the treatment of coupon payments made during the term of the transaction. In sale and buy-backs the coupon accrued during the term of the repo is returned to the seller through the repurchase price calculation (see Figure 4.1), but a coupon paid during the term of the repo is not recoverable by the seller because there is no document other than the bond trade tickets governing the transaction. Sellers must be careful to consider this question before entering into trades.

Repurchase agreement (repo)

A repo is merely a more sophisticated sale and buy-back governed by a written agreement rather than merely being evidenced by deal confirmations. The written agreement will normally govern all such

Fig 4.2

Repurchase agreement

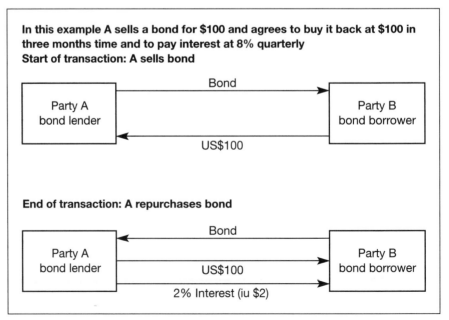

In this example A sells a bond for $100 and agrees to buy it back at $100 in three months time and to pay interest at 8% quarterly
Start of transaction: A sells bond

Bond

| Party A bond lender | → | Party B bond borrower |

US$100

End of transaction: A repurchases bond

Bond

| Party A bond lender | | Party B bond borrower |

US$100

2% Interest (iu $2)

transactions between the counterparties. The agreement will typically include the right to mark transactions to market and to ask for variation margin as well as the rights to terminate transactions in the event of a default and to set off one against another so as to net the exposure of the non-defaulting counterparty (see Figure 4.2).

A further difference of a practical nature is that the return to the supplier of cash is quoted separately.

Collateralized lending

A securities lending transaction involves one party agreeing to lend specified securities against collateral delivered by the other party who pays a fee for borrowing the securities. The supplier of the securities is known as the "lender" and the supplier of collateral is known as the "borrower" even if the collateral is cash and a rate of interest is payable on it. The securities and collateral do not change ownership, and the owner of the securities continues to receive all coupons paid on them (see Figure 4.3).

Collateralized lending

Fig 4.3

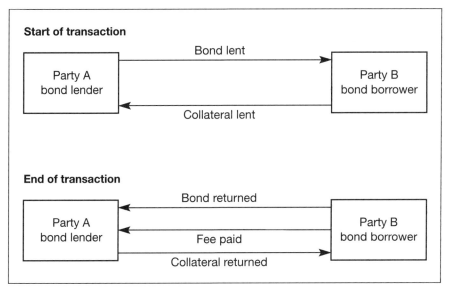

Start of transaction

Bond lent

Party A
bond lender

Party B
bond borrower

Collateral lent

End of transaction

Bond returned

Party A
bond lender

Fee paid

Party B
bond borrower

Collateral returned

Securities lending transactions may also be structured as "open" trades in which securities are lent for an unfixed period of time with the fee or interest being reset period of time with the fee or interest being reset periodically.

Types of collateral vary from market to market and may include government securities, eurobonds, certificates of deposit, commercial paper, bankers' acceptances, mortgage-backed securities and equities. In many markets dealers may specify whether they require a specific security as collateral or whether they are happy to accept any securities within a general category.

EXAMPLE OF REPO CALCULATION

Example Take the following transaction:

Trade date	10 May
Value date	12 May
Termination date	15 May
Term	3 days
Security	7.5% Bund 11.11.2004
Nominal amount	DM20 million
Clean price (excluding accrued interest)	109.00
Accrued interest	3.770833%
	DM754,166
Invoice price on trade date	112.770833
	DM22,554,166
Repo rate	3.5% pa

Sale and buy-back calculation

If the transaction is to be structured as a sale and buy-back then the cash flows will be as follows.

Example Party A agrees to sell DM20 million nominal against receipt of DM22,554,166 and agrees to buy back the bonds after three days. The clean price at which Party A repurchases the bonds is calculated as follows:

Repurchase clean price = Purchase clean price – (bond coupon – repo rate)

The bond coupon $= 7.5\% \times 20,000,000 \times 3/360$
$$= 12,500$$

Repo rate return $= 3.5\% \times 22,554,166 \times 3/360$
$$= 6,578$$

Therefore the repurchase clean price is

$$21,800,000 - (12,500 - 6,578) = 21,794,078$$

or a price of 108.970390

Accrued interest to the termination date is 3.833333% or DM766,666. The invoice price on the termination date will therefore be

$$108.970390 + 3.833333 = 112.803723$$

or $\qquad$ DM21,794,078 + DM766,666 = DM22,560,744

The difference between the invoice prices on the trade date and the termination date is

$$DM22,560,744 - DM22,554,166 = DM6,578$$

During the transaction the coupon of the bond continues to accrue to the benefit of the bond lender or seller while the cash repo rate accrues to the benefit of the borrower or buyer. The difference between the two represents the net benefit to the bond lender or seller.

"Classic" repo calculation

If the same transaction had been structured as a repo with the benefits conferred by a proper repo agreement the arithmetic would have been as follows.

Party A agrees to deliver DM20 million nominal value of bonds against receipt of DM22,554,166 and agrees to take back the bonds after three days against payment of the same amount together with an interest payment calculated as the repo rate applied to the cash amount.

Example

> "Because repos are collaterized loans they often represent a borrowing mechanism which is cheaper than unsecured money market borrowing."

In this case the payment on the value date would be DM22,554,166 and the payment on the termination date would be DM22,554,166 plus interest of DM calculated as

$$22,554,166 \times 3.50\% \times 3/360 = DM6,578$$

USES OF REPOS

Bond lenders

> "Repos can represent an opportunity for investors holding bonds to enhance the yield on their portfolios by borrowing cheaply through the repo market and then lending at higher rates so as to earn an interest margin."

Because repos are collaterized loans they often represent a borrowing mechanism which is cheaper than unsecured money market borrowing. This is particularly true for financial institutions which do not have direct access to the interbank deposit market. The open market operations of central banks may also provide low-cost funding to the repo market.

Certain bonds may become scarce when they are described as being "on special." This usually means that there are many market participants who want to borrow a particular bond and that in consequence the repo cash lending rate is very low for that particular security.

Repos can represent an opportunity for investors holding bonds to enhance the yield on their portfolios by borrowing cheaply through the repo market and then lending at higher rates so as to earn an interest margin. The structure of such a transaction would be as shown in Figure 4.4.

Bond borrowers

Bond borrowers may include cash lenders seeking a secured, short-term investment, or central banks which sometimes use the repo market to add liquidity to the money markets through their open market operations.

Repos for bond investors

Fig 4.4

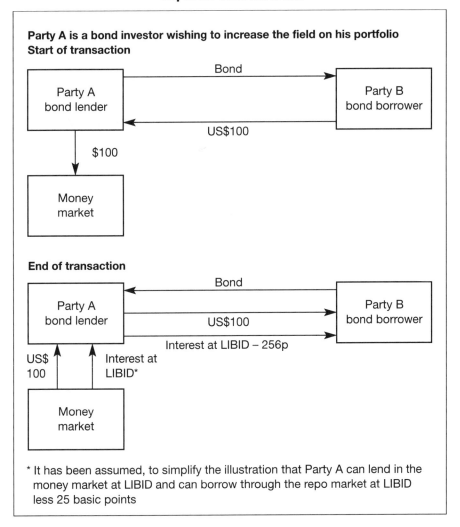

Party A is a bond investor wishing to increase the field on his portfolio
Start of transaction

End of transaction

* It has been assumed, to simplify the illustration that Party A can lend in the money market at LIBID and can borrow through the repo market at LIBID less 25 basic points

Very often bond borrowers are traders who use borrowed securities to short the market. Having sold securities which they do not own they need to borrow them to make delivery. Such a transaction might be as shown in Figure 4.5.

It should be noted that while all the cash flows under the repo are agreed in advance the price at which Party B repurchases the bonds in the bond market is not known in advance. This price may give rise to a profit if Party B has judged the market correctly. It may otherwise give rise to a loss for Party B if the market price of the bond has risen over the life of the repo transaction.

Fig 4.5

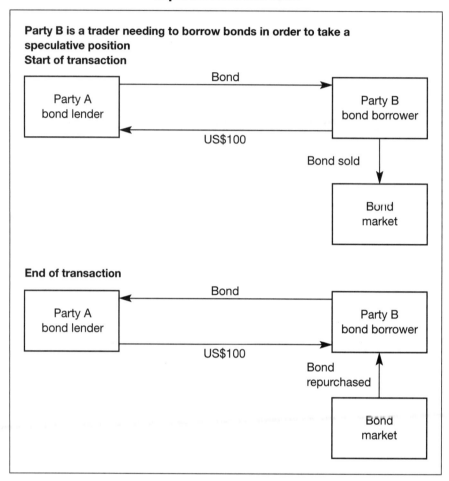

Repos for bond borrowers

Party B is a trader needing to borrow bonds in order to take a
speculative position
Start of transaction

Bond

| Party A bond lender | → | Party B bond borrower |

US$100

Bond sold

Bond market

End of transaction

Bond

| Party A bond lender | ← | Party B bond borrower |

US$100

Bond repurchased

Bond market

Repos and tax

The different circumstances of investors and the varieties of regulation
make a comprehensive survey impossible. In order to see the sort of
transaction which may be useful consider the following example.

Example

A portfolio manager owns a four-year UK gilt on which he has an
unrealized loss. He does not wish to recognize the loss for tax reasons
but expects the market to fall further. He decides that hedging his
position with the Long gilt future on LIFFE would not be satisfactory
because of the maturity mismatch between the deliverable bonds (ten
years plus) and his own holding of four-year bonds. The investor

decides to borrow the same four-year gilt under a repo agreement and simultaneously to sell the borrowed gilt in the market. If the market falls as the portfolio manager expects he will be able to buy back the gilt at a lower price, thus offsetting the loss in his portfolio. The transaction would be as described in Figure 4.5.

IMPLIED REPO RATE

There is a close parallel between the repo market and the futures market. We have seen above that often the same general objective may be achieved using futures or repos. We will now look in more detail at what governs the relationship between the two.

> *The **implied repo rate** is the break-even financing rate for an investor considering a cash/futures arbitrage transaction.*   **Definition**

Example

Suppose an investor was planning to buy a bond and sell an equivalent bond future, (known as a cash and carry position). The future contract would allow him to deliver the bond at a known price at the maturity of the future contract. The investor would sell the future and simultaneously buy the bond, financing the purchase by repoing the bond for a period coterminous with the future contract.

At maturity the investor would receive back the bond under the repo transaction and deliver it under the future contract. The investor would pay the repo rate to the repo counterparty and would receive the implied repo rate under the future contract. This can be illustrated as shown in Figure 4.6.

If the implied repo rate exceeds the repo rate then our investor can make a profit. This opportunity can be arbitraged away. The reverse condition, when the implied repo rate is less than the repo rate, cannot be arbitraged away because the investor is not certain which bond will be delivered into the future contract. This is why the implied repo rate is usually less than the repo rate.

The description of the cash flows has been simplified. In practice, for example, there would be margin calls on the futures position and the amount of the repo financing would be less than the market value of the bond by a sum equal to the margin required.

Fig 4.6

Cash and carry

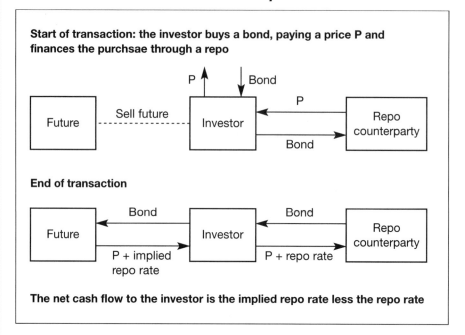

Start of transaction: the investor buys a bond, paying a price P and finances the purchsae through a repo

End of transaction

The net cash flow to the investor is the implied repo rate less the repo rate

Calculating the implied repo rate

The starting point is the breakeven concept which can be expressed as:

Cost to purchase and finance bond = receipt from contract delivery plus coupon & reinvested earnings

This can be expressed for cases with no or one coupon payment as:

$$(P + A_1)(1 + rD_1/360) = (DP + A_2) + C(1 + rD_2/360)$$

where P   = bond purchase price
A_1 = accrued bond interest at purchase value date
r   = implied repo rate (expressed as decimal)
D_1 = days from purchase value date to futures delivery date
C   = Coupon received (0 if none)
D_2 = days from coupon date to futures delivery date
DP = delivery price
A_2 = accrued bond interest at futures delivery date

Now this formula can be rearranged into the form

$$r = \frac{DP + A_2 - (P + A + C)}{(P + A_1)(D_1/360) - C(D_2/360)}$$

RISK

We need to consider two main areas of risk: market risk and credit risk.

"The two main areas of risk are: market risk and credit risk."

Market risk

Generally it is the case that market risk on the securities in a repo transaction are borne by the seller/lender of the securities who has contracted to buy them back at a fixed price, whatever the market price of the securities.

It is consequently true that the decision of the buyer/borrower of the securities to enter into a repo transaction is not influenced by the market price of the securities, or by their coupon, maturity or expected price performance, provided that the securities represent saleable collateral for an adequate amount in the event of a default by the counterparty.

Credit risk

This may be divided into two parts: counterparty risk and collateral risk.

Counterparty risk

Counterparty risk is the risk that the counterparty fails to perform on the termination date. If the counterparty fails to return the securities or the cash the risk is that the value of the securities at that point is less or greater than the repurchase price. This might be thought of as contingent market risk. It will be potentially greater with securities of longer duration and in volatile market conditions.

This risk can be reduced by agreeing suitable margining arrangements. However, there will always be a risk that margin calls are not paid by the counterparty so the risk can not be entirely eliminated.

> **"The obvious danger is that the same collateral may be used several times over or may not exist at all!"**

Collateral risk

The second part of credit risk is collateral risk, the danger that the issuer of the collateral might default during the term of the repo. This, too, is a contingent risk because the counterparty is still obliged to repurchase the securities whatever their market value. The risk is therefore only crystallized if both the issuer of the collateral and the repo counterparty default during the life of the repo.

Margining

Because the value of collateral will change with market conditions the counterparty looking to the collateral as security will often require a "margin" of value above the amount of cash advanced. This requirement is usually divided into "initial margin" required at the outset, and "variation margin" which is called for if the value of the collateral has fallen by an agreed amount. In order to manage this process in a sensible manner the repo documentation will often stipulate a minimum amount by which the value of the collateral must change in order for more collateral to be demanded or for surplus collateral to be returned.

In all of these arrangements it matters where the collateral is held. A "hold-in-custody" repo is one where the supplier of the collateral retains possession and merely segregates it in his books. In some markets this is pledged to the counterparty but even so is not always completely secure. The obvious danger is that the same collateral may be used several times over or may not exist at all!

The safest form of collateral arrangement is known as a "tri-party repo". It also saves on the expenses of transferring securities between depositaries. Collateral is held by an independent third party which manages the exchange of cash and securities, monitors value and manages margin calls and substitution of securities.

■ ■ ■

"Futures are relatively simple and quite intuitive. Options, on the other hand, are more complex and sometimes almost counter-intuitive in their behavior."

What are Derivatives?

INTRODUCTION

This chapter deals with two types of derivatives: futures and options. Of the two futures are relatively simple and quite intuitive. Options, on the other hand, are more complex and sometimes almost counter-intuitive in their behavior. Options are therefore dealt with at much greater length.

WHAT IS A FUTURE?

Because a future is a type of forward contract we will start with forward contracts.

Definition   *A **forward contract** obliges the forward buyer to purchase a specified financial instrument or commodity at a specified price on a specified future date, the settlement date. The seller of a forward contract is similarly obliged to deliver a specified financial instrument or commodity in settlement of his obligation.*

Generally no payments are made under a forward contract until the settlement date. Forward contracts therefore represent a credit risk for each party on the other from the inception of the contract until the settlement date.

Settlement of a forward contract may be by cash settlement. That is no delivery takes place but there is a cash payment from one party to the other of the difference between the contract value of the forward and the spot or current value on the settlement date.

If the forward contract relates to a reasonably liquid instrument or commodity then the forward price will be related to the cost of owning the underlying instrument or commodity less any income such ownership may bring. In the absence of any storage or other costs and in the absence of any income then the forward price will generally exceed the spot price by an amount equivalent to the cost of owning or carrying the underlying for the period of the forward contract. This net difference is one of the things called "basis".

A future has three important advantages. First, being exchange traded, the price is readily ascertainable. Second, futures are a robust mechanism for controlling and reducing credit risk. Third, futures are, for the most part, very liquid, traded instruments. so that the owner of a future can always sell it.

> "The counterparty to a futures contract is the exchange clearing house."

The credit point requires explanation. The counterparty to a futures contract is the exchange clearing house. This may be a preferable counterparty to many of the market participants. The clearing house can net the exposure of a member to the market and ensure that only net amounts need be paid. A clearing house controls its exposure to members by requiring initial margin and subsequently variation margin to be deposited at the inception of a contract and then in response to changes in the market value of that contract.

Futures contracts are standardized particularly the following terms:

- amount
- settlement date
- last trading date
- minimum price movement
- eligible deliverable securities.

How exchanges operate

Trading may be by open outcry on the floor of an exchange or by an automated screen-based trading system. Figure 5.1 shows how a trade is registered at LIFFE in London.

In Figure 5.1 the clearing house (at LIFFE it is The London Clearing House Ltd.) acts as the central counterparty. A fund manager, for example, would use a broker to execute or clear their trades at LIFFE. LIFFE members act as principals and not as agents on behalf of their clients. The fund manager's counterparty is the broker not the clearing house or LIFFE.

Fig 5.1

Trade registration at LIFFE, London

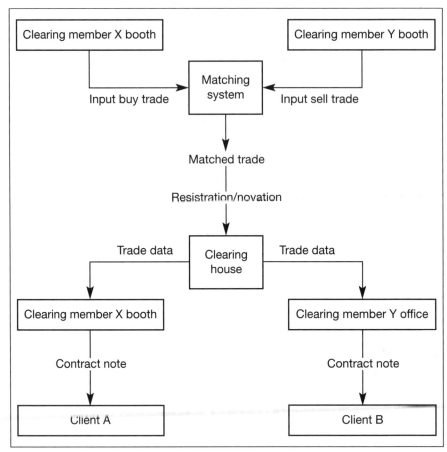

Source: LIFFE

Delivery

Delivery *is the obligation attached to a futures (or option) contract which has remained open at the end of trading in that contract and which is not specified to be cash settled.*

At LIFFE, for example the gilt, Bund and BTP futures are deliverable while the JGB future is cash settled. At some exchanges delivery is by a named counterparty who is assigned the obligation to deliver. Alternatively, as at LIFFE, delivery may be through the clearing house and therefore anonymous.

What is delivered is the cheapest to deliver bond from the basket of deliverable bonds specified by the exchange. Before a contract comes to be traded a basket of deliverable bonds is announced. These bonds will be of different maturities and coupons though all will have a certain minimum amount in issue. To each bond is attached a price factor intended to equalize their value for delivery when applied to the nominal amount.

At the end of each contract's trading life an Exchange Delivery Settlement Price (EDSP) for the future is set. The invoicing amount for delivery is therefore set as

Invoicing amount = (EDSP × price factor × nominal value) + accrued interest

Suppose that we are calculating the invoicing amount for a trade in a single Bund future for which the unit of trading is DM250,000. The EDSP is 97.875, the price factor for the CTD bond is 1.018976 and the accrued interest is DM1,987.65. The invoice amount is calculated as:

Example

$$((97.875/100) \times 1.018976 \times DM250,000) + DM1,987.65$$

which is   DM251,318.34.

Cheapest to deliver

> The **cheapest to deliver bond** *is the bond from the basket of deliverable bonds which provides the highest return on a cash and carry transaction.*

Definition

This is the calculation which ties the fair price of a future to the cash market in the underlying. So it is important to understand cash and carry.

Cash and carry

> A **cash and carry transaction** *is usually a long position in the underlying bond and a short position in the related future.*

Definition

The profit or loss calculation is as follows:

cash inflow *less* cash outflow,

or **short futures *le*ss long underlying bond,**

which is   (futures price × price factor + accrued interest at delivery + coupon income)
less   (long bond clean price + accrued interest at purchase + financing cost).

Who uses futures?

There are numerous ways to use futures and many possible users. Some of the more obvious users and their possible strategies are described in Table 5.1.

Table 5.1

Futures users and their strategies

User	Strategy	Application
Market-makers	Hedging cash book	Long bonds/sell futures Short bonds/buy futures
Institutional investors	Hedging	Long bonds/sell futures
	Investing future cash	Buy futures (sell when bonds bought)
	Change asset allocation	eg sell gilt futures and buy Bund futures
	Duration adjustment	Buy/sell futures to alter duration
Issuers of debt	Hedging future borrowing	Sell bond futures and close when debt is issued
Traders	Directional trades	Buy/sell bond futures
	Yield curve trades	Buy/sell bond futures and sell/buy short futures
	Bond spreading	Buy/sell bond futures and sell/buy other bond futures

Source: LIFFE

Example from LIFFE

A fund manager has a holding of £100 million of the Treasury 8.5 percent 2007 UK gilt. He is bearish about the gilt market and wishes to hedge his position. He knows that notional value of the gilt future is £50,000 and that (for this example) that the 8.5 percent 2007 gilt is the cheapest to deliver stock with a price factor of 0.9607523.

> **Example**

> **"So where are these futures traded?"**

The number of contracts needed for the hedge is calculated as

(amount of holding/contract size) × price factor

which in this case is

(£100,000,000/£50,000) × 0.9607523 = 1,922 contracts.

Note that the number of contracts is calculated to the nearest whole number of contracts. It is not always possible to hedge a position exactly. A second imperfection is that the asset being hedged may not be exactly replicated by the future. In this case the gilt being hedged was also the cheapest to deliver. If it had not been or had been outside the deliverable basket altogether there would have been a basis risk and the hedge would have been imperfect. (Note this is another use of the term basis which is different to the one described earlier in this chapter.)

Futures trading volumes

So where are these futures traded? Table 5.2 overleaf is arranged by nationality of the underlying and shows the leading government bond futures contracts in 1995.

> **"Care in this area will reduce the likelihood of career-threatening experiences."**

The terms of some of these contracts are set out in Part II in the relevant country chapters.

Last, as a guide to operational procedures it is useful to review a checklist of steps (suggested by LIFFE) which should precede the use of futures or options. Care in this area will reduce the likelihood of career-threatening experiences.

Table 5.2

Leading government bond futures contracts, 1995

Contract	Size	Exchange	Volume traded
USA			
US Treasury bond	$100,000	CBOT	86,375,916
US Treasury note 10 yr	$100,000	CBOT	22,445,356
US Treasury note 5 yr	$100,000	CBOT	12,637,054
UK			
Long gilt	£50,000	LIFFE	13,796,555
France			
Notional Bond 10 yr	Ffr500,000	MATIF	33,610,221
Germany			
German Bund	DM250,000	LIFFE	32,231,210
German Bund future	DM250,000	DTB	12,526,264
German Bobl	DM250,000	DTB	7,351,783
Japan			
10 year Government bond	¥100,000,000	TSE	14,010,374
Italy			
BTP	ITL200,000,000	LIFFE	9,612,899
10 year notional bond	ITL250,000,000	MIF	2,636,161
Other			
Australian 3-year T-bond	A$100,000	SFE	8,826,905
Australian 10-year T-bond	A$100,000	SFE	5,748,674
Canadian 10-year bond	C$100,000	MONTREAL	1,026,197
Danish long-term bond	DKK1,000,000	FUTOP	167,457
Spanish 10 year notional bond	PTS10,000,000	MEFFRF	13,095,805
Swedish 5-year government bond	Skr1,000,000	OM	909,793
Swedish 10-year government bond	Skr1,000,000	OM	954,881
Swiss government bond	Sfr100,000	SOFFEX	955,895

Source: *Futures & Options World*

Authorization

- Ensure that senior management permit the use of futures and options.
- Ensure that the firm is authorized to deal in futures and options and that client mandates, trust deeds scheme particulars, and so on permit their use.
- Identify any specific steps necessary to obtain authorization.
- Agree with trustees or senior management the circumstances in which

futures and options will be used; and

- Ensure that objectives are clear.

Back office

- Ensure that the back office is able to deal with futures and options.

- Decide whether new systems or staff are necessary, or whether existing staff need special training.

- If buying a new system decide between an off-the-shelf solution and a made-to-measure system.

- Identify how a new system will integrate with existing settlement and administration systems.

Broker services

- Identify services required in:
  execution and clearing
  portfolio risk management advice
  market research, either quantative or fundamental,
  statistics and charts.

- Identify which brokers to use for trade execution and for clearing.

- Agree commissions and fees with each firm.

Clearing

- Decide whether separate accounts with clearing broker are needed.

- Agree how to settle and reconcile accounts with the clearing broker each day.

Initial margin procedures

- Agree which forms of initial margin can be deposited with each broker.

- Agree the level of interest the broker will pay on the balance of the margin deposit.

- Agree multicurrency arrangements for margin.

- Agree how to deal with the varying margin requirements on different exchanges.

- Ensure that the firm is able to deal with sudden changes in margin levels triggered by changing market conditions.

Reporting structure

- Identify the types of trade reports and confirmations that are required.

- Identify all the reports needed for the company's internal administration.

- Ensure that an appropriate internal reporting structure is in place. In particular ensure separation between back office and front office with separate management responsibility.

WHAT IS AN OPTION?

Definition	*An* **option** *is a contractual agreement which gives the buyer of the option the right, but not the obligation, to purchase "call" (or to sell "put") a specified security, currency or commodity (the "underlying") at a specified price during a specified period of time (or on a specified date).*

The basic definitions

All options have certain features which may be summarized as follows.

Buyer and seller

The buyer of an option acquires the right but not the obligation to do something. The buyer risks only the premium he pays for the option but assumes the credit risk that the seller of the option will not be able to perform his obligations under the option contract.

The seller (sometimes called the writer or grantor) receives a premium but in return may have an unlimited risk. The seller cannot control the exercise of an option once it has been sold. The seller does not, however, run any credit risk on the buyer of an option once the premium has been received.

The underlying

The subject of a bond option may be a bond or a future. An option may carry the entitlement to receive or deliver the underlying or to receive or pay cash calculated by reference to the value of the underlying.

Premium

The price at which an option is purchased is called the premium. In theory this is the value of the option, the price required by the seller to take on the risk involved in writing the option.

Value

The value of an option may be divided into two parts: present value and potential future value.

The present value of an option is usually referred to as its intrinsic value. This is the profit which could be realised by exercising the option at once.

The potential for future value in an option depends chiefly on two things. The first is the price behavior of the underlying. If the price fluctuates considerably it is said to be volatile. High volatility increases the value of an option. This is because if the price of the underlying has seen large movements in the past it is thought more likely that similar large movements will occur in the future. Such large movements increase the chance that the option will come to have value, or more value, at expiry

The second component is the amount of an option's remaining life. This is the time value of an option.

Because "while there is life there is hope" an option always has some time value, however little. It is usually (but not always) better to sell an option rather than exercise it early for this reason since exercise captures only the intrinsic value of an option.

During its life an option's value will rise and fall. An option may be traded profitably over its life even though it may expire worthless.

Exercise or strike price

The specified price at which an option may be exercised is known as the exercise or strike price. When the exercise price is compared to the actual price of the underlying the option is said to be: "at the money" if the exercise price and the actual price are equal; "in the money" if the exercise price is so related to the price of the underlying that the holder of the option could realize an immediate profit by exercising the option and executing a transaction in the underlying; or "out of the money" if the exercise price is so related to the price of the under-lying that the holder of the option would realize a loss by exercising the option and executing a transaction in the underlying.

A call option is "in the money" and has intrinsic value if the price of the underlying is above the exercise price. A put option is "in the money" and has intrinsic value if the price of the underlying is below the exercise price.

The premium for an option which is "in the money" will be higher than that for a similar option which is "at the money". The premium for an option which is "out of the money" will be lower than that for a similar option which is "at the money".

Expiry date

The last business day on which an option may be exercised is known as the expiry date.

Exercise

Exercise of an option is the purchase or sale of the underlying at the strike price by the holder of a call or a put.

In the case of options on futures the holder of an option will be assigned a futures position. For example, the holder of a call option will be assigned a long futures position. The possible assignments are as follows:

Position in option	Futures position assigned
long a call	long futures
short a call	short futures
long a put	short futures
short a put	long futures

However some options are cash settled. That is to say that at expiry (or exercise) a reference price of the underlying is used to determine the value of the option and, if the value is positive, the cash amount is paid to the option holder. In the case of exchange-traded options it is usually assumed that the holder of an option which is in the money will want to exercise it and exercise is made automatic at expiry.

The decision to exercise is based on a calculation of whether exercise will afford a profit.

"American" and "European" options

The time at which an option may be exercised is usually specified as either a period of time or a specified date.

If exercise may be at any time within a specified period this is known as an "American" option.

If exercise may only be on a specified date this is known as a "European" option.

The price of two options, one European and one American, which are in all other respects identical, will be different. The American option will be worth more.

These terms are not indications of where the options are traded. Most options traded in Europe have American-style exercise provisions.

Calls and puts

A call (put) option gives the buyer of the option the right, but not the obligation, to buy (sell) the underlying security, currency, commodity or financial instrument at a specified price.

The buyer of a call (put) is said to be "long a call (put)" and the seller of a call (put) option is said to be "short a call (put)".

The value of a call (put) option rises (falls) as the value of the underlying security, currency or commodity rises and falls (rises) as the value of the underlying falls.

THE THEORY OF OPTION VALUATION

Probability and distribution

It is not possible to determine the future price of the underlying on the date when an option will expire. It is possible, however, to estimate the probability that the underlying will trade at a given price in the future. This is done by devising a model of the price behavior of the underlying.

Normal distributions

Following scientists observations of random events in nature the first model we could consider is a normal distribution. This is useful because it allows us to accomplish the key task which is to assign probabilities to possible future values of the underlying.

We make the assumption that the behavior of the underlying is random and that returns are normally distributed. This distribution is characteristic of many phenomena including, for instance, the results of throwing three dice. The shape of the graph is a curved bell falling on either side to two tails which are the extreme results. Throwing dice and getting three sixes or three ones is what makes the tails.

Standard deviation

This assumption allows the use of statistical concepts, particularly standard deviation. Standard deviation measures the spread of values around the mean. It is defined as the square root of the mean of the squared deviations of members of a population from their mean. In practise this is used as a measure of risk.

In a normal distribution 68.3 percent of outcomes fall within one standard deviation on either side of the mean and some 95 percent within two standard deviations.

Thus for a normally distributed sample of bond price returns if the mean return is +2.00 percent and the standard deviation is 6.00 percent, there is a 68.3 percent chance that the return will be between −4.00 percent and +8.00 percent. Similarly, the probability of a particular range of returns can be calculated and thus we have a method for calculating probabilities of future prices and thus for pricing options.

Distributions which are not normal

However for many securities, including bonds, the observed distributions are not normal. This presents us with a problem because if the distribution of results is not normal then our probability calculations will be unreliable. If the results were in fact tightly clustered around the mean the probability calculated in the example above would be an underestimate of the true probability of a return in the range −4.00 percent to +8.00 percent. Conversely, if the results were more widely dispersed then we would have overestimated the probability of a result within that range.

Lognormal distribution

A lognormal distribution is often used in pricing models. This is simply the normal distribution applied to the logarithms of the prices of the underlying.

Using logarithms we have a world where a bond price is as likely to halve as it is to double. This can be illustrated as follows:

Price	Logarithm	Difference
$100	4.60517	
$200	5.29832	+ 0.69315
$50	3.91202	− 0.69315

A lognormal distribution when plotted in price terms rather than in logarithm terms appears positively skewed. That is to say for a bond trading at $100, future prices of $200 (double) and $50 (half) would appear symetrically when plotted as logarithms on a lognormal graph but, clearly, are not symetrically placed when plotted in price terms.

Nonlognormal distribution

Options on fixed-income securities deal with a much less complicated underlying security than do, for example, equity options. First, the range of factors influencing a bond price is smaller than for an equity. The chief factor determining the price of a bond is the general level of interest rates. Second, the range of possible price movements is less for a bond than for an equity. Debt securities tend to approach their redemption value at maturity. Equities have no redemption value and no limit on possible upward movement in price. However the approach of maturity on a long-term bond hardly influences the value of, say, a three-month option on a twenty year bond.

Volatility of even long-term bond prices is often less than the volatility of an equity index and usually less than the volatility of a particular share. Only on long-term bonds are different estimates of volatility likely to be very significant

Duration

Duration is a crucial measure of bond price volatility. As we have seen duration is the weighted average life of the cash flows of a bond. Modified Duration is duration divided by $(1+ i/n)$ where i is the yield to maturity in decimal form and n is the number of interest payments per year. Modified Duration can be used to calculate the percentage price volatility of a bond for a given change in interest rates.

Generally it is the case that the longer the maturity of a bond the greater the volatility. For bonds with identical final maturity dates, the bond with the longer duration (eg a zero coupon bond) will be more volatile than the bond with shorter duration (eg a bond with annual coupon).

Path dependence

It must be noted that we may be interested in more than just a final price of the underlying. The underlying generates an income stream and it may be that an option is capable of exercise before expiry.

Events over the life of an option will often have to be incorporated into its valuation.

Binomial models

A third key concept is the binomial model. Such models assume a finite number of time periods with two (binomial) or sometimes three (trinomial) possible price movements in each period.

These models tend to approach the normal distribution as a limit and are therefore not very reliable when dealing with an underlying distribution which is not normal or lognormal.

This approach to option valuation is useful because it allows adjustments for cash flows or early exercise. It also permits the valuation of path-dependent options where not only the final outcome but also the route taken to get there is important.

Put/call parity

There is a relationship between the price of a put and the price of a call at the same strike price. This is because it is possible to construct a synthetic version of the purchase of either option by means of a combination of the other option and the underlying.

"The pricing of options must be consistent whatever the model used to do so. This is because of put/call parity."

For example, being long a call is equivalent to being long the underlying and long a put both at the same strike price as the call.

The first rudimentary test of an option pricing model is whether it gives option values that are in accord with put/call parity. This test works whatever the option pricing model being used.

"The theoretical fair value of an option is the price which an option writer would need to receive so as to be able to construct a risk-free hedge of his position."

Black–Scholes

In 1973 Fischer Black and Myron Scholes published a theoretical valuation formula for stock options. It was based on the idea of the cost of a riskless hedge.

A riskless hedge was closely defined and certain assumptions were made. The definition was that for small price changes close to the current price of the underlying it is possible to construct a hedge position in the underlying which will change in value exactly with the option being hedged. This is what we know as delta hedging.

Black

A modification of the Black-Scholes model was devised by Black for options on bond futures. The Black pricing model is used, for instance, at LIFFE. The interest rate component set to zero because these are options on futures contracts and because premium is not paid upfront but through futures-style margining.

$$C = F \times N (d_1) - X \times N(d_2)$$

where $d_1 = \dfrac{\ln(F/X) + 1/2 \times S^2 \times T}{S \times \sqrt{T}}$

$d_2 = d_1 - S \times \sqrt{T}$

C   = call premium
F   = price of the underlying contract
X   = strike price
S   = volatility measured by annual standard deviation
T   = time to expiration in years
N(.) = cumulative function of normal distribution.

Assumptions

This model makes various assumptions which need to be considered carefully. It will become clear from what follows that valuing options is not a precise science, however seemingly scientific the methods may be.

Price of the underlying
It is assumed that bond prices follow a random continuous walk and that at the end of a period the distribution of possible prices is lognormal. However market movements are not random and the returns are not always lognormally distributed. Prices do not always move continuously but can jump.

Volatility
Volatility is assumed to be constant. In practice the volatility of the underlying will change over the life of the option. It is also the case

that the volatility used to price an option differs according to whether the option is in, at or out of the money. Volatility does not remain constant.

Exercise

The formula values only European options exerciseable at maturity.

Commissions

It is assumed that there are no transaction costs in buying or selling either options or the underlying.

Many practitioners live with the defects, being content to increase their volatility assumptions when in doubt.

THE ELEMENTS OF VALUE IN AN OPTION

The theoretical fair value of an option is the price which an option writer would need to receive so as to be able to construct a risk-free hedge of his position. That is the theory which lies behind the Black–Scholes formula.

From the point of view of a holder of an option the value of an option has two parts: intrinsic value and/or the possibility of having intrinsic value during its life (usually referred to as time value). We will look at each in turn.

Intrinsic value

The first and main element of intrinsic value is the profit which could be made now by exercising an option and simultaneously executing an offsetting trade in the underlying. An option in this position is described as being "in the money".

Possible future value

An option which is "out of the money" and therefore has no intrinsic value still has value as it is possible that it will become "in the money" before it expires. The value given to the possibility that an option will have intrinsic value in the future (its current time value) is made up of two components: time and volatility.

> "Option values do not include any prediction about the direction of actual price movements of the underlying but include only a view about the likely size of those movements."

Time

The longer the period of time to expiry of the option the greater the chance that the option will come to be "in the money" before the expiry date.

Consequently longer term options are more valuable than shorter term options although not proportionately so. For example, a six-month option will be more expensive than a one-month option but not six times more expensive.

The time value of an option decreases as the time to expiry decreases but falls more sharply as an option approaches its expiry date.

Volatility

The likelihood of an option being profitably exercised in the future depends on the volatility of the price of the underlying. In an extreme case where the price of the underlying has changed only by small amounts over a period of time (ie its price volatility is low) it might be expected that an out-of-the-money option is unlikely ever to be in-the-money. Conversely with a very volatile underlying an option which was a long way out of the money might still be thought likely to be in the money before expiry. Consequently the higher the volatility of the underlying the greater will be the value of the option.

Option values do not include any prediction about the direction of actual price movements of the underlying but include only a view about the likely size of those movements.

Market conditions

In addition to the factors already identified which govern option values, option prices may be influenced by market-related factors. These may include illiquidity in the underlying or in the option itself, sudden changes in market levels causing widespread revision of volatility assumptions and temporary reductions in appetite for risk.

VOLATILITY

The key assumption in most pricing models is that made about future volatility. While most of the other inputs to an option pricing model can be tested or checked, the volatility figure is subjective.

Measuring volatility

Volatility is measured as the variance or annualized standard deviation of the underlying. Standard deviation is a measure of variation about a mean familiar to statisticians. It is defined as the square root of the mean of the squared deviations of a sample from its mean.

Volatility is expressed as a percentage. An annualized volatility of 8 percent means that over a period of one year the price of the underlying would be expected to be within one standard deviation (8 percent) of the current price 68 percent of the time and within two standard deviations (16 percent) 95 percent of the time.

Standard deviations are most useful when looking at normally distributed random variables. As we saw ealier normal distributions are not often observed in most financial markets.

Historic volatility

Historic volatility may be established objectively but the choice of period during which it is measured and the weighting given to each period will both affect the result.

The judgment of which period to use or how to weight the periods is subjective even though historic volatility purports to be an objective measure.

Implied volatility

Implied volatility is the volatility implicit in an option price. While the volatility implicit in an option price can be calculated from the price the choice of that volatility number by the writer of an OTC option is partly subjective. Other market participants will often have a different expected volatility. In the case of traded options the implied volatility represents a temporary market consensus.

MEASURES OF CHANGING VALUES AND RELATIONSHIPS

Delta

Of the measures which express the sensitivity of an option or portfolio of options to a change in one of the components of its value Delta is perhaps the most useful.

Delta is an expression of the correlation between price changes in the option and price changes in the underlying. It is a useful measure in determining the hedge needed to eliminate the market risk in an option position.

Gamma

Gamma is the measure of the rate of change of delta in relation to a movement in the underlying. From the analysis of delta we can see that gamma will tend to be lower when an option is deeply in the money or deeply out of the money. The gamma of an at-the-money option will be higher. As an option approaches expiry the gammas of deeply in- or out-of-the-money options will tend to decline while the gamma of an at-the-money option will increase. This is because the delta of at-the-money options is volatile.

Theta

Theta is the rate of change of an option's price for a given change in time. The theta of an option increases as expiry approaches. This is because the time value of an option declines at an accelerating rate as it comes closer to expiry in a manner related to the square root of the time remaining.

Vega

The vega of an option or portfolio is the rate of change in value in relation to a movement in the volatility of the underlying.

A portfolio of options which has been delta hedged with positions in the underlying will tend to have a high vega. This is because the value of the option positions is sensitive to changes in volatility while the value of the positions in the underlying is not affected at all by changes in volatility.

Rho

Rho is a measure of the sensitivity of an option to movements in interest rates. Currency options may have two rhos because option value is affected by changes in the interest rates in each currency.

VARIETIES OF OPTION STRUCTURE

These esoteric options modify what you thought you knew about expiry, strike price, and premium and serve to illustrate the variety of options available in the OTC market.

Path dependent options

The value of a path dependent option is determined not only by the value of the underlying at expiry but by the route the underlying takes to get there.

Such options have an expiry price as well as an expiry date. If the underlying reaches the expiry price then the option expires immediately.

The possibility that a path dependent option may expire worthless before its nominal expiry date causes such an option to cost less than a conventional option. If we think back to the binomial tree we can see why this is so. The structure effectively cuts off branches from the tree, reducing the range of possible outcomes at maturity.

One type of barrier option is sometimes called an "out option" (or knock-out option). These may be "down-and-out" or "up-and-out" options. Out options have both an expiry date and an expiry price or "outstrike". They expire if the underlying breaches the outstrike. In either case the further away the outstrike is from the current price of the underlying the closer the price of the out option will be to that of a standard option.

"In options" (or knock-in options) are option contracts which become conventional options once the underlying has reached an "instrike price". These may be "down and in" or "up and in" options. The strike price may be the same as the instrike or may be set at another level. An in option plus an out option with identical terms and the same instrike/outstrike equate to a conventional option.

Deferred strike options

As its name implies a deferred strike option is one where all the terms are set except the strike price. The level of the strike is then set subsequently according to an agreed mechanism within or at the end of a predetermined period. Afterwards the option becomes a normal option.

The main merit of such options is that they allow the buyer to take a view on volatility separately from taking a view on the underlying market. A buyer will purchase the right to an option at a lower volatility than she expects to have to pay when she wants to fix the strike price.

Contingent premium options

A contingent premium option is an option where the buyer pays no initial premium but agrees to pay a premium only if the option has any value at expiry.

Note that a deferred premium option is different. In that case the premium is always payable whatever the value of the option but actual payment is postponed.

The premium for a contingent premium option will be higher than for a conventional option even though the payoff will be the same.

The main use is where buyers are reluctant to hedge a position believing the hedge to be either unnecessary or merely a form of disaster insurance and therefore do not wish to pay for it up front.

> "The main use is where buyers are reluctant to hedge a position believing the hedge to be either unnecessary or merely a form of disaster insurance and therefore do not wish to pay for it up front."

Asian options

Also known as Average Rate or Average Price options, Asian options have a value which is determined by calculating the difference between the strike price (or rate) and the average price (or rate) during a selected period. The theoretical price will be less than that of a conventional option because the value starts to crystallize at the start of the averaging period, so shortening the effective life of the option.

An Asian option may be thought of as being like a series of smaller options each maturing on a different day of the selected period. However, the price of the Asian option will be less than that of such a series of options because in calculating the value of an Asian option negative values offset positive values, reducing its value. With a series of options there is no such offsetting.

Look-back options

As its name implies, a look-back option gives the holder the retrospective right to buy or sell the underlying at the most favorable price seen during a selected period. These are sometimes called "hindsight" options.

WHERE ARE OPTIONS OBTAINED?

Options are best thought of as being either "over-the-counter" (OTC) options or exchange-traded options.

OTC options

Originally all options were traded "over the counter" (OTC). The purchaser of an option dealt directly with one institution on terms agreed between them reflecting the buyer's requirements. The buyer of an OTC option must accept the credit risk of the option writer and may not always be easily able to sell or cancel the option contract at an acceptable cost. OTC options continue to have the advantage of being tailored to the needs of individual buyers which may not be satisfied by traded options.

One method of estimating the size and growth rate of OTC options activity is to look at the reports of the International Swaps and Derivatives Association (ISDA). ISDA reported that a survey of its members at 31 December 1995 showed outstanding interest rate options totalling US$3,704 billion, up 36% on the previous year. The figures include caps, floors, options on caps and floors, participations, combinations and swaptions.

Exchange-traded options

Exchange-traded options are standardized contracts with established settlement and clearance procedures. The buyer of an exchange-traded option cannot have the tailored terms of an OTC option but gains transparency of price and liquidity in most market conditions.

The credit risk assumed by the buyer of an option is transferred from a single company to the exchange clearing house. In an OTC contract the buyer of an option relies on the seller for performance. In the case of a long-dated or very volatile option the credit risk may be considerable. Thus transfering this risk from a single counterparty to a clearing house may seem attractive. It should be noted, however, that not all clearing houses operate in the same way and they represent, therefore, credit risks of varying quality.

Comparison of OTC and exchange-traded options

Comparison of OTC and exchange-traded options

Table 5.3

	OTC	Exchange traded
Contract terms	Flexible	Fixed
Strike prices	Flexible	Fixed
Expiration	Flexible	Fixed
Period	One day to very long term	Usually under twelve months
Contract amount	Flexible	Fixed, with small contract units
Secondary trading	No	Yes

	OTC	Exchange traded
Price transparency	Not always	Yes
Commissions	No	Yes
Trading hours	All	Market hours

Option trading volumes

Arranged by type of underlying the leading traded option contracts in 1995 are shown in Table 5.4.

Table 5.4

Leading traded option contracts, 1995

Contract	Size	Exchange	Volume
USA			
US Treasury bond	$100,000	CBOT	25,639,950
US Treasury note 10 yr	$100,000	CBOT	6,887,102
France			
Notional bond 10 yr	Ffr500,000	MATIF	9,517,932
Germany			
German Bund	DM250,000	LIFFE	6,988,666
German Bund future	DM250,000	DTB	194,036
German Bobl	DM250,000	DTB	123,019
Italy			
BTP option	ITL200,000,000	LIFFE	1,130,762
Other			
Australian 3-year T-bond	A$100,000	SFE	426,836
Australian 10-year T-bond	A$100,000	SFE	580,091
Danish long-term bond	DKK1,000,000	FUTOP	78,971
Spanish 10-year notional bond	PTS10,000,000	MEFFRF	1,888,547

Source: *Futures & Options World*

The bond-based contracts traded at LIFFE are shown in Table 5.5.

Table 5.5

Bond-based contracts, LIFFE

Contract	Future	Option
German Government bond (Bund)	*	*
Italian Government bond (BTP)	*	*
Japanese Government bond (JGB)	*	
UK Government bond (Long Gilt)	*	*

The Government futures and options traded at the Chicago Board of Trade are shown in Table 5.6.

Table 5.6

Government futures and options, Chicago Board of Trade

Contract	Future	Option
Two-year US Treasury note	*	*
Five-year US Treasury note	*	*
Ten-year US Treasury note	*	*
US Treasury bond	*	*

Derivatives on the Internet

Many of the derivatives exchanges have introduced internet sites. These include:

CBOT	http://www.cbot.com
LIFFE	http://www.liffe.com/
MATIF	http://www.matif.fr

■ ■ ■

"There are four basic positions which may be taken with a single option transaction. These are the building blocks for more elaborate strategies."

What can an Investor do with Options?

6

INTRODUCTION

In Chapter 5 we dealt with the theoretical basis on which options are valued. In this chapter we look at both the theory and the practice of using options. In the theoretical part we consider first synthetics – that is creating the equivalent of an option with either other options or positions in a mixture of options and the underlying. Then we analyze the basic option strategies identifying what each one risks and achieves. Then, turning to practice, we review some of the simple types of option trade which a bond portfolio manager might employ giving worked examples.

OPTION STRATEGIES

There are four basic positions which may be taken with a single option transaction. These are the building blocks for more elaborate strategies.

Long a call

The holder of a call enjoys profit potential if the underlying rises and risks only the premium he has paid.

Fig 6.1

Long a call

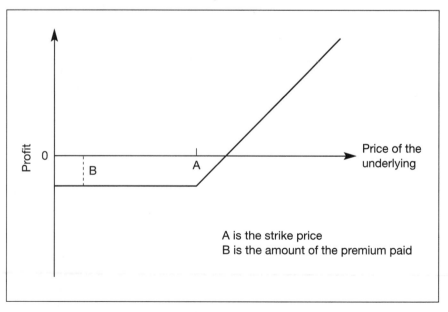

A is the strike price
B is the amount of the premium paid

Short a call

The writer of a call risks an unlimited loss if the underlying rises and will enjoy at best a profit equal to the premium he received.

Short a call

Fig 6.2

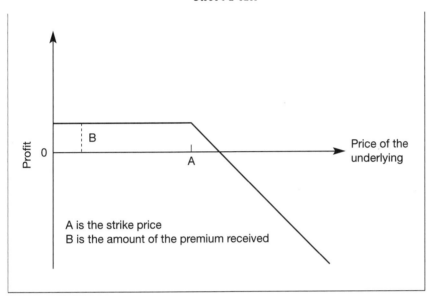

A is the strike price
B is the amount of the premium received

Long a put

The holder of a put enjoys profit potential if the underlying falls and risks only the premium he has paid.

Long a put

Fig 6.3

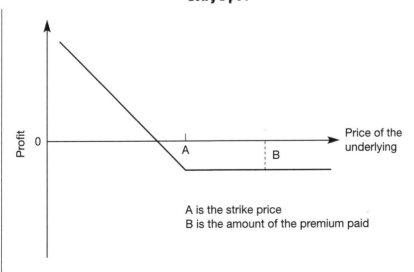

A is the strike price
B is the amount of the premium paid

Short a put

The writer of a put risks a large loss if the underlying falls and will enjoy at best a profit equal to the premium he received.

Fig 6.4

Short a put

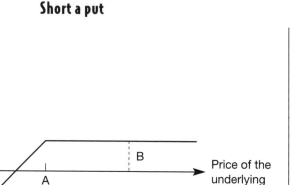

A is the strike price
B is the amount of the premium received

SYNTHETICS

It will be clear that certain option positions are equivalent to positions in the underlying or to positions which combine the underlying and other options. These are often referred to as synthetics. Their significance is that they establish a pricing equilibrium or, if not, then they offer arbitrage possibilities.

Figures 6.5 to 6.10 set out some of these equivalents.

(a) Position: Long a call

Fig 6.5

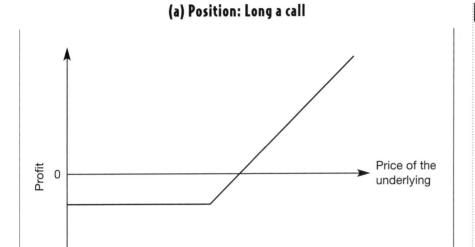

(b) Synthetic: Long the underlying; long a put

Fig 6.5

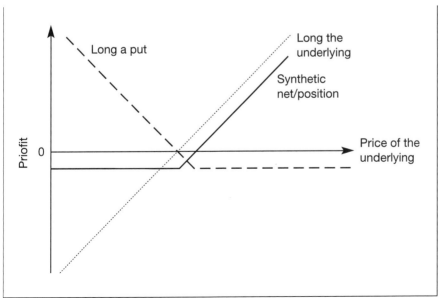

Fig 6.6

(a) Position: Short a call

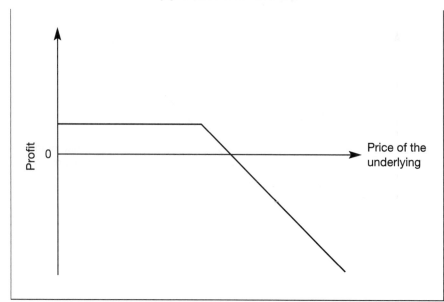

Fig 6.6

(b) Synthetic: Short the underlying; short a put

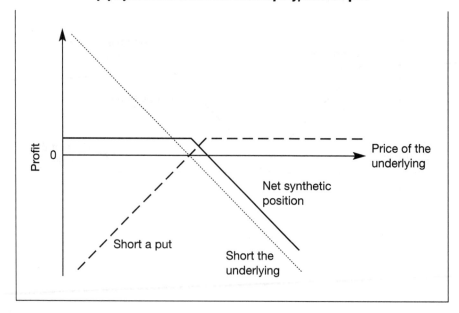

(a) Position: Long a put

Fig 6.7

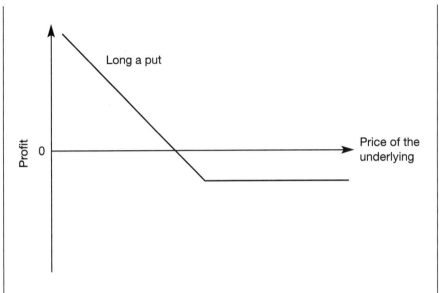

(b) Synthetic: Short the underlying; long a call

Fig 6.7

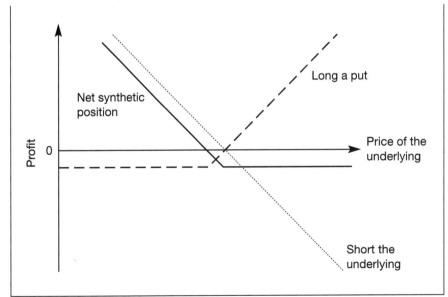

Fig 6.8

(a) Position: Short a put

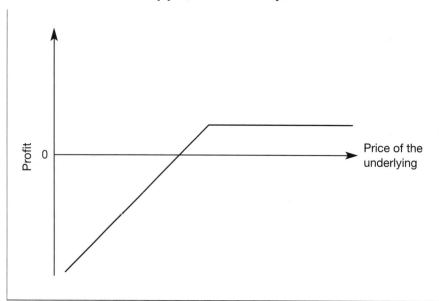

Fig 6.8

(b) Synthetic: Long the underlying; short a call

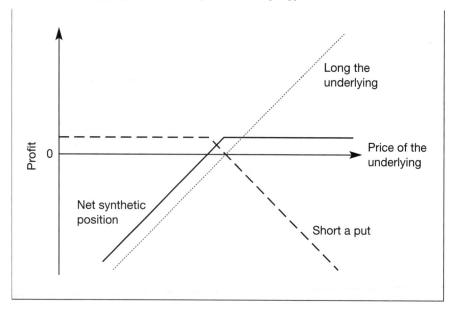

(a) Position: Long the underlying

Fig 6.9

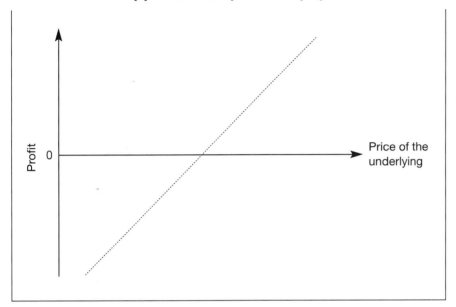

(b) Synthetic: Short a put at A; long a call at A

Fig 6.9

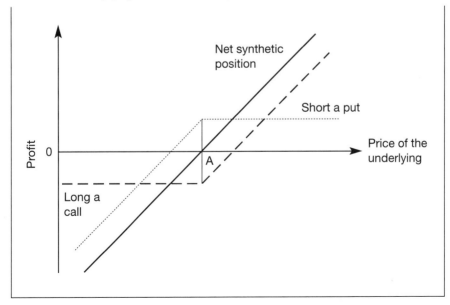

Fig 6.10

(a) Position: Short the underlying

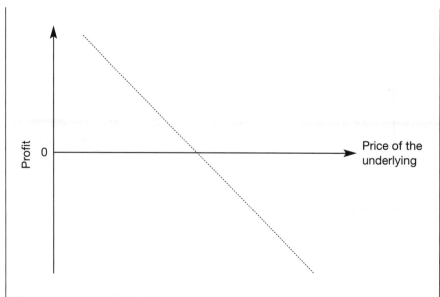

Fig 6.10

(b) Synthetic: Long a put at A; short a call at A

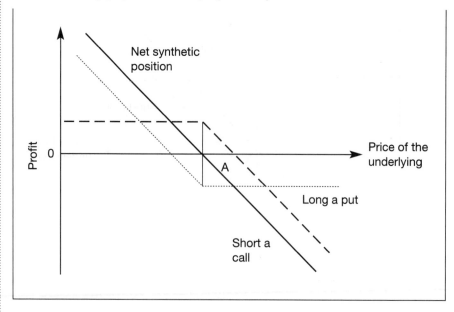

Now we turn to some of the ways in which option transactions can be combined. In each case we summarize the likely motive and the risk profile of each strategy.

The pay-off figures which follow ignore transaction costs which in reality may materially alter the attractiveness of certain strategies.

SIMPLE SPREADS

A vertical spread involves the simultaneous purchase of one option and the sale of another at different strike prices. The options will be either both puts or both calls and will have the same expiry date.

A horizontal spread (usually known as a calendar spread) involves the simultaneous purchase of one option and the sale of a shorter dated option at the same strike price.

A diagonal spread involves two positions with different expiry dates as well as different strike prices.

A spread is "bought" when there is a net premium cost and "sold" when there is net premium income on establishing the spread.

BULL AND BEAR SPREADS

Bull spreads and bear spreads are directional trades. That is to say that they are undertaken with a view of the probable direction of future price movements in the underlying.

Bull spread

Buy the bull spread. Buy a call at X and sell a call at Y. Both positions have the same expiry date. The strike price of the short position is higher than that of the long position. This is a vertical spread.

You believe that the price of the underlying will rise but want to limit your risk or you are only moderately bullish about the underlying. By giving away some of the upside potential of owning a call you reduce the cost of your position.

Advantages
Both potential profit and potential loss are limited. The maximum loss will be if, at expiry, the underlying is trading at or below X. Your

Fig 6.11

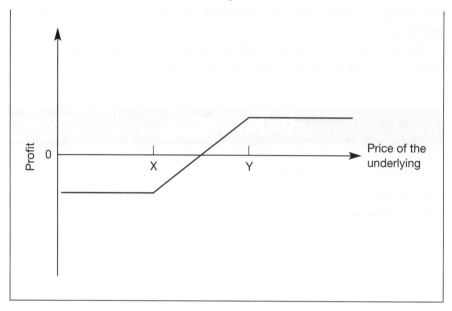

Bull spread

loss will be the net cost of your position (ie the cost of the long call position at a strike price of X less the premium earned by selling the call at Y). The maximum profit will be if, at expiry, the underlying is trading at or above Y. Your profit will be (Y – X) less the net cost of your position. Breakeven is when the underlying is trading at a price equivalent to X plus the net cost of your position.

Bear spread

Sell the bear spread. Buy a call at Y and sell a call at X. Both positions have the same expiry date. The strike price of the short position is lower than that of the long position.

You believe that the price of the underlying will fall or you are happy to earn premium while capping your downside risk.

Advantages
Both potential profit and potential loss are limited. The maximum profit will be if, at expiry, the underlying is trading at or below X. Your profit will be the net premium income received on establishing your position. The maximum loss will be if, at expiry, the underlying is trading at or above Y. Your loss will be (Y – X) less the net gain on establishing your

Bear spread

Fig 6.12

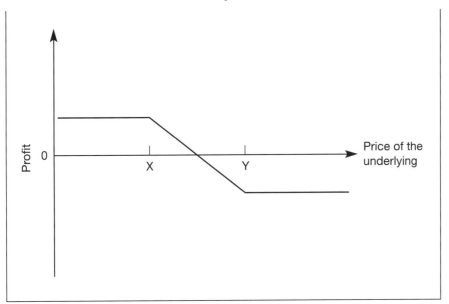

position. Breakeven is when the underlying is trading at a price equivalent to Y less the net gain on establishing your position.

CALENDAR SPREADS

A calendar spread involves the simultaneous purchase and sale of two options at the same strike price but with different expiry dates. The object is to exploit the different speeds of time decay of short- and long-dated options. The loss of time value becomes faster as an option approaches expiry. Shorter options therefore lose value faster than longer dated options, other things being equal. Therefore a calendar spread will involve the sale of a short-dated option and the purchase of a longer dated option. Often such spreads are at the money and are called neutral but can be combined with a view on the likely direction of the price of the underlying. A calendar spread will be most profitable when the price of the underlying is close to the strike price at the time that the shorter option expires.

Buy the March–June calendar spread. Buy a June call and sell a March call both at a strike price of X.

Example

Fig 6.13

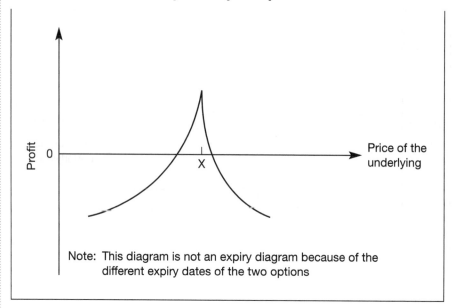

Calendar spread: expected profit or loss

Note: This diagram is not an expiry diagram because of the different expiry dates of the two options

The underlying is expected to be close to the strike price of the short option at the date of that option's expiry. This will allow the March option to expire at small or no expense while the June option may be sold at a price likely to generate a profit.

Advantages

At the expiry of the March option if the underlying is below X then the March option will expire worthless. The price of the June option will have fallen and a loss will be incurred. If the underlying is trading at X then the March option will be worthless but the June option will still have a value similar to its value when bought and will be sold to generate a net profit. If the underlying has risen sharply the March option will have to be repurchased for its intrinsic value while the June option, being deep in the money, will probably trade on a smaller spread than at inception. Deeply in the money options are expensive in terms of premium paid because of their high intrinsic value. They are less attractive because less geared than an at the money option.

BUTTERFLY SPREADS

A butterfly spread combines a vertical bull spread and a vertical bear spread with the same expiry dates for all the options and the same strike price for all short options. A "perfect" butterfly spread would require no net premium payment. The premium received on the options sold would equal the premium paid for the options bought. Butterfly spreads are rarely profitable.

Long butterfly spread

Buy a long butterfly spread. Buy calls at strike prices of A and C. Sell two calls at B. Assume A and C are equidistant from B.

You expect the underlying to move significantly but are not willing to take a view on the direction of that move.

Advantages
The maximum loss is the cost of the spread, whether the underlying moves up or down. The maximum profit will be earned if the underlying is trading below A or above C at expiry. The maximum loss will

Long a butterfly spread

Fig 6.14

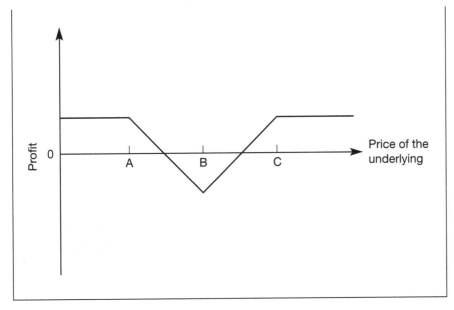

occur if the underlying closes at B. There are two breakeven points: prices equivalent to either A plus the cost of the spread, or C less the cost of the spread.

Short butterfly spread

Sell a short butterfly spread. Sell calls at A and C and buy two calls at B.

You expect the underlying to stay close to B but want to be protected should the underlying rise or fall substantially.

Advantages

The maximum profit is the net premium received on establishing the spread. The maximum profit occurs when the underlying closes at B. The maximum loss will be earned if the underlying is trading below A or above C at expiry. There are two breakeven points: prices equivalent to either A plus the initial credit, or C less the initial credit.

Short a butterfly spread

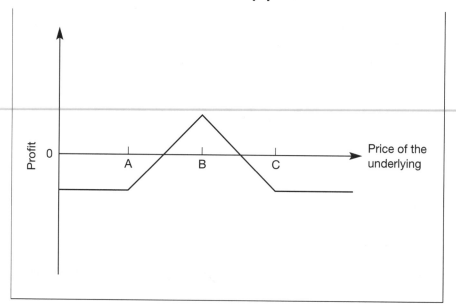

STRADDLES

Straddles are more aggressive than spread positions. Profit or exposure may be open ended.

Long straddle

Buy a call at A. Buy a put at A.

The underlying is close to A and you expect a significant movement but are not sure of the direction.

Advantages

Maximum profit is unlimited in either direction. If there is a substantial move in the underlying one of the options will expire worthless but the other will entitle you to benefit from all the movement in the underlying. Maximum loss is incurred if the underlying closes at A and will be the total premium paid for the straddle. Breakeven occurs at two prices equivalent to A plus the total premium paid for the straddle and A minus the total premium paid for the straddle.

Long a straddle

Fig 6.16

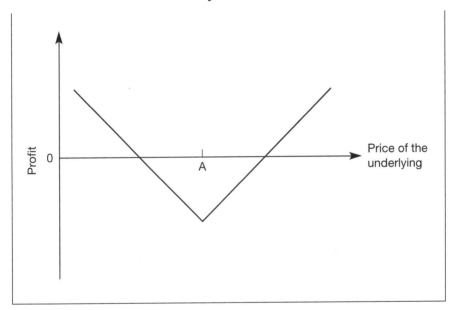

Short Straddle

Sell a call at A. Sell a put at A.

The underlying is close to A and you expect very little movement.

Advantages

This can be very dangerous. The maximum loss is unlimited in either direction. Maximum profit is achieved if the underlying closes at A and both options expire worthless. It is equivalent to the premium earned on selling the options. Breakeven occurs at two prices equivalent to A plus the premium received and A minus the premium received.

Fig 6.17

Short a straddle

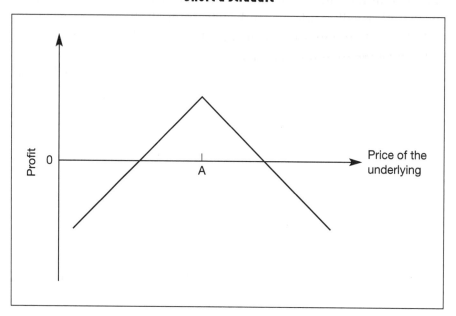

STRANGLES

Strangles are essentially straddles but with different strike prices for each option. Strangles are sometimes called spraddles.

Long strangle

Buy a call at B. Buy a put at A.

The underlying is between A and B and you expect a sharp movement but are not sure of the direction.

Advantages
Maximum profit is unlimited in either direction. Maximum loss is incurred if the underlying closes between A and B being the total premium paid. Breakeven occurs at two prices equivalent to A minus the total premium paid and B plus the total premium paid.

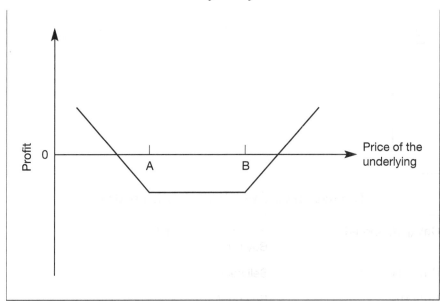

Long strangle

Fig 6.18

Short strangle

Sell a call at B. Sell a put at A.
   The underlying is between A and B and you expect very little movement.

Advantages
The maximum loss is unlimited in either direction. Maximum profit is achieved if the underlying closes between A and B and both options expire worthless. It is equivalent to the premium earned on selling the options. Breakeven occurs at two prices equivalent to A less the premium earned and B plus the premium earned.

Fig 6.19

Short strangle

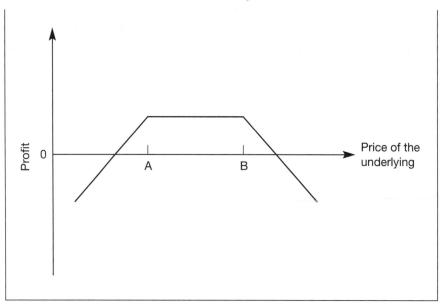

Table 6.1

Combinations and variations of option strategies

Call (put) spread	Buy call, sell call at higher strike. Buy put, sell put at lower strike.
Calendar spread	Sell near put (call), buy far put (call).
Butterfly	Buy put (call), sell two puts (calls) at higher strike, buy put (call) at a strike higher by the same amount again.
Straddle	Buy put, buy call at same strike.
Strangle	Buy put, buy call at higher strike.
Diagonal calendar spread	Sell near put (call), buy far put (call) at different strike.
Guts	Buy call, buy put at higher strike.
Iron butterfly	Buy straddle, sell strangle.
Ladder	Buy call, sell call at higher strike, sell call at equally higher strike.
Straddle calendar spread	Sell straddle in near month, buy straddle in far month at same strike.
Diagonal straddle calendar spread	Sell straddle in near month, buy straddle in far month at different strike.

SUMMARY

In order to summarize the above and to include some combinations and variations Table 6.1 on the previous page may be useful. It may be encouraging to know that these are not just invented to puzzle the reader. All are recognized as LIFFE option strategy trades and may be executed simultaneously as single trades at LIFFE.

> **"Bond options deal with a much less complicated underlying security than do equity options."**

CHARACTERISTICS OF BOND OPTIONS

We have noted that volatility of even long-term bond prices is often less than the volatility of an equity index and usually less than the volatility of a particular share. Only on long-term bonds are different estimates of volatility likely to be very significant

> **"Duration is a crucial measure of bond price volatility."**

Table 6.2 illustrates the comparative volatilities of bonds, equities and foreign exchange in seven major countries in the period 1990 to 1994:

Table 6.2   Comparative volalities of bonds, equities and foreign exchange, 1990–94

Country	Volatility of bond yields	Volatility of share prices	Volatility of exchange rates
USA	0.23	2.8	1.5
Japan	0.38	5.8	2.4
Germany	0.22	4.1	0.9
France	0.31	5.3	0.7
Italy	0.46	6.6	1.9
UK	0.36	3.7	2.0
Canada	0.31	3.5	1.1

Source: OECD, Economics Department Working Papers, No 154, 1995
Note: Volatility is measured as the standard deviation of monthly changes in percent

USING OPTIONS WITH A BOND PORTFOLIO

It is best to start with a simple trade: buying a call.

Example

Let us assume that an investor has bought a one month call on a bond. The face value is $25,000,000, the strike price is 99.00 and the premium is 15/32 percent.

The cost of this option may be shown as:

$$\$25,000,000 \times 15/32\% = \$117,187.50$$

The option premium is paid on the business day following the transaction.

At expiry if the bond is trading at 100.50 the investor will exercise the options. The profit will be:

$$(100.50 - 99.00) \times \$25,000,000 - \$117,187.50 = \$257,812.50$$

In other words he has bought bonds which are trading at 100.50 for an effective price of 99.00 and 15/32 option premium, or 99.46875.

So we can now look at some possible motivations.

An outright option trade

If a trader believed that the price of a particular bond future was going to rise he might decide to buy a call option. He would benefit from the expected price rise but would put at risk only the premium paid.

The price performance of the options bought would be positively affected by any increase in the price of the underlying future or by an increase in volatility of the underlying. The value of the calls would decrease with time as well as with any fall in the price of the underlying future or any decrease in its volatility.

Portfolio insurance

If an investor in government bonds wanted to protect his portfolio against an expected large fall in price he might hedge the risk with options.

Let us assume that he owns Lit25bn of Italian Government BTPs. The March futures price is 97.50 and the March 96.00 put option is quoted at 0.12 – 0.14. We will assume that the portfolio of BTPs will mirror exactly the futures contract and that the option is held to expiry. The nominal value of the future is Lit200 million and a tick is worth Lit20,000.

The investor buys 125 contracts at 0.14. This is calculated as 25 billion (the size of the portfolio) divided by 200 million (the nominal value of the future).

The investor is now protected from any decline in value below a futures price of 96.00.

In March the future is trading at 95.50 and the March 96.00 put is trading at 0.50 – 0.51. The investor sells 125 contracts at 0.50.

The result of the two option trades is as follows:

The profit per contract is 0.50 – 0.14 = 36 ticks

The overall profit is therefore 36 ticks × 125 contracts × Lit20,000 which equals Lit90,000,000.

Note that in reality there may be significant basis risk between the price of the futures and the value of the investor's portfolio. This is because the futures are based on government bonds while the portfolio is likely to contain a mixture of bonds with varying maturities. These bonds will not stay in a constant relationship to government bonds.

Income enhancement

Let us imagine an investor who holds DM30 million of German government bunds and does not expect the price to rise. He is under pressure to increase the income from his portfolio. One strategy would be to write calls against his portfolio.

The investor sees December 98.00 calls are trading at 0.38 – 0.40. He sells 120 calls at 0.38. (DM30,000,000 portfolio/DM250,000 nominal value). We assume the buyer holds the options to expiry. In December the futures price is below 98.00 and the option is not exercised.

The result of the option writing strategy is as follows:

The profit per contract is 38 ticks

The overall profit is therefore 38 ticks × 120 contracts × DM25 which equals DM114,000 or 0.38 percent of the portfolio.

Note that in reality there may be significant basis risk between the price of the futures and the value of the investor's portfolio as discussed above.

If the price of future had risen and the option had been exercised then the investor would have sacrificed the profit potential in his portfolio.

More aggressive trades (eg straddles and strangles) are also possible with the risk and reward characteristics described earlier in this book.

Managing option portfolios

For any participant in derivatives markets the 1993 Group of the 30 Report, *Derivatives: Practices and Principles*, though one of many reports published in recent years, is a useful guide. This report highlighted the following fundamental principles of good management which each dealer and end-user of derivatives should follow.

> **Determine at the highest level** of policy and decision-making the scope of its involvement in derivatives activities and policies to be applied.

> **Value derivatives positions at market,** on at least a daily basis for risk management purposes. Lower-of-cost-or-market accounting or accrual accounting are not appropriate for risk management. Intraday or even real time valuation may be appropriate for some option portfolios.
>
> The valuation should be based on mid-market levels less specific adjustments to allow for future costs such as unearned credit spread, closeout costs, investing and funding costs and administrative costs.

Quantify its market risk under adverse market conditions against limits, perform stress simulation, and forecast cash investing and funding needs. (This is dealt with in more detail below.)

Assess the credit risk arising from derivatives activities based on frequent measures of current and potential exposure against credit limits.

Reduce credit risk by broadening the use of multiproduct master agreements with closeout netting provisions. Aggregate credit exposures should be calculated across product areas taking into account enforceable netting agreements.

Establish market and credit risk management functions with clear authority, independent of the dealing function.

Authorize only professionals with the requisite skills and experience to transact and manage the risks, as well as to process, report, control and audit derivatives activities

Establish management information systems sophisticated enough to measure, manage and report the risks of derivatives activities in a timely and precise manner.

Voluntarily adopt accounting and disclosure practices for international harmonization and greater transparency.

RISK MEASUREMENT

"There are two components to be measured: market risk and credit risk."

There are two components to be measured: market risk and credit risk. Further considerations are liquidity risk, payment risk and operational risk.

Market risk

The market risk in a portfolio of options depends on the price behavior of the constituent parts of the portfolio when market conditions change. The assessment of market risk requires the components to be identified and their interrelationships to be understood. In an option portfolio the basic risks are as follows.

Absolute price or rate risk (delta)

This risk is familiar to us from the discussion of delta in the previous chapter. This risk is the exposure to a change in value of the portfolio resulting from change in the price of the underlying.

It will also be remembered that the sensitivity to this risk changes with changes in the underlying. As we have seen the hedging of such positions is a dynamic process which carries with it risks of unexpected hedging costs and sudden large price movements before hedges can be adjusted. Option positions are therefore sensitive to gaps in the price of the underlying as well as the direction of price movements.

Convexity risk (gamma)

We have seen that gamma is the measure of the expected change in delta. It is an expression of the risk described above where the relationship between an option and the underlying is not linear. The greater the gamma or convexity the more frequently the hedge in the underlying will need to be rebalanced and therefore the greater the risk.

Volatility risk (vega)

This is the risk that the value of an option will change with a change in the volatility of the underlying. The portfolio's value could change even if there was a negligible change in the price of the underlying.

Time decay risk (theta)

This is the exposure to a change in value arising from the passing of time. In the case of a single option the passing of time reduces the chance that the option will end up in the money (or further in the money). In a portfolio where options have been sold as well as bought the net exposure to time may be positive or negative.

Basis risk

This is the risk which relates to differences between the price change of an option and its hedge. This might arise where the hedge was not the same as the underlying of the option. In a portfolio where transactions are aggregated and the net exposure is hedged there may be maturity mismatches.

Interest rate risk (rho)

This is the risk that the value of a portfolio will change with a change in the interest rates used to value it.

Value at risk (VAR)

Market risk is best measured as "value at risk" (VAR). There are two main modelling techniques.

Variance/covariance analysis

This uses historic data on price volatilities and correlations within and between markets to estimate likely potential losses. Price changes are assumed to be normally distributed which allows a confidence level to be calculated.

This confidence level is calculated by reference to the standard deviation of historic price changes (volatility) multiplied by a scaling factor. If returns are normally distributed, there is a 1 percent chance that the return will be greater than 2,326 deviations from the mean. Thus if we wanted to have a 99 percent confidence interval we would multiply the historic volatility observed by 2.326.

The chief problem with this approach is that the assumption about distribution does not accord with observations in many markets where "fat-tailed" distributions and skewed distributions are frequently seen. The approach implicitly assumes that a portfolio's value changes linearly with changes in the underlying – in other words it ignores the effect of gamma.

Historical simulation

Here historical data are applied to a portfolio to calculate the changes in value which would have occurred if it had been in existence during that period. This allows the calculation of a 99 percent confidence interval without assuming a normal distribution by calculating the loss which would not have been exceeded on 99 percent of occasions. In this case the confidence interval is observed while before it was calculated statistically.

The simulation method can be adapted to deal with gamma and with basis risk.

Practical application

In practice a typical method of measuring "value at risk" for a portfolio of trading instruments might be as follows:

- Calculate volatilities and correlations from daily market data over the observation period (at least one year).
- Stochastically evolve today's market data forward over time at daily intervals for the "holding period" of, say, ten business days using the volatilities and correlations calculated.

- Recalculate the market value of the portfolio each day in the holding period and record the worst case.

- Repeat this calculation a large number of times (say 10,000).

- Rank the outcomes and take the appropriate percentile or confidence interval (say 99 percent) as the value at risk.

- Recalculate the monthly and quarterly rolling average value at risk.

Credit risk

Credit risk has two components: current exposure and potential exposure.

Current exposure

"Credit risk has two components: current exposure and potential exposure."

Current exposure to a counterparty in a single transaction is simply the cost of replacing the transaction. This may be positive or negative. If the cost is negative there will at least be no loss if the counterparty defaults.

With portfolios the calculation of current exposure depends on the extent to which exposures to a single counterparty across a range of transactions and product areas may be netted. If the sum of positive values can be reduced by the negative values the net risk will be lower.

The enforcability of netting provisions can be determined only on a jurisdiction-by-jurisdiction and case-by-case basis. In the absence of netting provisions only the positive should be used to calculate exposure.

Potential exposure

"Losses may occur because of human errors, inadequate systems or failures of management control."

Potential exposure is more difficult to establish. It requires an assessment of what the replacement costs could be in the future. Generally these modeling techniques produce both an "expected" and a "worst case" exposure.

Expected losses may be estimated by combining expected exposure with expected default rates.

With a portfolio potential exposures are easily overstated. Exposures may be offsetting or may peak at different times. Diversified portfolios with exposures to a wide range of counterparties will be unlikely to experience all the worst case outcomes at once.

Liquidity risk

This risk may take the form that a large transaction will affect the price of the instrument, or that in a thin or nervous market the bid-offer spread will widen. Liquidity may also be reduced by sudden price or volatility shocks or other unexpected events.

Option risk may be broken down into constituent parts so that risk liquidity is more significant than product liquidity. For example, a customized cap transaction might seem illiquid but the component risks might be liquid in other markets

Payment risk

Many transactions are not settled on a same-day basis. If market conditions change a counterparty may be unwilling or unable to make payment. Payment netting through clearing houses and through bilateral master agreements serves to reduce this risk.

Operational risk

Losses may occur because of human errors, inadequate systems or failures of management control. Six factors can be identified which reduce this risk:

- control by informed and involved senior management
- documentation of limits, policies and procedures
- independent risk-management function reporting to senior management
- independent internal audits which verify compliance with limits, policies and procedures
- back office equipped with proper technology and systems
- system of independent checks and balances at every stage of the transaction process from initiation to settlement.

Part Two

■ ■ ■

"UK Government bonds are known as gilts. They are marketable securities, denominated in sterling and issued by the government through the Bank of England."

United Kingdom

LEGAL FRAMEWORK

> "Trading in gilts is subject to the rules of the London Stock Exchange. Many of the major participants are supervised by the Bank of England, the Securities and Investments Board (SIB) and the Securities and Futures Authority (SFA)."

Form

UK government bonds are known as gilts. They are marketable securities, denominated in sterling and issued by the government through the Bank of England.

The obligations to pay principal and interest are a charge on the National Loans Fund, with recourse to the Consolidated Fund of the United Kingdom.

Some 95 percent of gilts by value are held in dematerialized book-entry form operated by the Central Gilts Office which is run by the Bank of England. These holdings are automatically registered with the Registrar's Department of the Bank of England.

Identification

UK securities, including gilts, are assigned a Stock Exchange Daily Official List (SEDOL) number. This seven-digit number is incorporated in the twelve-digit International Security Identification Number (ISIN) assigned to each gilt.

Regulation of the market

Trading in gilts is subject to the rules of the London Stock Exchange. Many of the major participants are supervised by the Bank of England, the Securities and Investments Board (SIB) and the Securities and Futures Authority (SFA).

TAXATION

STAR Accounts

Most holders of gilts who are not private individuals may receive interest gross without the deduction of withholding tax. This is achieved by holding gilts in gross paying STAR accounts at the Central Gilts Office.

To be eligible under the CGO STAR account system for gross payments of interest (referred to as "dividends" in the gilt market) bodies must be:

"The Inland Revenue maintains a list of 'recognized intermediaries' who hold stock on behalf of others."

- UK resident and subject to corporation tax
- companies not resident in the United Kingdom
- exempt bodies such as pension funds
- sovereign bodies not liable for UK tax.

An eligible market participant that is not a member of the CGO must make a declaration to a CGO member or to a "recognized intermediary" that it is an eligible body. This declaration will be inspected by the Inland Revenue. Such a declaration needs to be made only once for all current and future holdings of gilts, unlike the FOTRA declaration (see below) which must be made for each holding.

The Inland Revenue maintains a list of "recognized intermediaries" who hold stock on behalf of others. These will include Stock Exchange members, banks, building societies, and certain other UK and foreign intermediaries.

Taxation of UK entities

Those who are taxable in the UK must account quarterly for the tax due on gross interest received. This reporting requirement does not apply to overseas investors or exempt UK investors such as pension funds.

A fundamental reform of taxation affecting gilts and other bonds takes effect from April 1996. The total return on wholesale investors' holdings of gilts will be taxed as income.

Strippable gilts

One of the consequences of the planned introduction in 1997 of stripped gilts was that certain gilts would pay interest gross to all holders. The five stocks eligible for stripping initially, representing some £32.2 billion at 31 January 1996, were to pay interest gross to all holders, once the Treasury has made a direction under the Income and Corporation Taxes Act 1988. These five stocks are the 8% 2000,

> **"The UK has Double Taxation Agreements with some 75 countries which may permit the tax on interest deducted at source to be reclaimed in whole or in part by those who cannot benefit from the STAR account facility."**

8.5% 2005, 7.5% 2006, 8% 2015 and 8% 2021. They would not be subject to the quarterly accounting system described above.

FOTRA

A previously important distinction, that certain stocks are free of tax to residents abroad (FOTRA) on application to the Inspector of Foreign Dividends, is no longer meaningful for all corporate overseas investors and for most other investors. The FOTRA exemption applies to holdings and not to investors. An application must be made therefore for each holding. For this reason some overseas stockholders when selling their stocks kept very small holdings of each of their FOTRA stocks.

Double taxation treaties

The UK has Double Taxation Agreements with some 75 countries which may permit the tax on interest deducted at source to be reclaimed in whole or in part by those who cannot benefit from the STAR account facility.

Stamp duty and turnover tax

There is no stamp duty and no turnover tax.

PROFILE OF THE DEBT

Debt outstanding

At 29 December 1995 the nominal and market value of the sterling government bonds listed on the London Stock Exchange was as shown in Table 7.1.

Table 7.1

Nominal and market value of sterling government bonds listed on the London Stock Exchange, 29 December 1995

	No. of securities	Nominal value (£m)	Market value (£m)
Shorts (0–7 yrs)	31	78,516.8	83,253.0
Mediums (7–15 yrs)	26	74,193.0	80,896.2
Longs (over 15 yrs)	9	37,323.6	39,294.8
Undated	8	3,207.6	1,387.6
Index-linked	14	24,401.7	37,640.2
Variable rate	1	5,700.0	5,707.4
Bonds	5	11,061.0	11,231.8
Total	94	234,403.7	259,411.0

Source: London Stock Exchange

Debt maturity by year

At 7 February 1996 the outstanding government stocks matured as shown in Table 7.2. The first column excludes the index-linked stocks whose value at redemption is not known. These stocks are shown separately at their nominal amounts. It has been assumed that double dated stock are repaid on the latest date possible.

The yield curve

An inverted yield curve beyond 7–8 years is a frequent feature of the gilt market. In the 15 years to the end of March 1995 the average spread between the 10-year and the 20-year gilt yields was –25 basis points.

Possible reasons for this include the alleged preference of domestic institutional investors for long duration stocks, perhaps reflecting the UK"s highly developed long-term savings industry. Note that UK insurance companies own 30 percent of all gilts. The higher convexity of these bonds may also make them more attractive in volatile markets.

Another possible reason is to do with the behavior of speculative traders who may be most active in the 5–10 year maturities. This theory would have the hump becoming more pronounced in a falling market where such traders are selling their holdings.

Table 7.2

Maturity of government stocks, 7 February 1996

Year	Fixed amounts	Index linked
1996	5,359	1,200
1997	13,358	
1998	17,744	800
1999	20,300	2
2000	16,438	
2001	13,164	1,700
2002	6,738	
2003	11,170	1,700
2004	12,095	1,150
2005	15,965	
2006	11,906	1,950
2007	10,547	
2008	6,871	
2009	3,450	2,050
2010	4,750	
2011	5,273	2,500
2012	6,360	
2013	6,100	2,850
2015	10,300	
2016	78	3,050
2017	8,550	
2020		3,000
2024		2,700
2030		1,300
Total	232,469	

Source: Compiled from Bank of England information
Note: At this date there was a further £3,186 million of undated debt outstanding

INSTRUMENTS AND DERIVATIVES

Conventional stocks

These have a fixed coupon paid semi-annually and usually one fixed repayment date. There are eight undated stocks which have a fixed rate of interest but no repayment date. Three of these, $2\frac{1}{2}$ percent Consolidated stock, $2\frac{1}{2}$ percent Annuities and $2\frac{3}{4}$ percent Annuities have interest paid quarterly.

All gilts have a title. Some of these have no practical significance (eg Treasury, Exchequer, Funding) but some titles are significant. "Convertible" stocks give holders the right on specified terms and specified dates to convert all or part of their holding into one or more other specified stocks. "Conversion" is the title of stocks which came into being as a result of a conversion. "Loan" means that an investor may hold the stock in the form of bearer bonds.

"Double-dated" stocks (eg 8 percent Treasury Loan 2002–2006) give the government the right to redeem the stock at par on giving three months notice at any time after the first date. Such stocks must be redeemed by the second date.

New issues are sometimes in the form of 'Partly paid" stocks where the stock is paid for in two or three stages with interest accruing on the amount paid.

Index-linked stocks

Both the interest payments and the amount payable on redemption are adjusted in line with UK inflation as measured by the Retail Prices Index eight months in arrears.

Stockholders are protected against changes in the coverage of the index or its calculation. If the Bank of England considered that a fundamental change had been made which was materially detrimental to the interests of investors, then holders would be offered the right to require the Treasury to redeem their stock not later than seven months from the last month of publication of the old index.

Floating rate stocks

Interest payments are reset every three months by reference to sterling money market rates.

Treasury notes in ECU

Three-year notes have been issued in ECU.

Treasury bills in sterling

Discount bills in bearer form may be issued for any period not exceeding twelve months. Normally tenders are held on a weekly basis for 91-day bills (or sometimes for one or two days more or less to take account of public and bank holidays).

ECU treasury bills

These are issued by tender, normally with maturities of one, three and six months.

Derivatives

The London International Financial Futures and Options Exchange (LIFFE) is owned by its members – over 200 of whom about 30 percent are from the UK and 20 percent from each of the USA, Japan and continental Europe. Trades are cleared through the London Clearing House (LCH) which is owned by six clearing banks.

Long Gilt Future

The Long Gilt Future was the first government bond future in Europe.

Key features — **Long Gilt Future**

Contract unit	£50,000 nominal value notional gilt with 9 percent coupon.
Delivery months	March, June, September, December.
First notice day	Two business days prior to the first day of the delivery month
Last notice day	First business day after the last trading day
Delivery day	Any business day in the delivery month at the seller's choice.
Last trading day	Two business days prior to last business day in delivery month.

Quotation	Per £100 nominal.
Tick size	£1/32 per £100 nominal.
Tick value	£15.625 per £ 50,000 contract.
Trading hours	Pit 08.00–16.15 APT 16.30–18.00
Deliverable gilts	Any on the list published ten business days before the first notice day of the delivery month. The gilts will have 10–15 years to maturity with no call, will not be convertible, partly-paid or in bearer form but will have at least £500 million outstanding.
Exchange delivery settlement price (EDSP)	The LIFFE market price at 11.00 am on the second business day prior to Settlement Day.

Option on the Long Gilt Future

Contract unit	1 Long Gilt futures contract.
Delivery months	March, June, September, December plus additional months so that four expiry months include the three nearest calendar months.
Exercise price intervals	£1. 13 exercise prices are listed for each new series. Additional exercise prices are introduced when the Long Gilt Future settlement price is within £16/32 of the sixth highest or lowest existing exercise price.
Exercise	Exercise by 17.00 on any business day, extended to 11.30 on Last Trading Day.
Delivery	Delivery on the first business day after the exercise day.
Expiry	11.30 on the Last Trading Day.
Last trading day/time	10.00 on day six business days prior to first day of delivery month.
Tick size	£1/64 per £ 100 nominal.
Tick value	£7.8125 per £ 50,000 contract.
Trading hours	08.02–16.15.

MARKET-MAKING SYSTEM

Gilt-edged market-makers (GEMMs)

Gilt-edged market-makers (GEMMs) are primary dealers and are required to quote firm two-way prices in all conditions at all times. GEMMs may deal directly with the Bank of England, they have access to a secured late lending facility at the Bank of England and access to Inter-Dealer Brokers (IDBs) in order to trade anonymously with other GEMMs.

As part of its relationship with the GEMMs the Bank of England makes bids in index-linked stocks, in conventional stocks close to maturity and in stocks where there is only a small amount outstanding.

There were eighteen GEMMs in early 1996:

ABN Amro Hoare Govett Sterling Bonds Limited
Barclays de Zoete Wedd Gilts Limited
CS First Boston Gilts Limited
Daiwa Europe (Gilts) Limited
Deutsche Bank Gilts Limited
Goldman Sachs Government Securities (UK)
HSBC Greenwell
J.P. Morgan Sterling Securities Ltd.
Kleinwort Benson Gilts Limited
Lehman Brothers Gilts Limited
Merrill Lynch Gilts Limited
NatWest Gilts Limited
Nikko Gilts Limited
Salomon Brothers UK Limited
Société Générale Gilts Limited
SBC Warburg Securities (Gilt-Edged) Ltd.
UBS Gilts Limited
Winterflood Gilts Limited

Aitken Campbell, Bankers Trust, Barings, Nomura and Yamaichi withdrew as GEMMs during 1995–1996, December 1995 and February 1996. The introduction of a full repo market in 1996 which removed one of the advantages enjoyed by GEMMs was thought likely to lead to the resignation of one or two more firms.

The Bank of England is anxious that these firms should be robust and regularly reports their aggregate capital which was, for example, £815 million at 31 December 1995. New supervisory arrangements, implementing the Capital Adequacy Directive, has enabled GEMMs to support higher levels of business with less capital so that in the first quarter of 1996 the aggregate capital was reduced to £616 million. Their aggregate profitability has been volatile with an aggregate operating loss in 1994 of £60 million being followed by an operating profit in 1995 of £13 million. The Bank of England noted that "a profit was reported by nearly half the GEMMs which were active throughout 1995". In fact the seven most prominent GEMMs have a market share of about 70 percent according to the Bank of England. These leading firms are BZW, Goldman Sachs, HSBC, Lehman Brothers, Salomon Brothers, Nat West and SBC Warburg.

Stock Exchange Money Brokers (SEMBs)

The eight SEMBs in existence at the end of 1995 became unnecessary with the introduction of the repo market in 1996.

Inter-dealer brokers (IDBs)

Inter-dealer brokers (IDBs) provide a means by which GEMMs may trade with each other anonymously. At 4 September 1995 they were:

Garban Gilts Limited
Williams, Cooke, Lott and Kissack Limited
Cantor Fitzgeralds Gilts

Dealing costs

Total dealing costs for large transactions fell by about 60 percent in the two years following the establishment of the GEMMs in 1986.

Spreads are typically 1/32 for short-dated benchmark issues and rise up to 1/8 for longer dated off-the-run issues.

Commission charges are often negligible. Settlement charges through the CGO are £5 per sale. There is no turnover tax or stamp duty.

TRADING

Benchmark issues

In some markets benchmarks are designated by the issuing authorities. In the gilt market benchmarks are chosen by market participants. The Bank of England's declared policy has been to create large liquid issues capable of being benchmarks and usually there are benchmarks in the 5-year, 10-year and long-dated maturities.

Table 7.3

Largest fixed-rate issues outstanding, 6 February 1996 (£ millions)

Stock	Redemption date	Amount issued
$8\frac{3}{4}$% Treasury Loan 1997	01-Sep-1997	5,550
$7\frac{1}{4}$% Treasury Stock 1998	30-Mar-1998	8,150
6% Treasury Stock 1999	10-Aug-1999	6,600
9% Conversion Stock 2000	03-Mar-2000	5,358
8% Treasury Stock 2000	07-Dec-2000	7,800
7% Treasury Stock 2001	06-Nov-2001	7,750
$9\frac{3}{4}$% Treasury Stock 2002	27-Aug-2002	6,527
8% Treasury Stock 2003	10-Jun-2003	8,600
$6\frac{3}{4}$% Treasury Stock 2004	26-Nov-2004	6,500
$8\frac{1}{2}$% Treasury Stock 2005	07-Dec-2005	8,900
$7\frac{1}{2}$% Treasury Stock 2006	15-Nov-2006	6,000
$8\frac{1}{2}$% Treasury Loan 2007	16-Jul-2007	7,397
9% Treasury Loan 2008	13-Oct-2008	5,621
9% Conversion Loan 2011	12-Jul-2011	5,273
9% Treasury Stock 2012	06-Aug-2012	5,360
8% Treasury Stock 2013	27-Sep-2013	6,100
8% Treasury Stock 2015	07-Dec-2015	9,500
$8\frac{3}{4}$% Treasury Stock 2017	25-Aug-2017	7,550

Source: Bank of England

At the end of 1995 the 18 largest stocks accounted for 60 percent of conventional stocks outstanding.

The largest fixed-rate issues (above £5,000 million) outstanding at 6 February 1996 are shown in Table 7.3 in £ millions.

Turnover figures in gilts

Turnover figures in gilts, 1990–95

Table 7.4

Year	Shorts 0–7 yrs	Mediums 7–15 yrs	Others over 15 yrs	Index-linked	Variable Rate	Total -by stock type
1990	367,461	335,035	242,047	28,642		973,184
1991	411,779	434,726	237,618	28,590		1,112,714
1992	520,722	460,421	211,844	45,802		1,238,790
1993	738,785	576,182	214,797	68,652		1,598,417
1994	721,799	557,296	197,142	50,341	18,613	1,545,191
1995	740,128	484,968	278,970	52,334	19,923	1,576,323

Source: Stock Exchange, Quality of Markets department

Turnover figures in gilts 1990–95 – number of bargains

Table 7.5

Year	Total number of bargains	Average value per bargain	Average no. of bargains per day	No. of business days
1990	653,962	1,488,136	2,585	253
1991	617,747	1,801,245	2,442	253
1992	799,431	1,549,590	3,147	254
1993	790,405	2,022,276	3,124	253
1994	702,333	2,200,083	2,787	252
1995	646,010	2,440,091	2,564	252

Source: Stock Exchange, Quality of Markets department

In 1995 turnover was as shown in Table 7.6, expressed in £ millions.

Table 7.6

Turnover in gilts, 1995 (£ millions)

Type of business	Shorts 0–7 yrs	Mediums 7–15 yrs	Others over 15 yrs	Index-linked	Variable rate	Total
Customer	364,224	272,751	155,842	33,035	11,666	837,519
Intra-market	375,904	212,217	123,128	19,299	8,257	738,804
Total in 1995	740,128	484,968	278,970	52,334	19,923	1,576,323

Source: Stock Exchange, Quality of Markets

By month the 1995 turnover was as shown in Table 7.7 expressed in £ millions.

Table 7.7

Turnover in gilts by month, 1995 (£ millions)

Month	Total £ m	Total bargains	No. of days
January	141,889	55,257	21
February	122,384	56,903	20
March	135,766	67,605	23
April	105,620	43,897	18
May	139,084	58,002	21
June	177,723	59,081	22
July	119,089	55,100	21
August	106,865	48,665	22
September	138,608	52,172	21
October	148,941	54,114	22
November	138,505	56,209	22
December	101,850	39,005	19

Source: Stock Exchange, Quality of Markets

Turnover figures in derivatives

Long Gilt Futures contracts 1995

Table 7.8

Contracts 1995	Monthly volume	Month-end open interest	Trading days
January	1,028,106	98,100	21
February	1,305,774	105,856	20
March	1,370,411	84,443	23
April	730,816	80,911	18
May	1,432,070	141,813	21
June	1,402,012	97,152	22
July	963,671	99,206	21
August	1,005,111	109,465	22
September	1,309,632	99,800	21
October	1,164,680	106,298	22
November	1,261,971	141,995	22
December	822,301	132,540	19
Total for 1995	13,796,555		252
Total for 1994	19,048,097		252

Source: LIFFE
Note: 1995 volume was down 27.57 percent on 1994.

Long Gilt Options contracts, 1995

Table 7.9

Contracts 1995	Monthly Volume	Month-end open interest	Trading days
January	154,726	98,770	21
February	203,526	49,709	20
March	211,262	82,119	23
April	123,743	74,866	18
May	209,051	54,271	21
June	187,531	83,499	22
July	125,192	65,022	21
August	104,056	28,451	22
September	122,056	57,374	21
October	115,726	64,881	22
November	130,892	36,921	22
December	68,772	30,853	19
Total for 1995	1,756,533		252
Total for 1994	2,357,348		252

Source: LIFFE
Note: 1995 volume was down 25.49 percent on 1994.

ISSUANCE

A key document was the joint Treasury and Bank of England *Report of the Debt Management Review* (DMR) published in July 1995. This confirmed that auctions would be the primary means of issuance for conventional stock and announced plans for greater transparency in tap issuance.

An important change was the intention to remove in 1996–7 the prohibition on new issues of less than three years maturity. Any maturity will now be possible within a set maturity structure to be announced each year.

Debt issuance is now focussed on the Central Government Borrowing Requirement (CGBR), which is what is in fact funded by gilt issuance, and away from the previously emphasized Public Sector Borrowing Requirement (PSBR).

Towards the end of March the Treasury publishes a funding remit to the Bank of England setting out the planned annual funding requirement and an auction calendar for the following twelve months. Typically the Bank of England plans to fund evenly over the year. Since September 1995 the Bank has held quarterly meetings with market-makers and end investors to discuss new issue policy with regard to maturities. The minutes of these meetings are published.

Gilts

In 1995–6 eight auctions were planned to be held on the last Wednesday of the first and third month of each calendar quarter. The December auction follows the Chancellor's annual budget statement and is subject to change.

Before the beginning of each calendar quarter there is an announcement of the likely maturity of stocks to be sold in that quarter together with a report on the progress of the funding. The maturity ranges for auctions in a quarter are announced at 3.30 pm on the last business day of the previous quarter.

Auction terms are announced at 3.30 pm on the Tuesday of the week preceding the auction and a prospectus is published in certain newspapers. Each auction is planned to be for £2–3 billion of stock. An auction may sometimes be split between more than one stock, in which case auctions may be held on successive days for each stock.

Applicants may bid on a competitive or non-competitive basis. There is no minimum price set. Competitive bids must be for a minimum of £500,000. Non-competitive bids must be for a minimum of £1,000 and a maximum of £500,000. GEMMs may each make a single non-competitive bid of up to 0.5 percent (nominal value) of the amount on offer.

Each auction closes at 10.00am. GEMMs may bid by telephone directly to the Bank of England's dealing room in multiples of £1 million. Others may bid directly by delivering a completed application form by 10.00am to the Bank's Central Gilts and Moneymarkets Office in London (or to the Bank's Registrar Department in Gloucester, or by 3.30pm the previous day to any of the Banlk's branches or agencies).

The Bank aims to publish the result of an auction by 10.45am. If any of the stock on offer is not allotted it will not be subsequently sold to the market at a price below the lowest accepted price for a period of two months after the auction.

"When-issued" trading begins once the terms are known seven days beforehand. Settlement of these trades is the day after the auction when trading in the new stock begins.

Taps

The programme of auctions is accompanied by sales of gilts "on tap" through GEMMs. Index-linked gilts are usually issued by tap. Taps of conventional gilts are not intended to be a routine method of financing but are used as a market management mechanism at times when there is temporary excess demand in a stock or sector or when there is an exceptionally sudden rise in the market. Tap issues are announced at 10.15 am for bids at 10.45 am and details of the amount sold at the initial and any subsequent mini-tenders are published.

Larger amounts are issued in tranches without accrued interest and are designated by a letter until the first ex-dividend date when the new tranche becomes fungible with the existing issue.

In the case of auctions of partly paid stocks the first payment is fixed and it is the last payment which varies according to the allotment price.

Mini-tenders

After an initial tender the Bank allows bids to be made either as "blue sky" bids by individual GEMMs or as common price mini-tenders open to all GEMMs for a five minute period. Mini-tenders are held automatically each day between 8.45 and 8.50 am with the results published before 9.00 am if sales have been made.

Shop window

Small amounts of stock acquired in the course of its official operations by the Bank are offered to be resold to the market through a "shop window". At 8.30 am each day the Bank posts on its screen pages a list of the amount of each stock available for sale. A necessary condition is that any successful bid must be at or above the current market price.

Treasury Notes in ECU

Issued by tender quarterly under a calendar announced at the beginning of the year. An announcement is made on the second Tuesday of the month if there is to be an issue with the tender taking place on the following Tuesday. Bids are submitted by 10.30 am and the result is published at 01.00 pm. Settlement is seven days later though a change to three-day settlement is being considered.

Treasury bills

Tenders are on the last business day of each week. The amount and maturity of bills to be offered is announced one week in advance at around 1.15 pm. Bids are submitted by 12.30 pm and the result is published around 1.15 pm. Any person or institution may tender for bills. Tenders must be for a minimum nominal amount of £50,000 and be expressed in terms of the net amount per £100 nominal the bidder will pay. Bills are allotted at the prices bid. Settlement is on any day of the following week at the buyer's choice.

Treasury bills in ECU

These are issued monthly under a calendar announced at the beginning of the year. An announcement on the first Tuesday of the month leads to a tender on the second Tuesday. Bids must be submitted by 10.30 am and the result is published at 1.00 pm. Settlement is two days later.

Issuance volume

During the last ten years the changes in the UK Public Sector Borrowing Requirement can be seen from Table 7.10.

The new issue activity of 1995 may be summarized as follows. Table 7.11 illustrates clearly the Bank's intention to auction £2–3 billion of stock at each auction and to build up existing issues with fungible new issues. Seven of the nine auctions in 1995 added to existing stock. The average level of cover (the ratio of bids to gilts auctioned) was 1.65.

It may be noted that, despite "when issued" trading the market did not operate with complete efficiency. The September auction was not fully covered and the tail was 7 basis points. The December auction with a tail of 11 basis points also resulted in questions about the effectiveness of price discovery in the "when issued" period.

Changes in UK PSBR, 1986–95
Table 7.10

Year	No.	Issues amount £m	No.	Redemptions value £m	No.	Net amount £m
1986	81	16,811	8	6,139	73	10,671
1987	51	15,242	7	7,807	44	7,435
1988	37	7,007	7	7,501	30	(494)
1989	8	0	9	10,220	(1)	(10,220)
1990	10	0	10	8,700	0	(8,700)
1991	35	15,607	6	6,517	29	9,090
1992	75	36,514	8	9,471	67	27,043
1993	88	57,230	6	6,265	82	50,965
1994	52	32,640	7	9,290	45	23,350
1995	41	29,720	5	7,620	36	22,100

Source: Stock Exchange, Quality of Markets department
Note: For the years 1986 to 1992 non-money raising issues are included. From 1993 only money raising issues are shown.

Table 7.11

New issue activity, 1995

Date 1995	Stock	Status	Amount issued £ bn	Average yield %	Times covered	Tail[1]
25 Jan	8% 2015	New	2.0	8.58	1.79	0
22 Feb	8.5% 2005	Fungible	2.0	8.72	2.08	0
29 Mar	8% 2015	Fungible	2.0	8.40	1.24	2
26 Apr	8% 2000 A	Fungible[2]	2.0	8.30	2.17	0
29 June	8.5% 2005	Fungible	2.5	8.42	2.00	0
26 July	8% 2015	Fungible	2.5	8.33	1.42	1
27 Sept	7.5% 2006	New	3.0	8.02	0.99	7
25 Oct	8% 2015 A	Fungible[3]	3.0	8.33	2.00	0
6 Dec	7.5% 2006	Fungible	3.0	7.45	1.12	11

Source: The Bank of England
Notes:
[1] Tail is the difference in basis points between the average yield and the highest yield at which bids were allotted.
[2] Fungible after 5 days.
[3] Fungible after 6 days.

Looking in more detail at maturities and all other issuance as well as auctions, a typical quarter's new issues may be summarized as shown in Table 7.12.

New issues of index-linked gilts were planned in a pilot series of auctions in the 1996–7 financial year together with a possible separate list of index linked market makers. These proposals were under consultation in early 1996.

Table 7.12

New issues, typical quarter

October – December 1995	No. of issues	Nominal value (£m)	Money raised (£m)
Shorts (0–7 yrs)	1	3,250	3,217
Mediums (7–15 yrs)	2	250	255
Longs (over 15 yrs)	1	3,000	2,887
Index-linked	8	1,000	1,584
Variable rate	1	600	601
Bonds	1	229	229
Total	14	8,329	8,774

Source: Stock Exchange, Quality of Markets department

SETTLEMENT AND DELIVERY

The CGO

Gilt trades are settled through the Bank of England's Central Gilts Office (CGO). The CGO provides a facility which allows investors to hold stock in dematerialized form. About 95 percent by value of gilts are so held. The CGO also offers an automatic stock transfer and assured payment system. Transfer forms and paper certificates are not required. Stock moves electronically between members of the CGO. The process requires a simultaneous positive acceptance of the stock by the purchaser and commitment by the purchaser's settlement bank to make the payment, thus achieving delivery versus payment.

In exchange for the undertaking to make payments a CGO member's settlement bank will usually require a floating charge over the stock held in the CGO by that member.

In November 1995 the Bank announced that three international centralized depository institutions would be members of the CGO and offer settlement and custody services from March 1996. These three institutions are Bank of New York, Cedel Bank and Euroclear.

The Bank of England's Registrar Department

The register of stock holders is automatically updated two days after trades settled through the CGO. Besides maintaining the register for each issue (once a new stock is fully paid) the Registrar's Department is also responsible for issuing certificates where required and for making payments of interest and principal with funds provided by the Treasury.

Delivery by Value

The CGO also offers a facility for transferring collateral known as Delivery By Value (DBV). A member wishing to borrow money overnight using gilts as collateral may pledge stock from his CGO account in return for an assured payment from the lender's bank. The next morning the stock is returned and the money is repaid automatically

Trade dates

Settlement is usually T+1 but trades between a Stock Exchange member and a non-member may be settled later under Stock Exchange Rules. This feature is useful, for example, for those who have matching foreign exchange trades to execute.

Planned changes

In early 1997 certain changes to the CGO system were planned to be introduced. These included an amendment to the Assured Payment System under which the settlement bank acting for a CGO member would be able to set a cap, being the maximum net debit available to a member at any point during the day. These debit caps were planned to have collateralized and uncollateralized elements. The settlement bank would continue to be able to take stock held in the member's account as collateral against any CGO exposure incurred by the bank on the member's account.

The CMO

The Central Moneymarkets Office (CMO) provides for money market instruments including Treasury Bills a computerized book entry transfer service and linked payment mechanism equivalent to that provided by the CGO for Gilts.

The European Settlements Office provides a book-entry transfer system for Ecu-denominated securities and same day settlement facilities.

INVESTORS

The distribution of the sterling national debt at 31 December 1995 at market value was as shown in Table 7.13.

Table 7.13

**Distribution of sterling national debt,
31 December 1995**

£ billions	Total	%
UK market holdings	251.1	85.6
of which:		
Public sector	4.6	1.8
Banking sector[1]	24.9	9.9
Building societies	2.1	0.8
Insurance companies	80.5	32.0
Pension funds	52.4	20.8
Other financial institutions	22.4	8.9
Industrial and commercial companies	3.5	1.4
Persons	24.7	9.8
Overseas holders	36.3	14.4
Total market holdings	251.4	100.0
Official holdings	7.9	
Total debt at market value	259.3	

Source: Bank of England
Note: [1] Includes nominee companies

QUOTATIONS, INTEREST AND YIELD CALCULATIONS

Prices

Prices are quoted per £100 nominal of stock and excluding accrued interest. The usual tick size is £1/32 per £100 nominal.

A buyer must calculate the interest accrued to know the total consideration to be paid.

Let us suppose that on 27 March 1997 (for settlement on 28 March 1997) the 9% Treasury Stock 2012 was quoted at £109 3/8 (offer price) and that the last interest payment date was 6 February 1997.

Example

The number of days from the last interest payment date to the settlement date is 50 days. The gross interest accrued can be calculated as the coupon times the number of days divided by 365:

$$£9.00 \times 50/365 = £1.2329 \text{ per } £100 \text{ nominal of stock}$$

Therefore the total price payable is £109.375 + £1.2329 = £110.61 after rounding per £100 nominal of stock.

Yield

Interest is calculated on a 365-day year and on 182.5 days for semi-annual coupons.

Two yields are usually quoted in the newspapers. The first, less useful, is the "flat" or "running" yield which is calculated by dividing the coupon by the price and multiplying by 100. The more useful measure is redemption yield which reflects both the interest received and the capital gain or loss incurred if the gilt is bought at a quoted price and held to redemption.

The redemption yield formula used by the Bank of England is as follows:

$$P + AI = v^f \times [d + c/y(1-v^n)] + 100v^t$$

where
P = Clean price of the stock
AI = Accrued interest on the stock
v = $1/(1+y/2)$
f = (actual number of days from settlement to next receivable interest payment)/182.5
d = Value per £100 nominal of next receivable interest payment
c = Annual coupon per £100 nominal
y = redemption yield on stock
n = number of half-yearly payments after the next one
t = (actual number of days from settlement to maturity) /182.5.

Adjustments are made for stocks trading ex-dividend, partly-paid stocks, index-linked stocks and double-dated stocks.

Double-dated stocks

In the case of double-dated stocks the market convention is that where a stock is trading below par (100) the further date is used to calculate yield to redemption. This is because such a stock must have a coupon below current market yields which the Bank of England could not refinance more cheaply. Where a double-dated stock is trading above par the nearer redemption date is used to calculate redemption yield because it is assumed that the Bank of England will refinance this stock more cheaply as soon as it can.

Ex-dividend

Since the beginning of 1996 transfers of gilts have been made ex-dividend from seven working days before the interest payment date. Similarly transfers of a maturing gilt are not accepted after seven working days before redemption. This is known as the shutting date. One exception is the 3.5 percent War Loan for which the period is ten days in each case.

Special Ex-dividend

Except 3½% War Loan, stocks of more than five years maturity may be traded, for a three-week period before the ex-dividend date, cum or ex-dividend at the request of the buyer. Ex-dividend trades in this three-week period are known as "special ex-dividend". There are Stock Exchange rules to prevent dividend manufacture which, among other things, prohibit the sale of a stock cum-dividend which has been bought special ex-dividend.

Rebate interest

Negative accrued interest is called rebate interest. It occurs when a gilt is bought ex-dividend before the dividend date. The seller pays the buyer rebate interest to compensate the buyer for the period in which the stock is held without earning interest.

Let us suppose that on 22 April 1997 (for settlement on 23 April 1997) the 9.5% Conversion Stock 2004 is quoted at £112 xd. The next interest payment is due on 25 April 1997.

The amount of rebate interest is calculated as the coupon rate times the number of days from the day after settlement date to the interest payment date (both inclusive) divided by 365. In this case

$$£9.5 \times 2/365 = £0.05205 \text{ per } £100 \text{ nominal of stock}$$

Therefore the total price paid by the buyer is £112 − £0.05205 = £111.95 (after rounding) per £100 nominal of stock.

Accrued interest on partly-paid stock

By convention when a partly-paid stock is issued by auction it is assumed, for the purpose of calculating gross interest accrued, that the fully paid price is £100 per £100 nominal. When a stock is issued by tender, however, it is assumed that the fully paid price is the minimum price, that is the sum of the price at which the stock was originally issued by the government and all the subsequent calls.

9% Conversion Loan 2011 "C" tranche was issued to the Bank at £15 per £100 nominal on 16 February 1993. A call of £35 was paid on 11 March 1993, with a final call of £54.50 due on 4 May 1993.

If the stock had been traded on 31 March 1993 for settlement on 1 April 1993, the gross interest accrued calculation would have been as follows:

The number of days after issue that the stock traded at £15 paid was 23 days (16 February to 11 March). The number of days before settlement that the stock traded at £50 paid was 21 days (11 March to 1 April). The gross interest accrued was therefore:

$$(£9 \times 23/365 \times 15/104.5) + (£9 \times 21/365 \times 50/104.5) = £0.3292$$
per £100 nominal of stock

That is annual coupon multiplied by the proportion of the year elapsed multiplied by the proportion paid of the placement price of the stock.

Note: The author is indebted to the Bank of England for this example.

Index-linked interest

It was noted above that index-linked stocks pay a coupon and that this coupon and the principal at redemption are increased in line with increases in the retail price index (RPI). The specific measure of the index is that which is eight months in arrears on any calculation date.

The 4 1/8% Index-Linked Treasury Stock 2030 was issued on 12 June 1992. Interest is payable on each 22 January and 22 July until 22 July 2030. The base month for the RPI was October 1991, eight months before June 1992. In October 1991 the RPI was 135.1.

Interest calculation

Each semi-annual coupon (except in this case the first which was for a seven-month period) is £ 2.0625 (half the 4 1/8% coupon) adjusted for the movement in the RPI on each £100 nominal of stock. Thus the payment on 22 July 1993 was calculated as follows:

The RPI in November 1992 (eight months before the payment) was 139.7. The coupon is therefore

$$£2.0625 \times 139.7/135.1 = £2.1327 \text{ per } £100 \text{ nominal of stock}$$

Principal repayment calculation

Let us suppose that the RPI in November 2029 had risen by about 3% per annum to 411.8. Then the redemption amount of the stock would be calculated as:

$$£100 \times 411.8/135.1 = £304.8112 \text{ per } £100 \text{ nominal of stock}$$

Note: The author is indebted to the Bank of England for this example.

RECENT AND FUTURE DEVELOPMENTS

Three reforms of the gilt market have been introduced or are planned. The first was more transparent and predictable issuance, through the introduction of an auction calendar and maturity schedule. The second reform, an open gilt repo market, took effect from 2 January 1996. The third, the introduction of a strip mechanism, follows on from a consultative paper published in May 1995 called *Strips and New Instruments in the Gilt-Edged Market* and is likely to take effect in early 1997.

Repos and securities lending

By mid 1996 it was estimated that repo outstandings were over £50 billion with daily traded volume thought to be averaging £12 billion. The Bank of England's money market operations were still focused on eligible bills and Treasury bills rather than repo operations.

Spreads between bid and offer in the repo market in its first months were about 5 basis points with gilt repo trading about 5–7 basis points below the interbank market.

Delivery By Value (DBV) was trading 2–3 basis points over General Collateral, because the lender of cash versus DBV does not have the use of the bonds for the term of the trade; 80 percent of trading was estimated to be under one month in maturity.

The reforms introduced on 2 January 1996 have two components:

- changes to the structure of the market
- changes to the taxation regime.

Market structure

The chief structural change was that any market participant became free to enter into gilt-repo or stock-lending transactions. Any group is free to offer intermediation services in gilt repos, whether on a name-passing, agency or matched-principal basis.

Discount houses are free to trade repos for any maturity. Groups which own both a discount house and a Stock Exchange Money Broker (SEMB) have merged the SEMB's operations into the discount house. Discount houses are required to be kept separate, however, from any bank treasury operations in the same group. Inter-dealer brokers are also free to offer intermediation services to GEMMs in gilt repos.

Taxation

The chief tax change which took effect on 2 January 1996 was that withholding tax ceased to be applied to dividend payments on most holdings of gilts.

As regards repos a question arose about the treatment of manufactured dividends. A manufactured dividend is a payment of an amount equal to a dividend payment made by the borrower of stock to the lender of stock so that the lender receives the income that would have been received if it had not lent or repaid out the stock. Under the tax changes all manufactured dividends are payable gross.

Institutions wishing to benefit from these changes had to open STAR accounts with the CGO. If, as planned, Cedel and Euroclear join the CGO then gilts held in those settlement systems by eligible persons will also receive gross dividends so long as the settlement systems hold their gilts in STAR accounts.

As regards regulatory status, gilt repos are "financial instruments" for the purposes of the Investment Services Directive and the Capital Adequacy Directive.

Documentation is intended to be under the PSA/ISMA Global Master Repurchase Agreement with an annexe which covers certain matters specific to the gilt market such as deliveries-by-value. This documentation provides for, among other things:

- absolute transfer of title to the securities being repoed
- remargining during the life of a contract or for close-out and repricings
- close-out and set-off in event of default of all transactions.

Strips

It was expected that gilt strips would be introduced in early 1997. While the authorities are uncertain of the demand for zero-coupon securities direct issuance of zero-coupon debt is unlikely. The chief features of the proposed stripping facility were as follows:

Gilt strips

Issues to be stripped	8% 2000, 8.5% 2005, 7.5% 2006, 8% 2015 and 8% 2021. Further issues may be designated.
Limits	No limit on amount of each issue which may be stripped.
Minimum amount	The minimum strippable amount will be £10,000 nominal, increasing in units of £10,000 nominal.
Duration	The duration of the principle strip of the 8% 2021 would be about 25 years (in 1996) more than twice the duration of the coupon bond.
Form	Registered securities held in the CGO book entry system.

Fungibility	The five named stocks have common interest payment dates (7 June and 7 December). Legislation will permit fungibility between coupon strips. Principal and coupon strips will not be fungible initially.
Information	The Bank of England envisages publishing weekly information on the amount of each gilt which has been stripped or reconstituted.
Market-making	As for ordinary gilts. No separate list of market-makers is anticipated.
Redemption	Coupon strips will be repaid as if they were redemptions of principal and not according to mandated dividend instructions.

It was expected that by the end of the 1996/97 financial year the amount of strippable gilts outstanding would have risen to over £50 billion.

SOURCES OF FURTHER INFORMATION

Internet
The Bank of England's Internet address is www.bankofengland.co.uk.

Screen pages
Information on the Bank of England's operations may be found on all screen services.

Gilts

Bloomberg	NH BOE
Cognotec	62251-62258
Knight-Ridder	3302-3309
Reuters	GEDR-Y
Telerate	22550-22557
Topic	44700-44721

Treasury Bills

Bloomberg	NH BOE
Cognotec	62241-62242
Knight-Ridder	3889-3891
Reuters	RTCD-RTCF
Telerate	3871-3873
Topic	44735-44736

ECU Treasury Bills and Notes

Bloomberg	NH BOE
Cognotec	62261-62269
Knight-Ridder	3292-3301
Reuters	GBAA-GBAJ
Telerate	6473-6478, 6556-6559
Topic	44751-44762

LIFFE has the following pages:

Bloomberg	G<comdty>
Knight-Ridder	GTL, 052G
Quick	LIF12, LIF66-69
Quotron	G + month code LF
Reuters	LIFK-S
Telerate	994, 15990-1
Topic	20011, 19999

Addresses

Bank of England
Gilt-Edged and Money Markets
Division
Threadneedle Street
London EC2R 8AH
Tel: 44 71 601 4540

HM Treasury
Accounts Division
Parliament Street
London SW1P 3AG
Tel: 44 71 270 5137

The Securities and Futures Authority
Cottons Centre
Cottons Lane
London SE1 2QB
Tel: 44 71 378 9000

Central Gilts Office
Central Moneymarkets Office
1 & 2 Bank Buildings
Princes Street
London EC2R 8EU
Tel: 44 71 601 3798/4782

London Stock Exchange
Quality of Markets department
Old Broad Street
London EC2N 1HP
Tel: 44 71 797 1000

The Securities and Investments
  Board
Gavrelle House
2-14 Bunhill Row
London EC1Y 8RA
Tel: 44 71 638 1240

■ ■ ■

"The management of the French national debt has been modernized since 1985. The market is now simple, liquid and transparent."

France 8

INTRODUCTION

> "The French government is the leading issuer of ECU-denominated securities."

The management of the French national debt has been modernized since 1985. The market is now simple, liquid and transparent. The government issues three main types of debt: long-term, medium-term and short-term. Of the long-term securities there were five issues with more than Ffr100 billion outstanding at 31 December 1995. New issues are managed under an annual calendar and auctions are held under a precise timetable for each type of security. The French government is the leading issuer of ECU-denominated securities.

LEGAL FRAMEWORK

Form

> "In December each year the French parliament approves the Finance Act which authorizes the Minister of the Economy to borrow in French francs or in ECU to cover the needs of the Trésor (Treasury)."

In December each year the French parliament approves the Finance Act which authorizes the Minister of the Economy to borrow in French francs or in ECU to cover the needs of the Trésor (Treasury). This is a general authorization without a limit. All debt is issued by the Trésor and is in book entry form.

Identification

OATs are identified by a SICOVAM number of four or five digits.

Regulation of the market

Besides the Ministry of the Economy which has a general supervisory role over the markets, the following entities have regulatory responsibilities.

Banque de France
The newly independent Banque de France is responsible for defining and implementing monetary policy. It is also responsible for supervis-

ing the money market and has operational involvement through keeping Treasury bill current accounts via the Saturne system.

Comité de la Réglementation Bancaire (CRB)

The banking regulations committee is chaired by the Minister of the Economy. It formulates general banking rules, accounting rules, prudential and risk ratios, market rules and particularly rules governing the inter-bank market and markets in negotiable debt securities.

Comité des Établissements de Credit (CEC)

The lending institutions committee is chaired by the Governor of the Banque de France. It licenses lending institutions (other than those supervised by the Commission Bancaire) and money brokers (*agents des marchés interbancaires*) under the Banking Act and under regulations laid down by the Comité de la Réglementation Bancaire.

Commission Bancaire

Under the Act of 24 January 1984 the Commission is responsible for ensuring compliance by lending institutions operating in France with all legislation and regulations. The Commission has wide powers to obtain information, to impose measures and to punish erring institutions.

Conseil des Bourses de Valeurs (CBV)

The CBV [Stock Exchange Supervisory Council] draws up and enforces stock market regulations. For example, trading in the secondary market in government securities is governed by Title IX of the Conseil's general regulations.

Société des Bourses Françaises (SBF)

The SBF is responsible for daily operations and development of the market under the rules of the CBV.

Conseil des Marchés à Terme (CMT)

An advisory body for the futures market. It formulated general regulations which were published in March 1990 and which make up the regulatory document for the derivatives market.

Matif SA

The Matif SA operates the market and the clearing mechanism for futures.

> "Residents of a state which does not have a double taxation treaty with France must provide proof of non-resident status for each interest payment."

Commission des Opérations de Bourse (COB)

The Commission is responsible for investor protection. It supervises investor information, operation of the securities market, listed financial products and traded futures. It approves prospectuses and licenses mutual funds (Sicavs) and investment trusts.

TAXATION

Corporations which are liable to corporate income tax in France pay tax on interest, redemption premiums and capital gains at the standard corporate tax rate.

Exemption from French tax is available if the investor's country has a tax treaty with France and if a single proxy form is completed by the investor and submitted to a custodian bank. This system also applies to corporate members of Cedel and Euroclear.

Residents of a state which does not have a double taxation treaty with France must provide proof of non-resident status for each interest payment.

PROFILE OF THE DEBT

Debt outstanding

The amounts outstanding at year-end may be summarized as shown in Table 8.1 (Ffr bn).

Table 8.1

Amounts outstanding at year-ends, 1991–5 (Ffr bn)

	1995	1994	1993	1992	1991
OATs	1,655	1,421	1,215	978	761
Other long-term debt			138	79	149
BTF	292	239	189	259	139
BTAN	760	682	592	456	418
Total negotiable debt	2,826	2,480	2,134	1,772	1,467

Source: Ministère de l'Économie et des Finances

It is instructive to look at the total government debt as a percentage of GDP (see Table 8.2). Total debt excludes securities issued on behalf of the FSR.

Table 8.2

Total French government debt as percentage of GDP, 1984–94.

Year	Total-debt Ffr bn	Total debt/GDP %
1984	915.4	21.0
1985	1,067.5	22.7
1986	1,194.6	23.6
1987	1,281.7	24.0
1988	1,474.8	25.8
1989	1,622.4	26.4
1990	1,782.4	27.5
1991	1,867.1	27.6
1992	2,111.3	30.2
1993	2,461.7	34.5
1994	2,903.8	39.3
1995	3,251.0	42.4

Source: Ministère de l'Économie et des Finances

Debt maturity by year

The negotiable public debt outstanding at 31 December 1995 may be divided into three sections according to instrument (see Tables 8.3, 8.4 and 8.5).

Table 8.3

OATs as at 31 December 1995

Year	OATs Ffr (Ffr m)	OATs ECU (ECU m)
1996	55,092	
1997	173,862	967
1998	73,666	
1999	84,307	
2000	98,594	2,124
2001	106,554	1,033
2002	103,709	4,113
2003	200,809	1.210
2004	217,982	3,054
2005	211,154	1,458
2006	52,656	
2008	64,666	
2012	35,984	
2019	62,238	
2022		1,500
2023	87,952	
2025	47,330	
Totals	15,458	1,676,555

Source: Ministère de l'Économie et des Finances

INSTRUMENTS AND DERIVATIVES

Bons du Trésor à Taux fixe et Interêt Précomptés (BTFs)

BTFs are the Treasury bills of the French market. They are issued in minimum denominations of Ffr1m. Initially maturities are from 13, 26 and 52 weeks. New issue maturities may be adjusted so as to attach new sales to existing issues. Sometimes, therefore, short-dated notes of 4 to 6 weeks are issued, or notes of 24 to 29 weeks, or notes of 42 to 52 weeks, in order to match an existing issue.

Interest is in the form of a discount and the bills are quoted on a yield to maturity basis on a 360-day year to two decimal places. At

Table 8.4

BTAN as at 31 December 1995

Year	BTAN Ffr (Ffr m)	BTAN ECU (ECU m)
1996	194,867	
1997	166,531	1,225
1998	134,991	2,831
1999	119,045	1,726
2000	108,688	
Totals	724,122	5,782

Source: Ministère de l'Économie et des Finances

Table 8.5

BTF as at 31 December 1995

Month of maturity 1996	Amount (Ffr m)
January	75,373
February	61,389
March	74,175
April	7,749
May	7,982
June	36,151
September	21,320
December	7,488

Source: Ministère de l'Économie et des Finances

31 December 1995 Ffr291.6 billion of BTFs were outstanding with an average remaining life of 88 days.

Bons du Trésor à Taux Fixe et Interêt Annuel (BTANs)

BTANs are interest-bearing fixed rate Treasury notes. They are issued in minimum denominations of Ffr1m., though smaller amounts may be added to an existing holding of the same issue.

Maturities are either two- or five-year bullets. Every six months the Treasury issues new two-year and five-year BTANs and subsequent monthly issues add to the amount outstanding. Maturities and coupons are usually set to fall on the twelfth of the month.

Coupons are paid annually and notes are quoted on a yield to maturity basis on a 365-day year. The notes are not listed on the Stock Exchange. At 31 December 1995 Ffr724, 1 billion of BTANs were outstanding with an average remaining life of 2 years and 90 days.

ECU-denominated BTANs

These were first issued in February 1993. Issues have been syndicated rather than auctioned. Three issues existed at 31 December 1995, the largest of which is the ECU2.83 billion 7.25 percent issue maturing on 16 March 1998. The total of ECU BTANs outstanding at 31 December 1995 was ECU5.78 billion.

Obligations Assimilables du Trésor (OATs)

OATs are in minimum denominations of Ffr2,000. Initial maturities are from seven- to thirty-year bullets. Coupons are paid annually. Notes are quoted on a price basis excluding accrued interest. Bonds are traded on screen and on the Stock Exchange. At 31 December 1995 Ffr1,676 billion of OATs were outstanding with an average remaining life of 8 years and 354 days.

ECU-denominated OATs

These were issued first in 1989 and regularly thereafter. Denominations are ECU500. At 31 December 1995 there were nine issues totalling ECU15.46 billion outstanding. The largest of these was the 6 percent of April 2004 with ECU3.05 billion.

Other OATs

Besides the fixed-rate bullet maturity OATs there are some older less-traded issues which are convertible or were issued with warrants.

Floating rate OATs

There were no issues of floating rate OATs between November 1990 and April 1996. The amount outstanding at the end of 1995 was Ffr87.5 bn. However a new variable rate OAT based on a new index, the TEC was issued in April 1996 (see below). The different variable rate issues are known by their initials.

TMB
The rate is the arithmetic mean of the monthly average of the 13-week T-bill auctioned weekly throughout the year prior to the coupon payment.

TRB
The rate is reset quarterly as the yield of the 13-week T-bill auctioned prior to the payment of the coupon.

TRA
The rate is the arithmetic mean of the monthly average of yields on fixed-rate Emprunts d'État with maturities greater than seven years. This rate is published by the Caisse des Dépots et Consignations.

TME
The rate is the monthly average yield on a weighted sample of 7 to 30- year bonds on the secondary market recorded over the twelve months prior to payment of the coupon.

TEC

In March 1996 the Trésor announced the creation of "Taux de l'Echéance Constante", a ten-year constant maturity yield index. The TEC is published daily in the form of the yield to maturity of a hypothetical OAT with a maturity of exactly ten years. The yield is interpolated from the yields of the two nearest maturities of government bonds based on mid-prices quoted at 10.00 am in Paris by OAT market-makers, rounded to two decimal places. In April 1996 there was the first issue of 10.5-year OATs with quarterly coupons set in advance based on the TEC. These bonds, like other floating rate bonds, are not very sensitive to absolute rate changes. However, they are sensitive to changes in the yield curve. They will gain in value from any steepening of the curve and will fall on any flattening of the curve. The initial issue of TEC 10 OATs was via a syndicate led by BNP and the Caisse des Dépôts, but the intention was that subsequent issues would be auctioned.

Emprunts d'Etat (EEs)

EEs were issued regularly until 1985 and revived as the "Grand Emprunt d'Etat" known as the Balladur bond which had an initial issue amount of more than Ffr110 billion.

Stripped OATs

Since May 1991 the Trésor has permitted certain OATs to be stripped. The intention is to have liquid zero-coupon instruments maturing in April and October in several years. Authorization has been given to strip eleven Ffr issues. These are the OATs maturing in April and October of the years 2003, 2004, 2005, April 2006, October 2008, October 2019, April 2023, and October 2025. Since the beginning of 1994 the Trésor has permitted the stripping of ECU OATs maturing in April 2000, April 2002, April 2003, April 2004, April 2005 and April 2022.

Since June 1993 the par value of a stripped coupon has been Ffr5 so as to achieve fungibility between all interest certificates of a given maturity derived from OATs of different maturities. Strips are quoted in terms of yield unlike other government securities which are quoted in terms of price.

The par value of ECU-stripped coupons is ECU1.25.

SVTs may strip or reconstitute eligible OATs at any time. At 31 December 1995 a total of Ffr149,697 million was outstanding in strips. The three most stripped issues were as shown in Table 8.6.

In ECU OATs the total outstanding in strips was ECU308 million of which ECU217 million was of the 8.25% 2022 issue.

Table 8.6

Three most stripped issues

OAT (amounts in Ffr m)	Amount in issue	Amount stripped
8.50% April 2023	87,952	46,920
8.50% October 2019	61,328	43,360
7.50% April 2005	108,157	13,734

Source: Ministère de l'Économie et des Finances

Derivatives

Key features

Notional Bond Future

Underlying	Government bond with a remaining maturity of 7 to 10 years with a theoretical 10% coupon.
Trading unit	Ffr500,000.
Quotation	Percentage of nominal rounded to two decimals.
Tick	Two basis points (ie Ffr100).
Delivery months	March, June, September, December.
Last trading day	Fourth business day prior to the last business day of delivery month.
Delivery	7- to 10-year fixed income French Government bonds, selected from a basket of deliverable bonds.
Price change limits	Plus or minus 300 basis points from previous settlement price.

Option on Notional Bond Future

Underlying	Notional Bond Future contract.
Trading unit	1 Notional Bond Future contract.
Quotation	Premium in percent of nominal rounded to two decimals.
Tick	One basis point (ie Ffr50).
Delivery months	One front month plus three or four successive quarterly maturities from March, June, September, December. If the front month is a quarterly contract month no monthly contract is listed.
Last trading day	Last Thursday of the month preceding the Notional Bond delivery month.
Delivery	Notional Bond Future contract.
Strike price	Nine bracketing the at-the-money price.

Medium-term Futures Contract

Underlying	Government bonds with a remaining maturity of 3 to 5 years with a 6% coupon.
Trading unit	Ffr500,000.
Quotation	Percentage of nominal rounded to two decimals.
Tick	One basis point (ie Ffr50).
Delivery months	March, June, September, December.
Last trading day	Second business day prior to the third Wednesday of delivery month at 11.00 am Paris time.
Delivery	3- to 5-year fixed income French Government bonds, selected from a basket of deliverable bonds by the seller.
Price change limits	Plus or minus 150 basis points from previous settlement price.

Key features

Treasury Bond Future

Underlying	Government bonds with a remaining maturity of at least 15 years with an 8% coupon.
Trading unit	Ffr500,000.
Quotation	Percentage of nominal rounded to two decimals.
Tick	Two basis points (ie Ffr100).
Delivery months	March, June, September, December.
Last trading day	Fourth business day prior to the last business day of delivery month.
Delivery	15-year and over fixed income French Government bonds, selected from a basket of deliverable bonds by the seller.
Price change limits	Plus or minus 350 basis points from previous settlement price.

MARKET-MAKING SYSTEM

Specialistes en Valeurs du Trésor (SVTs)

Since February 1987 the Trésor has issued through a group of primary dealers. This group undertakes to maintain a liquid market. The regulations governing the SVTs were revised in the spring of 1994. SVTs are now appointed for a period of three years.

In the primary market SVTs are required to ensure that the auctions proceed smoothly, conveying information to the Trésor and bidding for reasonable amounts at each auction. SVTs are required to buy at least 2 percent of the annual volume issued in each of the four categories of security (BTFs, BTANs, OATs and ECU BTANs and OATs). The arithmetical mean of the three percentages relating to French franc securities must be at least 3 percent.

The SVTs are required to trade at least 3 percent each of the total volume traded by SVTs in each category of security in the secondary market (BTFs, BTANs and OATs) and 2 percent of such trading in ECU-denominated securities (combining ECU BTANs and ECU OATs). SVTs are also required to make continuous bid and offer prices in the principal issues and to show the amounts for which these are firm prices.

SVTs have two privileges: the right to make bids in non-competitive bidding rounds and the right to reconstitute stripped OATs.

Qualification for SVT status is earned by serving a period as Correspondant en Valeurs du Trésor (CVT) during which time a firm's competence is assessed. The Minister of the Economy may then grant them SVT status provided the firm meets certain structural and operational requirements. The minimum capital requirement is Ffr300 million. Each SVT must have a stable establishment in Paris from which all trading in French government securities must be conducted for the group to which the SVT belongs. The SVT must have a locally based sales team and appropriate mid-office and back office resources.

The 20 SVTs quote on Reuters and Telerate in amounts from FFr50m upwards. Spreads are 5–15bp in price. The SVTs in early 1996 were:

Banque Internationale de Placement–Dresdner Bank
Banque d' Escompte
Banque Indosuez
Banque Nationale de Paris
Banque Lehman Brothers S.A.
Banque Paribas
Caisse des Dépôts et Consignations
Caisse Nationale de Crédit Agricole
C.P.R. Intermédiation
Crédit Commercial de France
Crédit Lyonnais
Deutsche Bank
Goldman Sachs
JP Morgan & Cie S.A.
Louis Dreyfus Finance
Morgan Stanley S.A.
Merrill Lynch Finance S.A.
Société Générale
UBS France S.A.
Union Euro péenne de C.I.C.

Prominnofi

The inter-SVT broker which deals exclusively with SVTs on a no-names basis in government securities. It also handles securities lending.

Correspondants en Valeurs du Trésor (CVT)

These firms are the equivalent of reporting dealers. In March 1996 there were two such firms:

Compagnie Financière de B.Z.W.
ABN Amro Finance S.A.

These two firms were expected to be considered for promotion to SVT in early 1997.

Other authorized intermediaries

The market is open to brokerage houses and to credit institutions authorized to operate as banks, mutual banks and other specialized institutions.

Matif

There are five market-makers in the Option on the Notional Bond Future: Banque d'Escompte, BNP, Indosuez, Société Générale and Transoptions Finance. They must continuously display prices for the strike prices surrounding the at-the-money price for the front-month and the first three quarterly expirations. On request they must quote the other strike prices. For up to 100 contracts they must quote a maximum bid/offer spread of 10 basis points for the 9 strike prices surrounding the ATM price for the front-month and the first two quarterly expirations. For the other strike prices and the third and fourth quarterly expirations the spread must be not more than 20 basis points.

TRADING

Benchmark issues

At 31 December 1995 some of the most important issues were as shown in Table 8.7.

Dealing costs

OATs are usually quoted on a spread of 5 to 15 centimes. ECU OATs are typically quoted on a 15 centime bid/offer spread. All prices are net of tax and costs.

Important issues, 31 December 1995

Table 8.7

Type of bond	Coupon %	Maturity date	Amount in Ffr m
BTAN	4.75%	12.04.99	60,343
OAT	8.50%	25.11.2002	103,709
OAT	8.50%	25.04.2003	101,706
OAT	6.75%	25.10.2003	99,103
OAT	5.50%	25.04.2004	101,121
OAT	7.50%	25.04.2005	108,157
OAT	7.75%	25.10.2005	102,997
OAT	8.50%	25.10.2008	64,666
OAT	8.50%	25.10.2019	61,328
OAT	8.50%	25.04.2023	87,952
OAT	6.00%	25.10.2025	47,330

Source: Ministère de l'Économie et des Finances

Turnover

All OATs are tradeable on the Paris Bourse but are traded over-the-counter through SVTs. Trades are typically for amounts between Ffr50 and Ffr200 million.

ECU OATs are traded in blocks of ECU10 to ECU25 million.

BTANs and BTFs are traded in a similar way but are not traded on the Paris Bourse. The Banque de France publishes a daily list of prices and rates in the secondary market.

OAT liquidity indicator

The government has established a liquidity indicator which is published monthly. The indicator tracks the average daily volume for the five most actively traded Franc or ECU-denominated OATs in each of the three clearing systems.

It will be clear from Table 8.8, that the majority of trades in franc denominated securities are settled through SICOVAM as might be expected. As to the international clearing houses there seems to be a pattern that franc trades are more often settled through Cedel and ECU trades through Euroclear.

During 1995 the daily average turnover in the five most liquid Ffr and ECU OATs was as illustrated in Table 8.10 which also shows where the transactions were settled in Ffr billions:

Table 8.8

Daily average turnover in the five most liquid Ffr and ECU OATs

1995	CEDEL	SICOVAM	EUROCLEAR
January	5.571	44.127	3.613
February	5.764	46,146	5.899
March	5.187	47.805	6.093
April	5.663	56.801	6.557
May	6.448	51.263	8.348
June	3.604	53.449	6.597
July	5.246	50.294	6.843
August	8.507	51.969	6.494
September	10.430	72.437	9.248
October	7.099	60.901	7.627
November	16.895	71.395	5.912
December	8.168	60.136	6.016

Source: Direction du Trésor, Bureau A1

BTAN liquidity indicator

There is a similar indicator for BTANs which shows the average daily volume in the four most liquid BTANs traded in the Banque de France's SATURNE system. This average daily volume indicator includes repos and free-of-payment operations.

Matif

The trading totals of the last five years show a recent reduction in trading similar to that experienced by many other exchanges (see Tables 8.9 and 8.10).

Table 8.9

Matif volumes, 1991–5

	Notional future	Notional option
1991	21,087,899	8,411,903
1992	31,062,844	10,047,391
1993	36,804,824	11,572,671
1994	50,153,150	18,024,502
1995	33,610,221	9,517,932

Source: Matif SA

Cumulative volume and daily averages for 1995

Table 8.10

1995	Notional future	Notional option
Total volume in contracts	33,610,221	9,517,932
Daily average	135,525	38,379
Change vs 1994	–33.0%	–47.2%
Average open interest	138,506	304,005
Change vs 1994	–10.7%	–48.7%

Source: Matif SA

ISSUANCE

The Minister of the Economy and Finance announces an annual indicative financing programme for each year. As an example, that for 1996 was in summary as follows:

The total volume of long and medium term issues was to be Ffr520 billion (1995 Ffr503 billion) divided into Ffr270 billion of OATs (1995 Ffr263 bn) and Ffr250 billion of BTANs (1995 Ffr240 bn). The average maturity of total negotiable government debt is intended to remain between 6 and 6.5 years.

On the first Thursday of each month the Trésor will auction at least Ffr1 billion of 10-year OATs either of an existing issue or another new issue dated 2006 or 2007. If market conditions permit further issues may be made, particularly of the 6% 2025 OAT.

On the second Thursday of each month the Trésor will auction at least ECU100 million of ECU-denominated BTANs or OATs. Any change to this calendar will be announced on the preceding Friday at the latest.

On the third Thursday of each month the Trésor will auction at least Ffr1 billion of at least one 2- or 5-year BTAN.

The Trésor may execute securities swaps or repurchases as well as currency or interest rate swaps either by asking for bids or by syndication. The volume of securities outstanding or cancelled as a result of these operations will be published at the end of each month. Repurchases or exchanges may be part of the debt management activity.

The Trésor reserves the right to cancel or change any of the above in the light of exceptional market circumstances or its requirements.

OAT auctions

Two business days before the auction the government announces the bonds to be issued and sets upper and lower limits on its borrowing. Auctions of OATs are held on the first Thursday of the month and settlement is on twenty-fifth of the month.

OATs can be traded in the primary market from five days before the monthly auction and afterwards until the settlement date. The value date for all such trades is the settlement date with accrued interest to that date.

Auctions are by the multiple price sealed bid method. This is known in France as an "adjudication à la hollandaise" which is not to be confused with a "Dutch auction." Any institution holding an account with SICOVAM, Saturne and the Banque de France is eligible to bid. However the SVTs typically account for 90 percent of securities bought at auction.

Bids are handed to the Banque de France ten minutes before the time of auction or, more usually, are made by the Telsat remote bidding system direct from dealing desks. The whole process takes less than one hour until results are announced. Results are announced between 11.00am and 11.30am on Reuters TRFD and on Telerate 20068.

Bids for OATs are expressed as a percentage of par value to two decimal places with a spread of 0.02 percent between prices. The auction unit is Ffr50 million.

The twenty SVTs (Specialistes en Valeurs du Trésor) have the ability to make bids at the average price accepted for a limited amount, depending on market share and previous auctions. Non-competitive bids (ONC) may be made before the auction for an amount up to 10 percent of the auctioned volume (ONC 1) or on the following day before 4 pm up to 15 percent of the auctioned volume (ONC 2). These bids are satisfied at the weighted average price of the auction.

BTAN auctions

Two business days before the auction the government announces the bonds to be issued and sets upper and lower limits on its borrowing. Auctions of BTANs are held on the third Thursday of the month and settlement is on fifth of the following month for 2-year BTANs and twelfth of the following month for 5-year BTANs.

BTANs can be traded in the primary market. The value date for all such trades is the settlement date with accrued interest to that date calculated on a 365-day year.

The Trésor tends to issue the same two- and five-year BTANs during a six-month period to increase liquidity. Bids are accepted until 10.45am and must be expressed in price terms, excluding accrued interest, expressed to two decimal places. There is a gap of 0.01 percent between prices. The auction unit is Ffr1 million.

Results are announced between 11.00am and 11.30am on Reuters TRFB, on Telerate 20067 and on Bloomberg. Non-competitive bids from SVTs are accepted until 4.00pm on the following day. Bidding rules limit the size of bids at any one price so as to maintain an orderly market.

BTF auctions

The list of bills and amounts to be offered is announced on the Thursday preceding the weekly Monday auction. In the case of BTFs the amounts announced are precise and not given as a range as in the case of longer term securities. A 13-week BTF is auctioned each week often with a longer 26- or 52-week BTF. Bids are accepted until 2.50pm Paris time (until 2.55 pm for non-competitive bids) and must be expressed in yield-to-maturity terms to two decimal points on a 360-day year. This calculation basis is called "postcompte" in France.

Results are announced between 3.00pm and 3.15pm on Reuters TRFC, on Telerate 20067 and on Bloomberg. Non-competitive bids from SVTs are accepted until 4.00pm on the following day. Settlement takes place on the following Thursday except for 26- and 52-week BTFs where settlement takes place ten days after auction. Issues are often fungible to improve liquidity.

Bids at the marginal rate are scaled down on a pro-rata basis, rounded up to the nearest million which is the minimum unit.

Example

For example, the auction of the 13-week BTF on 27 January 1994 was announced for Ffr8 billion. The marginal discount rate was 6.07 percent. The percentage accepted at this marginal rate was 37.70434 percent. Thus a bid for Ffr100 million at the marginal rate would have been accepted for Ffr38 million. The total issued was Ffr8.008 billion, the excess over the announced amount being due to such rounding up.

SETTLEMENT AND DELIVERY

OATs

Domestic trades in Ffr and ECU OATs are cleared in the Relit (Reglement Livraison Titres) system managed by the Paris Bourse SICOVAM clearing house which automatically and simultaneously clears securities and cash. SICOVAM is the central custodian for OATs.

Buy/sell trades may be cleared through the Système de Livraison par accord Bilatéral (SLAB), a part of the Relit system, or by exchanging a transfer of funds from the Banque de France against a transfer of securities from SICOVAM. Trades between SVTs are cleared through a module reserved for them in Relit.

Repos are cleared through the Sico-Pensio module which operates a delivery-versus-payment system.

BTANs

BTAN trades are cleared through the Banque de France Saturne system. (Its full name is Système Automatisé de Traitement Unifié des Règlements de Créances Négociables.) The Banque de France acts as central custodian for BTANs (and BTFs).

The system operates with two-way notification. Failure to deliver by the last clearing session of the day leads to fines on the defaulting party of Ffr700 per Ffr1 million nominal for securities with less than two years to maturity and Ffr1,500 for longer term securities.

BTFs

BTF trades are settled in the same way as BTAN trades through the Banque de France's Saturne system.

International clearing systems

Both Saturne and SICOVAM have direct links with Cedel and Euroclear.

INVESTORS

At the end of November 1995 foreign investors held Ffr604.4 billion of French government securities, including Ffr340.7 billion of OATs. This is well below the figure at the end of 1993. It is interesting to note, however, that in 1989 the total was Ffr180 billion and only Ffr32 billion in 1987. The way in which these holdings fluctuate is illustrated by the following table which is in Ffr billion:

Non-resident holdings of French government securities

Table 8.11

	Dec 93	Jun 94	Dec 94	Jun 95	Nov 95
BTF	36.9	34.7	47.1	51.9	35.8
BTAN	228.4	165.2	144.4	178.1	227.9
OAT	521.7	371.6	333.1	350.1	340.7
Total	787.0	571.5	524.6	580.1	604.4

Sources: Balance des paiements

At the beginning of 1995 it was estimated that the main holders of OATs were UCITS (collective funds) 30 percent, insurance companies 20 percent, non-residents 20 percent and banks 13 percent.

QUOTATIONS, INTEREST AND YIELD CALCULATIONS

The market conventions may be summarized as shown in Table 8.12.

Market conventions

Table 8.12

	Quotation	Days basis
BTF	YTM	360/360
BTAN	Price ex accrued	actual/actual
OAT	Price ex accrued	actual/actual
Strips	YTM	actual/actual

Accrued interest with OATs

There is an important difference between domestic and international trades in the calculation of accrued interest. In the domestic market accrued interest is calculated to the trade date. In the international market accrued interest is calculated to the settlement date.

Example

A domestic trade

Suppose you have bought Ffr50 million of the 9.5% 25 January 2001 OAT on 31 January 1997 at a price of 130.0 for value 3 February 1997. The last coupon date was 25 January 1997.

The number of days accrued interest is 6 (31–25). The calculation is:

$$[9.5\% \times 6/365 = 0.156\%]$$

The amount due is calculated as:

$$(Ffr50,000,000 \times 130.0\%) + (Ffr50,000,000 \times 0.156\%)$$
$$= Ffr65,078,000$$

Repos and securities lending

The legal framework for repo business was established by the Act of 31 December 1993, augmented by the Decree of 2 May 1994 and the Paris money market agreement approved by the Governor of the Bank of France on 15 December 1994. The Act of 8 August 1994 permits netting of repo transactions between two parties.

There are two main types of repurchase agreement: the "pension livrée", and the borrowing or lending facility "prêt de titres" .

Pension livrée

A *pension livrée* is sale and repurchase agreement at a predetermined price and date. This has become the most common type of transaction following the passing of a law clarifying the legal position. This is a temporary sale of securities with a real transfer of ownership and ownership rights.

Prêt de titres

Prêt de titres is a form of stock lending which does not generally involve the movement of cash except for the remuneration paid at maturity.

SPVTs

The SPVTs (Spécialistes de la Pension sur Valeurs du Trésor) were originally appointed in July 1994 and the list was expanded in April 1995. In March 1996 the SPVTs and the SVTs were unified into a single group. SPVTs act as specialist repo dealers and are obliged to quote rates for certain maturities and amounts as follows:

Overnight	Ffr500 million
One week	Ffr500 million
One month	Ffr200 million
Three months	Ffr100 million

The Banque de France publishes daily rates based on these quotations.

A picture of the repo market may be had from the following table which shows the volume and maturity of fixed repos reported monthly by the primary dealers.

Fixed rate repo transaction by maturity

Table 8.13

(In Ffr bn) 1995	1–3 days	4–11 days	12–35 days	over 35 days
March	1,026,789	162,638	111,093	93,229
April	1,033,408	329,475	80,260	56,785
May	1,044,829	433,148	107,210	77,257
June	1,626,723	297,121	124,866	88,090
July	1,606,699	289,940	149,637	95,005
August	2,454,798	458,760	221,100	165,978
September	2,356,047	305,566	234,958	133,034
October	2,742,117	314,703	293,755	124,014
November	2,252,814	211,635	146,329	143,039
December	1,691,170	455,988	175,387	59,707

Source: Statement by the Primary Dealers in Treasury Repos

RECENT AND FUTURE DEVELOPMENTS

The Trésor pursues an active debt management policy. The prime instrument is the Fonds de Soutien des Rentes (FSR) which was reactivated in 1986. Recent legislation has widened the possible actions to include reverse auctions, repurchases or swaps of securities and the use of derivatives.

The policy has three main purposes. The first is to smooth the debt maturity profile and avoid concentrations of maturing debt. The second is to maintain liquidity in the secondary market by retiring debt which is no longer well traded. The third is to reduce the cost of the debt.

SOURCES OF FURTHER INFORMATION

Internet
The Ministère de l'Économie et des Finances has a site of elegance at http://www.tresor.finances.fr/oat/.

The Matif site is at http://www.matif.f

Screen pages

	Reuters	Telerate
Banque de France	SVTF-H	20018-19
Trésor	TRES	20067
SVTs collectively	SVTC/BTFF	

Addresses
Banque de France
39 rue Croix des Petits Champs
75049 Paris
Tel: 331 42 92 42 92
Fax: 331 42 96 04 23

La Bourse de Paris
4 place de la Bourse
75080 Paris Cedex 15
Tel: 331 40 26 85 90
Fax: 331 49 27 13 71

Matif SA (Marché à Terme International de France)
115 rue Réaumur
75083 Paris Cedex 02
Tel: 331 40 28 82 82
Fax: 331 40 28 80 01

Matif SA New York Office
67 Wall Street, Suite 1810
New York
NY 10005, USA
Tel: 212 425 2626
Fax: 212 425 3190

Ministère de l'Économie
Direction du Trésor, Bureau A1
139 rue de Bercy
75572 Paris Cedex 12
Tel: 331 44 87 71 11
Fax: 331 40 04 29 47

Societé des Bourses Francaises (SBF)
39 rue Cambon
75001 Paris
Tel: 331 49 27 10 00
Fax: 331 49 27 14 33

■ ■ ■

"The amount of out-standing German public debt securities doubled between 1991 and 1995."

Germany

LEGAL FRAMEWORK

Form

> "The market is overseen by the Deutsche Bundesbank. Bunds, Bobls, and Schätze are listed on the eight German stock exchanges. "

Bonds and Treasury Notes are issued as shares in a collective Debt Register claim entered in the Federal Debt Register in the name of Deutscher Kassenverein AG, Frankfurt am Main. Investors may have their holdings inscribed in their names in the Federal Debt Register.

Treasury Certificates are issued in book-entry form as shares in a collective certificate deposited with the Deutscher Kassenverein AG. Treasury Certificates are not converted into either physical securities or Debt Register claims.

Regulation of the market

The market is overseen by the Deutsche Bundesbank. Bunds, Bobls, and Schätze are listed on the eight German stock exchanges. BULIS and Finanzierungs-Schätze are not listed.

TAXATION

There is a 32.25 percent withholding tax (including solidarity surcharge) on interest payments which has been in place since 1 January 1993. Banks and non-German taxpayers are exempt.

PROFILE OF THE DEBT

Besides the Federal Government, significant public sector borrowers include the Federal States (Länder), the Treuhandanstalt (which no longer issues), the Federal Post Office (Bundespost), the German Unity Fund (Fonds "Deutsche Einheit") and the Federal Railways (Bundesbahn).

The total indebtedness of all the public entities together rose from DM1,053.5 billion at 31 December 1990 to DM1,875.6 billion at   30

June 1995. This amounted to an increase of 78 percent. In the same period the volume of public debt securities outstanding rose from DM555.4 billion to DM1,251.3 billion, an increase of 125 percent (Table 9.1 sets out the details).

Outstanding public debt securities (DM bn), 1991–5 — Table 9.1

Amounts in DM bn	1995*	1994	1993	1992	1991
Federal Government, of which:	716.3	681.3	638.8	537.8	493.7
Bundesobligationen	172.4	186.6	198.2	161.2	137.7
Bundesschatzbriefe	77.2	59.3	46.1	35.5	34.8
German Unity Fund	54.0	54.0	54.0	52.0	26.0
Currency Conversion Fund	65.0	64.4	59.0	50.3	0.7
ERP Special Fund	11.0	11.0	10.9	5.0	0
Treuhandanstalt	161.8	160.9	101.9	17.1	0
Länder	120.7	112.2	103.8	76.6	47.6
Local authorities	1.6	0.6	0.3	0.2	0.2
Federal Railways	39.4	42.6	42.2	37.4	31.2
Federal Post Office	100.6	102.0	64.4	56.0	43.9
Total	1,270.5	1,229.0	1,075.4	832.4	643.2

Source: Deutsche Bundesbank Kapitalmarktstatistik, January 1996
* as at 30 November 1995

It is also noticeable that the growth of debt with maturity of less than four years has been faster than the growth of debt with maturity over four years. However, the shorter debt is still only a small percentage of total public debt securities, having risen from 3.8 percent in 1991 to 7.4 percent in 1995 (see Table 9.2).

Turning to the Federal debt itself, and including debt not classified as public debt securities, the picture is as shown in Table 9.3.

> "It is also noticeable that the growth of debt with maturity of less than four years has been faster than the growth of debt with maturity over four years."

Outstanding public debt securities by maturity (DM bn), 1991–5 — Table 9.2

Amounts in DM bn	1995*	1994	1993	1992	1991
Maturity					
Four years and under	90.1	98.9	73.6	55.2	24.6
More than four years	1,171.0	1,130.2	1,001.8	777.1	618.7
Total	1,261.1	1,229.0	1,075.4	832.4	643.2

Source: Deutsche Bundesbank Kapitalmarktstatistik
* as at 30 November 1995

Table 9.3

Indebtedness of the Federal Government (DM bn), 1991–5

Amounts in DM bn	1995*	1994	1993	1992	1991
Bundesbank advances	0	0	0	4.4	0
Treasury discount paper	8.1	15.9	23.3	24.3	19.9
Federal treasury paper	65.4	67.0	60.6	50.5	47.9
Bundesobligationen	168.5	181.7	188.8	153.8	133.7
Bundesschatzbriefe	77.2	59.3	46.1	35.4	34.7
Debt securities	395.7	359.8	325.2	289.0	278.7
Lending by credit institutions	20.6	16.7	26.1	37.1	52.7
Owed to social security funds	0	0	0.7	1.5	1.6
Owed to other non-bank	0.9	0.9	3.2	3.7	5.7
Owing to German unification	1.4	1.4	1.4	1.5	1.5
Equalization claims	9.2	9.6	9.7	9.8	9.9
Others	0.2	0.2	0.2	0.2	0.2
Total	747.2	712.5	685.3	611.1	586.5

Source: Deutsche Bundesbank Monthly Report, January 1996
* as at 30 November 1995

Debt maturity by year

At 31 December 1995 the maturity profile of public sector debt was as shown in Table 9.4 (DM millions).

Table 9.4

Maturity profile of public sector debt (DM m), 31 December 1995

	DM mio
1996	120,234
1997	149,936
1998	152,266
1999	117,099
2000	135,011
2001	100,875
2002	119,100
2003	120,282
2004	81,936
2005	64,292
2006	470
2007	275
2008	450
2009	900
2010	0
2011 and later	97,965

Source: Deutsche Bundesbank Kapitalmarktstatistik

INSTRUMENTS AND DERIVATIVES

Bundesanleihen
(Bunds)

Bunds are generally fixed rate bonds with annual coupons, bullet maturities and no calls or puts. Minimum denomination is DM1,000. Some floaters have been issued which pay interest quarterly and which have call provisions.

The Treuhandanstalt, the German Unity Fund, the Economic Recovery Programme (ERP), the Federal Railway (the Bundesbahn) and the Federal Post Office (the Bundespost) also issue Anleihen. The first three carry the explicit guarantee of the Federal Government. The agencies (Bahn and Post) are backed by the full faith and credit of the Federal Government.

Bundesobligationen
(Bobls)

Bobls are fixed rate bonds with annual coupons, a five-year bullet maturity and no calls or puts. Minimum denomination is DM1,000.

Bundesschatzanweisungen
(Federal Treasury Notes or Schätze)

These are fixed rate bonds with annual coupons and a four-year maturity (since May 1991). Denominations are DM5,000.

Bundesbank Unverzinsliche Liquiditäts Schatzanweisungen (Discounted Treasury Certificates or " BULIS')

These are discounted bills with maturities from one to two years. The minimum denomination is DM500,000 (from March 1983 to December 1993 DM100,000). The Deutsche Bundesbank ceased issuing BULIS in September 1994.

The Bundesbank has been opposed to the issuance of short-dated Federal Government money market instruments, fearing that such activity might reduce the Bundesbank's control of money market rates. In May 1996 the German finance ministry announced the intention of issuing short term securities again. These were expected to be quoted instruments in large denominations only. An issuance level of DM50 billion per year was foreseen.

Finanzierungs-Schätze (Treasury financing bills)

These are discounted bills with maturities from one to two years. DM1,000 is the minimum denomination. These are not listed and may not be sold to credit institutions or to foreign investors.

Bundesschatzbriefe (Federal Savings Notes)

These are issued for six years with interest paid annually (type Λ) or for seven years with interest rolled up and paid at maturity (type B). Designed for private investors the type A notes have a DM100 minimum investment and the type B notes a DM50 minimum.

Treasury Bills

Treasury Bills have not been issued since 1968. They were discounted promissory notes sold under article 75 of the Bill of Exchange Act in minimum denominations of DM100,000 for maturities usually from 30 to 90 days, though sometimes very short maturities were issued.

Derivatives

The following contracts are traded on the Deutsche Terminbörse.

Medium-term Notional Bond Future (Bobl Future)

Underlying security	Medium-term notional debt security issued by the German Federal Government or the Treuhandanstalt with a term of 3.5 to 5 years and a coupon of 6%.
Contract size	DM250,000.
Quotation	In percentage of par value to two decimal places.
Minimum price change	0.01 percent, representing a value of DM25.
Delivery months	The three nearest quarter-end months in the cycle March, June, September, December.
Last trading day	Two exchange trading days prior to the delivery day of the relevant quarter-end month. Trading ends at 12.30 pm Frankfurt time.
Delivery day	The tenth calendar day of the quarter-end month if this is an exchange trading day, otherwise the next succeeding exchange trading day.
Daily settlement	The value of open positions is determined at the end of the post-trading-period each day and the difference from the previous day's value (or the trade price for trades on that day) is credited to or debited from the internal cash clearing account.
Daily settlement price	The average of the prices of the last five trades or, if more than five trades have occurred during the final minute of trading, the average of the prices of all trades during this period. If it

is not possible to determine a price or the price does not reflect true market conditions, the DTB will fix the settlement price.

Exchange delivery settlement price

Calculated in the same manner as the daily settlement price but at 12.30 pm Frankfurt time on the last trading day.

- Medium term Notional Bond Future (Bobl Future)
- Long-term Notional Bond Future (Bund Future)
- Very long-term Notional Bond Future (BUXL Future)
- Option on Bobl Future
- Option on Bund Future

Settlement

A delivery obligation may only be performed by delivering securities designated by the DTB. These are Federal Debt Obligations (Bobls), Federal Treasury Bills or, to the extent that they are guaranteed by the Federal Republic, listed debt securities of the Treuhandanstalt – with an original term of not more than 5.25 years, a remaining life of at least 3.5 years and a mini mum issue amount of DM 4 billion. Delivery is made through Deutscher Kassenverein AG.

Key features

Long-term Notional Bond Future (Bund Future)

Underlying security

Long-term notional debt security issued by the German Federal Government or the Treuhandanstalt with a term of 8.5 to 10 years and a coupon of 6%.

Contract size

DM250,000.

Quotation

In percentage of par value to two decimal places.

Minimum price change	0.01 percent, representing a value of DM25.
Delivery months	The three nearest quarter-end months in the cycle March, June, September, December.
Last trading day	Two exchange trading days prior to the delivery day of the relevant quarter-end month. Trading ends at 12.30 pm Frankfurt time.
Delivery day	The tenth calendar day of the quarter-end month if this is an exchange trading day, otherwise the next succeeding exchange trading day.
Daily settlement	The value of open positions is determined at the end of the post-trading-period each day and the difference from the previous day's value (or the trade price for trades on that day) is credited to or debited from the internal cash clearing account.
Daily settlement price	The average of the prices of the last five trades or, if more than five trades have occurred during the final minute of trading, the average of the prices of all trades during this period. If it is not possible to determine a price or the price does not reflect true market conditions, the DTB will fix the settlement price.
Exchange delivery settlement price	Calculated in the same manner as the daily settlement price but at 12.30 pm Frankfurt time on the last trading day.
Settlement	A delivery obligation may only be performed by delivering securities designated by the DTB. These are Federal Government Bonds or, to the extent that they are guaranteed by the Federal Republic, listed debt securities of the Treuhandanstalt – with a remaining life of 8.5 to 10 years. Delivery is made through Deutscher Kassenverein AG.

Very long-term Notional Bond Future (BUXL Future)

The BUXL future has not traded since June 1995.

Underlying security	Long-term notional debt security issued by the German Federal Government or the Treuhandanstalt with a term of 15 to 30 years and a coupon of 6%.
Contract size	DM250,000.
Quotation	In percentage of par value to two decimal places.
Minimum price change	0.01 percent, representing a value of DM25.
Delivery months	The three nearest quarter-end months in the cycle March, June, September, December.
Last trading day	Two exchange trading days prior to the delivery day of the relevant quarter-end month. Trading ends at 12.30 pm Frankfurt time.
Delivery day	The 10th calendar day of the quarter-end month if this is an exchange trading day, otherwise the next succeeding exchange trading day.
Daily settlement	The value of open positions is determined at the end of the post-trading-period each day and the difference from the previous day's value (or the trade price for trades on that day) is credited to or debited from the internal cash clearing account.
Daily settlement price	The average of the prices of the last five trades, or if more than five trades have occurred during the final minute of trading, the average of the prices of all trades during this period. If it is not possible to determine a price or the price does not reflect true market conditions, the DTB will fix the settlement price.

Exchange delivery settlement price	Calculated in the same manner as the daily settlement price but at 12.30 pm Frankfurt time on the last trading day.
Settlement	A delivery obligation may only be performed by delivering securities designated by the DTB. These are Federal Government Bonds or, to the extent that they are guaranteed by the Federal Republic, listed debt securities of the Treuhandanstalt – with a remaining life of 15 to 30 years and a minimum issue amount of DM4 billion. Delivery is made through DeutscherKassenverein AG.

Option on Bobl Future

Underlying security	Future on a notional medium-term debt security.
Unit of trading	One Bobl futures contract.
Quotation	In points with two decimal places.
Minimum price change	0.01 point, representing a value of DM25.
Expiration months	The next three in the cycle February, May, August and November.
Expiration day	The exchange trading day following the last trading day of each option series.
Last trading day	Six exchange trading days prior to the first calendar day in the delivery month of the Bobl future.
Exercise period	American style. An option may be exercised up to the end of the post-trading period on any exchange trading day during the life of the option.

Settlement	Exercise of an option gives rise to a futures position.
Daily settlement price	The price of the last trade in an option series during the last hour of trading on an exchange trading day. If no trades have occurred in this time or the traded price does not reflect true market conditions, the DTB will fix the settlement price.
Exercise prices	Nine exercise prices are introduced for each contract month with price gradations of 0.25.
New exercise prices	New strike prices are introduced if the daily settlement price of the Bobl future has, on the two preceding exchange trading days, exceeded or fallen below the average of the fifth and fourth highest or fifth and fourth lowest strike prices. A new series is not usually introduced if it would expire in fewer than ten exchange trading days.
Option premium	The premium is settled "futures style". The premium payment is not made at purchase of the option but as part of the daily settlement process during the duration of the option position based on a mark-to-market valuation of the position on each trading day.

Key features

Option on Bund Future

Underlying security	Future on a notional long-term debt security.
Unit of trading	One Bund futures contract.
Quotation	In points with two decimal places.
Minimum price change	0.01 point, representing a value of DM25.
Expiration months	The next three in the cycle February, May, August and November.

Expiration day	The exchange trading day following the last trading day of each option series.
Last trading day	Six exchange trading days prior to the first calendar day in the delivery month of the Bund future.
Exercise period	American style. An option may be exercised up to the end of the post-trading period on any exchange trading day during the life of the option.
Settlement	Exercise of an option gives rise to a futures position.
Daily settlement price	The price of the last trade in an option series during the last hour of trading on an exchange trading day. If no trades have occurred in this time or the traded price does not reflect true market conditions, the DTB will fix the settlement price.
Exercise prices	Nine exercise prices are introduced for each contract month with price gradations of 0.25.
New exercise prices	New strike prices are introduced if the daily settlement price of the Bund future has, on the two preceding exchange trading days, exceeded or fallen below the average of the fifth and fourth highest or fifth and fourth lowest strike prices. A new series is not usually introduced if it would expire in fewer than ten exchange trading days.
Option premium	The premium is settled "futures style". The premium payment is not made at purchase of the option but as part of the daily settlement process during the duration of the option position based on a mark-to-market valuation of the position on each trading day.

The following contracts are traded on LIFFE. A Bobl futures contract was delisted in September 1994.

Bund Future

Unit of trading	DM250,000 nominal value of a notional Government bond with a 6% coupon.
Delivery months	March, June, September, December.
Delivery day	Tenth calendar day of delivery month. If such a day is not a working day in Frankfurt, then the delivery day will be the next Frankfurt working day.
Last trading day	11.00 Frankfurt time, three Frankfurt working days prior to delivery day.
Quotation	Per DM100 nominal value.
Minimum price change	DM0.01, DM25 in value.
Trading hours	07.30–16.15 London time. APT 16.20–17.55 London time.
Contract standard	Delivery may be made of any Bund (including Unity Fund bonds and Treuhand bonds issued before 31 December 1994) with between 8.5 and 10 years remaining life as at the tenth calendar day of the delivery month, as listed by LIFFE. Any ELF bond issued on or after 1 January 1995 is not deliverable.
Exchange delivery settlement price	LIFFE market price at 11.00 Frankfurt time on the last trading day.

Option on Bund Future

Unit of trading	One Bund futures contract.
Delivery months	March, June, September, December plus additional serial months such that four expiry months, including the three nearest calendar months, are always available for trading.
Exercise day	Exercise by 17.00 on any business day, brought forward to 11.30 on last trading day.
Expiry day	18.30 on last trading day.
Delivery day	Delivery on the first business day after the exercise day.
Last trading day	10.00 six business days prior to the first day of the expiry month.
Quotation	Multiples of DM0.01.
Minimum price change	DM0.01, DM25 in value.
Trading hours	07.32–16.15 London time.
Contract standard	Assignment of 1 Bund future.
Exercise prices	Nine prices are listed for each series. Additional exercise prices are introduced on the business day after the Bund futures settlement price is within DM0.25 of the fourth highest or lowest exercise price. Exercise price intervals are DM0.50.
Option price	The contract price is not paid at the time of purchase. The contract price is payable on exercise, netted against the daily variation margin balance.

MARKET-MAKING SYSTEM

"Trading takes place over-the-counter, on the eight German stock exchanges of which Frankfurt is the most important, and on the IBIS domestic electronic dealing system."

Trading takes place over-the-counter, on the eight German stock exchanges of which Frankfurt is the most important, and on the IBIS domestic electronic dealing system. The majority of trading is OTC. The members of the Federal Konsortium are not obliged to make markets.

Trading hours are as follows:

Stock Exchange	10.30 – 13.30
OTC	09.00 – 17.00
IBIS	08.30 – 17.00 (quotes may be obtained from 08.00)

The benchmark issues generally trade on an 0.05 bid/offer spread with other issues trading on a spread of 0.10. The average OTC transaction size is about DM25 million.

TRADING

Only the Stock Exchange publishes turnover of domestic bonds which is an inadequate measure of the market as a whole.

Derivatives

During 1995 the trading on the DTB can be summarized as shown in Tables 9.5, 9.6, 9.7, 9.8, and 9.9.

Trading at LIFFE may be summarized as shown in Tables 9.10 and 9.11.

Bund Future, DTB 1995

Table 9.5

1995	Volume	Month-end open interest
January	1,130,570	191,731
February	914,524	184,022
March	1,219,969	142,601
April	741,640	150,746
May	957,913	149,441
June	1,333,395	140,942
July	942,898	180,799
August	910,154	147,135
September	1,422,958	139,917
October	1,088,564	170,342
November	1,085,469	165,621
December	777,210	123,321
Total 1995	12,525,264	
Daily average 1995	49,901	

Source: Deutsche Börse AG, Securities Standards Department

Option on the Bund Future, DTB 1995

Table 9.6

1995	Volume	Month-end open interest
January	16,554	19,959
February	17,439	5,135
March	13,279	8,333
April	9,927	10,296
May	17,705	4,507
June	14,497	9,549
July	13,018	12,987
August	20,641	3,277
September	7,801	6,977
October	12,567	15,084
November	37,555	16,629
December	13,053	19,556
Total 1995	194,036	
Daily average 1995	773	

Source: Deutsche Börse AG, Securities Standards Department

Table 9.7

Bobl future, DTB 1995

1995	Volume	Month-end open interest
January	404,345	104,782
February	518,933	185,887
March	630,674	129,106
April	376,148	113,984
May	588,121	161,413
June	703,084	134,204
July	524,166	132,433
August	678,182	178,420
September	769,880	163,096
October	734,416	190,156
November	785,513	175,072
December	638,321	103,523
Total 1995	7,351,783	
Daily Average 1995	29,290	

Source: Deutsche Börse AG, Securities Standards Department

Table 9.8

Option on the Bobl Future, DTB 1995

1995	Volume	Month-end open interest
January	4,222	6,079
February	3,346	1,430
March	3,538	3,739
April	1,581	4,827
May	1,832	975
June	2,529	2,746
July	3,456	4,571
August	3,415	1,568
September	20,678	12,247
October	21,302	23,035
November	44,957	22,507
December	12,163	21,104
Total 1995	123,019	
Daily Average 1995	490	

Source: Deutsche Börse AG, Securities Standards Department

BUXL Future, DTB 1995

Table 9.9

1995	Volume	Month-end open interest
January	736	312
February	1,011	300
March	1,040	160
April	968	203
May	798	338
June	31	0
July	0	0
August	0	0
September	0	0
October	0	0
November	0	0
December	0	0
Total 1995	4,584	

Source: Deutsche Börse AG, Securities Standards Department

Bund Future, LIFFE 1995

Table 9.10

1995	Monthly volume	Month-end open interest
January	2,599,020	213,761
February	2,718,023	222,460
March	3,447,437	170,153
April	1,911,124	173,598
May	2,652,651	182,136
June	3,481,739	193,407
July	2,252,745	200,657
August	2,400,187	216,415
September	3,333,215	185,570
October	2,720,675	206,907
November	2,787,993	230,547
December	1,926,401	201,842
Total 1995	32,231,210	
Daily Average 1995	127,902	

Source: LIFFE

Table 9.11

Option on the Bund Future, LIFFE 1995

1995	Monthly volume	Month-end open interest
January	571,312	319,263
February	540,824	210,415
March	527,434	263,153
April	434,561	302,206
May	548,510	212,211
June	716,532	313,977
July	578,741	317,291
August	557,795	220,853
September	708,546	337,661
October	591,814	330,467
November	725,806	275,709
December	486,780	275,416
Total 1995	6,988,655	
Daily average 1995	27,733	

Source: LIFFE

ISSUANCE

The 110 members of the Federal bond syndicate include 50 foreign firms. Each firm has a predetermined quota for the first tranche of each Bund issue.

Bundesanleihen (Bunds)

A first tranche of each new issue (about 40 percent) is sold to the 95 members of the Federal Bond Consortium (Bundesanleihekonsortium) who receive a placement commission of 0.875 percent. A second tranche (about 40 percent) is auctioned by a "US-style" auction. A third tranche (about 20 percent) is always kept by the Bundesbank for market support operations.

Bids may be submitted only by members of the Consortium and must be received by 11.00 am on the day of the auction. Bids must be in an amount of DM100,000 or multiples thereof and expressed in percentage to two decimal places. Non-competitive bids are possible and are satisfied at the average price of the competitive bids accepted.

A floating-rate bond was issued by tender in 1990.

New issues are announced on the Bundesbank's Reuters page BBK01/15 and on Telerate pages 22223/22229.

Bundesobligationen (Bobls)

Bobls are sold as tap issues in tranches. The total amount of each series is not fixed in advance. When market conditions require a new coupon the old series is closed and then is listed and traded on the Stock Exchange.

Purchases in the primary market are restricted to individuals and resident non-profit, charitable or church entities. Once admitted to the Stock Exchange anyone is allowed to buy the bonds.

Bundesschatzanweisungen (Federal Treasury Notes)

These are sold quarterly by tender. Only credit institutions holding a giro account with a Land Central Bank may participate in the tender. Bids must be submitted by 11.00 am in an amount of DM5,000 or a multiple thereof and be expressed in percentage to two decimal places. Non-competitive bids are possible. Issues have been usually at least DM4bn.

Bundesbank Liquiditäts Unverzinsliche Schatzanweisungen (Discounted Treasury Certificates) "BULIS"

These were not issued after September 1994. Only credit institutions holding a giro account and/or a safe custody account with a Land Central Bank were able to participate in the tender. Bids were required to be in an amount of DM500,000 or a multiple thereof and be expressed in percentage to two decimal places. Non-competitive bids were possible.

Finanzierungsschätze (Treasury financing bills) and Bundesschatzbriefe (Federal Savings Notes)

Both instruments are sold to retail clients through banks and do not have a special issuance procedure

New issue volumes

Table 9.12 gives the net borrowing figures for 1994 and the first half of 1995 by type of instrument. These figures may be lower than the increase in indebtedness due to the assumption of debts.

Table 9.12 **Net borrowing figures by instrument, 1994 and first half 1995**

Amounts in DM millions	1994 12m	1995 6m
Treasury discount paper	-10,082	-9,144
Treasury notes	+15,544	+9,735
Five-year special federal bonds	-7,030	-12,136
Federal savings bonds	+13,24	+8,840
Debt Securities	+33,967	+17,923

Source: Deutsche Bundesbank Monthly Report, January 1996

SETTLEMENT AND DELIVERY

Trades on Stock Exchanges settle on T+2. International trades settle on T+7. In OTC trades the settlement date may be negotiated.

Bonds are usually cleared through the Kassenverein but Bunds and bonds of the Post Office and Railways together with Bobls and Schätze may be settled through Cedel and Euroclear which are linked by the Auslandskassenverein to the Kassenverein.

INVESTORS

Table 9.13 illustrates the growth of non-resident investment in government securities during a five year period during which the total public debt more than doubled.

Holdings of public debt securities in 1989 and 1994 (at 31 December), amounts in DM billions

Table 9.13

	1989 Value	1989 %	1994 Value	1994 %
Households, of which	85.5	26.0	143.4	17.9
Individuals	75.8	23.1	129.6	16.2
Non-profit organizations	9.7	2.9	13.8	1.7
Non-financial enterprises	18.5	5.6	36.9	4.6
Public sector, of which	11.4	3.5	29.1	3.6
Social security funds	2.1	0.6	2.9	0.4
Central, regional and local authorities	9.3	2.8	26.2	3.3
Institutional investors, of which	53.7	16.3	112.3	14.0
Insurance enterprises	35.5	10.8	49.4	6.2
Funds of investment cos	18.2	5.5	62.9	7.9
Non-residents	159.5	48.5	477.7	59.8
Totals	328.6	100.0	799.4	100.0

Source: Deutsche Bundesbank Monthly Report, August 1995

QUOTATIONS, INTEREST AND YIELD CALCULATIONS

Bond prices are quoted in decimals and trade on a clean price basis.

Bond yields are calculated on a 30/360 day basis. ISMA methods are used for international transactions, and usually in the Bund market. There are two domestic conventions known as Moosmüller (used by pension funds and by the Düsseldorf and München exchanges) and Braess/Fangmeyer used by the Sparkassen) which differ in the calculation of compound interest in a broken period.

Treasury bill yields are calculated on an actual/360 day money market basis.

Federal government bonds do not trade ex-dividend.

Repos and securities lending

The repo market is not active in Germany. Most activity is in the form of securities lending. Repo is only available with the central bank which uses it to manage monetary policy.

In London there is a large repo market. It has been estimated that about DM100 billion or more is outstanding in repo transactions in London.

SOURCES OF FURTHER INFORMATION

Screen pages

	Reuters
Treasury bills	AVSJ-M
	BUNE
Bunds	AVSB-I
	DBFC-E
	BUNG

Addresses

Deutsche Borse AG
Borsenplatz   7-11
60284 Frankfurt am Main
Tel: 49 69 21 01 59 73
Fax: 49 69 21 01 39 51

Deutsche Bundesbank
6000 Frankfurt   50,
Wilhelm-Epstein str.   14
Tel: 4969   15 81
Fax: 4969   56 01 07 1

Ministry of Finance
Graurheindorfer Str. 108
5300 Bonn 1
Tel: 49 22 86 82-0
Fax: 49   22 86 82 44 20

■ ■ ■

"The fact to note is that the amount of new money being borrowed each year is not much different to the sums being borrowed ten years ago. What has changed is the refinancing need each year which now exceeds US$2,000 billion."

United States

LEGAL FRAMEWORK

> **"Each Treasury note or bond has a unique CUSIP number."**

Form

Since 1 August 1986 Treasury notes and bonds have been issued in book-entry form only.

The Secretary of the Treasury is authorized under Chapter 31 of Title 31, United States Code, to issue Treasury Securities and to prescribe terms and conditions for their issuance and sale (31 U.S.C. § 3121). The Secretary may issue bonds under 31 U.S.C. § 3102, notes under 31 U.S.C. § 3103 and bills under 31 U.S.C. § 3104.

Identification

Each Treasury note or bond has a unique CUSIP number. This is a nine-digit identifier (seven numbers and two letters) developed by the Committee on Uniform Securities Identification Procedures (CUSIP) under the auspices of the American Bankers Association. When an issue is stripped the principal strip is given another CUSIP number and the coupon strips are assigned a generic CUSIP number common to all stripped interest coupons due on a specific date.

Regulation of the market

The Treasury, the Justice Department, the Federal Reserve, the Securities and Exchange Commission and the self-regulatory organizations (SROs) have various responsibilities. Brokers and dealers in the secondary market are regulated under the Government Securities Act of 1986. Broker-dealers also are regulated by the Securities Exchange Act of 1934 and banks are subject to the banking laws.

US Treasuries are traded over-the-counter by government securities broker/dealers and are also listed on the New York Stock Exchange but trading takes place by telephone.

Government agencies (such as the Government National Mortgage Association, the Small Business Administration and the Tennessee Valley Authority) either issue marketable debt or guarantee debt.

Government-sponsored enterprises (such as the Federal National Mortgage Corporation, Farm Credit System, Federal Home Loan Bank System and Student Loan Marketing Association) also issue marketable debt, subordinated debt, and guarantee asset-backed securities.

TAXATION

Domestic US investors must provide a tax identification number to avoid 31 percent withholding tax. For non-resident investors there is no withholding tax on most issues provided that they have filed proof of beneficial ownership. Without such a filing a 30 percent withholding is levied.

PROFILE OF THE DEBT

Debt outstanding

The US government has no foreign currency debt. The Public Debt outstanding at 31 December 1995 could be summarized as shown in Table 10.1.

US Public Debt outstanding, 31 December 1995 (US$ bn)

Table 10.1

Amounts in US$ bn	31 Dec 1995	31 Dec 1994
Interest-bearing marketable debt of which:	**3,307.2**	**3,126.0**
Bills	760.7	733.8
Notes	2,010.3	1,867.0
Bonds	521.2	510.3
Other securities	15.0	15.0
Interest-bearing nonmarketable debt	**1,657.2**	**1,643.1**
Non-interest-bearing debt	**24.3**	**31.0**
Total Public Debt	**4,988.7**	**4,800.1**

Source: Bureau of the Public Debt, Department of the Treasury

The debt ceiling

By Act of 10 August 1993 the Statutory Debt Limit was permanently increased to US$4,900 billion. At 31 December 1995 there was US$25 million of room under this limit.

There was a much publicized impasse over the US budget in late 1995. Congress did not raise the debt ceiling as the Treasury Secretary had hoped. There was no real risk of default however. This was because the Treasury controlled a large amount of trust fund assets. Among the 160 trust funds which the Treasury administers were two retirement funds for federal employees which usually hold their assets in the form of special government bonds which count under the debt ceiling. The Treasury replaced some of these bonds with another form of obligation and thus created room under the debt ceiling. The Civil Service Retirement fund had assets of over US$300 billion so that the government was in a position to continue in this way for some time (see Table 10.2).

Table 10.2

Outstanding level of US public and private debt, 1980–95 (US$ bn)

Year	Municipal	Treasury	Agency mortgage-backed	US corporate
1980	365.4	616.4	110.9	471.5
1981	398.3	683.2	126.4	495.8
1982	451.3	824.4	176.3	527.5
1983	505.7	1,024.4	244.3	564.6
1984	564.4	1,176.6	289.4	627.3
1985	743.0	1,360.2	372.1	719.8
1986	789.6	1,564.3	534.4	860.9
1987	873.1	1,675.0	672.1	958.8
1988	939.4	1,821.3	749.9	1,071.1
1989	1,004.7	1,945.4	876.3	1,159.3
1990	1,184.4	2,195.8	1,024.4	1,231.9
1991	1,272.2	2,471.6	1,160.5	1,332.5
1992	1,302.8	2,754.1	1,273.5	1,430.6
1993	1,377.5	2,989.5	1,349.6	1,606.5
1994	1,348.2	3,126.0	1,441.9	1,656.6
1995	1,300.0	3,307.2	1,515.4	1,792.5

Source: Public Securities Association, derived from the US Treasury, Federal Reserve System, FNMA, GNMA and FHLMC

Notes: Treasury debt is interest-bearing public debt. Agency mortgage-backed includes only FNMA, GNMA, and FHLMC.

INSTRUMENTS AND DERIVATIVES

Treasury bills

Bills are issued with maturities of 13, 26 and 52 weeks. They are auctioned at a discount. Short-term cash management bills are also auctioned when required by the Treasury's cash-flow needs. Bills are in book-entry form held for investors through the Treasury Direct system and by financial institutions and Federal Reserve Banks through the commercial book-entry system. Minimum purchase amount is US$10,000 with larger amounts in multiples of US$1,000.

Treasury notes

Notes are coupon-paying securities issued with maturities of two, three, five, and ten years. Seven-year notes were issued until April 1993 and four-year notes were issued until December 1990. All notes have fixed coupons and bullet maturities. Minimum denomination is US$1,000. Minimum purchase is US$5,000 for notes of less than four years to maturity and US$1,000 for longer notes with larger amounts in multiples of US$1,000.

Treasury bonds

Bonds are coupon-paying securities issued with maturities over ten years. All bonds have fixed coupons and (for bonds issued since 1984) bullet maturities. Minimum denomination is US$1,000 with larger amounts in multiples of US$1,000.

Separate Trading of Registered Interest Principal (STRIPS)

At 31 December 1995 there were 65 issues of Treasury securities which were partly held in stripped form. US$221.6 bn in nominal value was held in stripped form by secondary market participants, being just over 25 percent of the nominal value of the issues concerned. These have been eligible to be reconstituted to their unstripped form since 1 May 1987.

Other debt

The Treasury issues non-marketable securities such as savings bonds.

In May 1996 the US Treasury secretary announced plans to issue inflation protected bonds with either a ten- or thirty-year life.

Derivatives

Summary

The following contracts are traded at the Chicago Board of Trade:

- Two-year US Treasury Note Futures
- Five-year US Treasury Note Futures
- Ten-year US Treasury Note Futures
- US Treasury Bond Futures
- Options on Two-year US Treasury Note Futures
- Options on Five-year US Treasury Note Futures
- Options on Ten-year US Treasury Note Futures
- Options on US Treasury Bond Futures.

Key features | ## Two-year US Treasury Note Futures

Trading unit	US Treasury Note having a face value at maturity of US$200,000 or multiple thereof.
Contract months	March, June, September and December.
Deliverable securities	US Treasury Notes with an original maturity of not more than 5 years 3 months and a remaining maturity of not less than 1 year 9 months from the first day of the delivery month but not more than two years from the last day of the delivery month. The two-year Treasury Note issued after the last trading day of the contract month will not be eligible for delivery into that month's contract.
Quotation	In points (US$2,000) and one quarter of 1/32 of a point (US$15.625). For example 91.162 equals 91 and 16.25/32.

Daily price limit	1 point above or below the previous day's settlement price (expandable to 1.5 points).
Last trading day	Seventh business day preceding the last business day of the delivery month. Trading ends at noon, Chicago time.
Delivery method	Federal Reserve book-entry wire transfer system.
Last delivery day	Last business day of the delivery month.
Trading hours	07.20 to 14.00 Chicago time Monday to Friday. Evening trading is from 17.00 to 20.30 (Central Standard Time) or 18.00 to 21.30 (Central Daylight Saving Time) Sunday to Thursday.

Five-year US Treasury Note Futures

Key features

Trading unit	US Treasury Note having a face value at maturity of US$100,000 or multiple thereof.
Contract months	March, June, September and December.
Deliverable securities	US Treasury Notes with an original maturity of not more than 5 years 3 months and a remaining maturity of not less than 4 years 3 months from the first day of the delivery month. The five-year Treasury Note issued after the last trading day of the contract month will not be eligible for delivery into that month's contract.
Quotation	In points (US$1,000) and one half of 1/32 of a point (US$15.625).
Daily price limit	3 points above or below the previous day's settlement price (expandable to 4.5 points).
Last trading day	Seventh business day preceding the last business day of the delivery month. Trading ends at noon, Chicago time.

Delivery method	Federal Reserve book-entry wire transfer system.
Last delivery day	Last business day of the delivery month.
Trading hours	07.20 to 14.00 Chicago time Monday to Friday. Evening trading is from 17.00 to 20.30 (Central Standard Time) or 18.00 to 21.30 (Central Daylight Saving Time) Sunday to Thursday.

Ten-year US Treasury Note Futures

Trading unit	US Treasury Note having a face value at maturity of US$100,000 or multiple thereof.
Contract months	March, June, September and December.
Deliverable securities	US Treasury Notes with remaining life between 6.5 years and 10 years from the first business day of the delivery month.
Quotation	In points (US$1,000) and thirty-seconds of a point (US$31.25).
Daily price limit	3 points above or below the previous day's settlement price (expandable to 4.5 points).
Last trading day	Seventh business day preceeding the last business day of the delivery month Trading ends at noon, Chicago time.
Delivery method	Federal Reserve book-entry wire transfer system.
Last delivery day	Last business day of the delivery month.
Trading hours	07.20 to 14.00 Chicago time Monday to Friday. Evening trading is from 17.00 to 20.30 (Central Standard Time) or 18.00 to 21.30 (Central Daylight Saving Time) Sunday to Thursday.

US Treasury Bond Futures

Trading unit	US Treasury Bond having a face value at maturity of US$100,000 or multiple thereof.
Contract months	March, June, September and December.
Deliverable securities	US Treasury Bonds that, if callable, are not callable for at least 15 years from the first day of the delivery month or, if not callable, have a maturity of at least 15 years from the first business day of the delivery month.
Quotation	In points (US$1,000) and thirty-seconds of a point (US$31.25).
Daily price limit	3 points above or below the previous day's settlement price (expandable to 4.5 points).
Last trading day	Seventh business day preceding the last business day of the delivery month. Trading ends at noon, Chicago time.
Delivery method	Federal Reserve book-entry wire transfer system.
Last delivery day	Last business day of the delivery month.
Trading hours	07.20 to 14.00 Chicago time Monday to Friday. Evening trading is from 17.00 to 20.30 (Central Standard Time) or 18.00 to 21.30 (Central Daylight Saving Time) Sunday to Thursday.

Options on Two-year US Treasury Note Futures

Trading unit	One CBOT 2-year US Treasury Note futures contract of a specified delivery month having a face value at maturity of US$200,000 or multiple thereof.
Tick size	One half of one sixty-fourth of a point (US$15.625 per contract) rounded up to the nearest cent per contract.

Strike prices	At quarter point intervals to bracket the current future price.
Daily price limit	1 point (US$2,000 per contract) above or below the previous day's settlement price for all trading days except the last.
Contract months	The front month of the current cycle plus the next three contracts of the regular quarterly cycle. If the front month is a quarterly month no monthly contract will be listed. The monthly options contract exercises into the current quarterly futures contract.
Last trading day	Options cease trading at noon on the last Friday preceding by at least five business days the last business day of the month preceding the option contract month. That is, options cease trading in the month prior to the delivery month of the underlying futures contract.
Exercise	On any business day prior to expiration by notice to the Board of Trade Clearing Corporation by 18.00 Chicago time. Options at least 1 point in the money on the last day of trading are automatically exercised.
Expiration	Unexercised options expire at 10.00 Chicago time on the first Saturday following the last day of trading.
Trading hours	07.20 to 14.00 Chicago time Monday to Friday. Evening trading is from 17.20 to 20.05 (Central Standard Time) or 18.20 to 21.05 (Central Daylight Saving Time) Sunday to Thursday.

Options on Five-year US Treasury Note Futures

Trading unit

One CBOT 5-year US Treasury Note futures contract of a specified delivery month having a face value at maturity of US$100,000 or multiple thereof.

Tick size

One sixty-fourth of a point (US$15.625 per contract) rounded up to the nearest cent per contract.

Strike prices

At half point intervals to bracket the current future price.

Daily price limit

3 points (US$3,000 per contract) above or below the previous day's settlement price for all trading days except the last.

Contract months

The front month of the current cycle plus the next three contracts of the regular quarterly cycle. If the front month is a quarterly month no monthly contract will be listed. The monthly options contract exercises into the current quarterly futures contract.

Last trading day

Options cease trading at noon on the last Friday preceding by at least five business days the last business day of the month preceding the option contract month. That is, options cease trading in the month prior to the delivery month of the under-lying futures contract.

Exercise

On any business day prior to expiration by notice to the Board of Trade Clearing Corporation by 18.00 Chicago time. Options at least 2 points in the money on the last day of trading are auto-matically exercised.

Expiration

Unexercised options expire at 10.00 Chicago time on the first Saturday following the last day of trading.

| Trading hours | 07.20 to 14.00 Chicago time Monday to Friday. Evening trading is from 17.20 to 20.05 (Central Standard Time) or 18.20 to 21.05 (Central Daylight Saving Time) Sunday to Thursday. |

Options on Ten-year US Treasury Note Futures

Trading unit	One CBOT 10-year US Treasury Note futures contract of a specified delivery month having a face value at maturity of US$100,000 or multiple thereof.
Tick size	One sixty-fourth of a point (US$15.625 per contract) rounded up to the nearest cent per contract.
Strike prices	At one point intervals to bracket the current future price.
Daily price limit	3 points (US$3,000 per contract) above or below the previous day's settlement price for all trading days except the last.
Contract months	The front month of the current cycle plus the next three contracts of the regular quarterly cycle. If the front month is a quarterly month no monthly contract will be listed. The monthly options contract exercises into the current quarterly futures contract.
Last trading day	Options cease trading at noon on the last Friday preceding by at least five business days the last business day of the month preceding the option contract month. That is, options cease trading in the month prior to the delivery month of the underlying futures contract.
Exercise	On any business day prior to expiration by notice to the Board of Trade Clearing Corporation by

18.00 Chicago time. Options at least 2 points in the money on the last day of trading are automatically exercised.

Expiration — Unexercised options expire at 10.00 Chicago time on the first Saturday following the last day of trading.

Trading hours — 07.20 to 14.00 Chicago time Monday to Friday. Evening trading is from 17.20 to 20.05 (Central Standard Time) or 18.20 to 21.05 (Central Daylight Saving Time) Sunday to Thursday.

Options on US Treasury Bond Futures

Key features

Trading unit — One CBOT US Treasury Bond futures contract of a specified delivery month having a face value at maturity of US$100,000 or multiple thereof.

Tick size — One sixty-fourth of a point (US$15.625 per contract) rounded up to the nearest cent per contract.

Strike prices — At two point intervals to bracket the current future price.

Daily price limit — 3 points (US$3,000 per contract) above or below the previous day's settlement price for all trading days except the last.

Contract months — The front month of the current cycle plus the next three contracts of the regular quarterly cycle. If the front month is a quarterly month no monthly contract will be listed. The monthly options contract exercises into the current quarterly futures contract.

Last trading day — Options cease trading at noon on the last Friday preceding by at least five business days the last business day of the month preceding the option contract month. That is, options cease trading in

	the month prior to the delivery month of the underlying futures contract.
Exercise	On any business day prior to expiration by notice to the Board of Trade Clearing Corporation by 18.00 Chicago time. Options at least 2 points in the money on the last day of trading are automatically exercised.
Expiration	Unexercised options expire at 10.00 Chicago time on the first Saturday following the last day of trading.
Trading hours	07.20 to 14.00 Chicago time Monday to Friday. Evening trading is from 17.20 to 20.05 (Central Standard Time) or 18.20 to 21.05 (Central Daylight Saving Time) Sunday to Thursday.

MARKET-MAKING SYSTEM

Primary dealers

There are thirty-eight primary dealers who are large underwriters of debt even though they no longer have exclusive access to auctions. Primary dealers provide liquidity in the market and are the means by which the Federal Reserve conducts open market operations.

To remain a primary dealer a firm must satisfy the Federal Reserve Bank of New York (FRBNY) that it makes reasonably good markets, provides the FRBNY with market information, bids at auctions, and has adequate capital.

Interdealer brokers

There are seven inter-dealer brokers of whom three trade only with primary dealers. The others variously include other members of the Government Securities Clearing Corporation (GSCC), other dealers, banks, pension funds, and other institutions.

TRADING

Benchmark issues

The most recently issued bills, note and bonds are said to be the "on-the-runs" or "benchmarks."

Volumes

Average daily trading volume of US Treasury Securities, 1981–95 (reported by Primary Dealers)

Table 10.3

US$ bn	Broker/ dealer transactions	Customer transactions	Total
1981	13.3	11.2	24.5
1982	17.4	14.8	32.2
1983	23.3	18.8	42.1
1984	28.5	24.3	52.8
1985	39.6	35.8	75.4
1986	53.3	42.3	95.6
1987	64.6	45.6	110.2
1988	63.0	39.2	102.2
1989	69.8	43.1	112.9
1990	68.7	42.5	111.2
1991	78.5	49.0	127.5
1992	95.7	56.4	152.1
1993	107.7	65.9	173.6
1994	116.1	75.2	191.3
1995	112.7	80.5	193.2

Source: Public Securities Association quoting the Federal Reserve Bank of New York

Trading volume

Tables 10.4, 10.5, 10.6, 10.7, 10.8, 10.9, 10.10 and 10.11 summarize the 1995 trading.

Table 10.4

Two-year US Treasury Note Futures,1995

1995	Monthly volume	Month-end open interest
July	34,095	19,300
August	68,673	18,547
September	37,775	16,274
October	34,282	19,804
November	83,571	24,444
December	49,048	17,127
Jan–Dec 1995	744,866	
Change vs 1994	–20.7%	

Source: CBOT

Table 10.5

Five-year US Treasury Note Futures, 1995

1995	Monthly volume	Month-end open interest
July	828,559	177,336
August	1,100,490	168,190
September	1,008,739	158,351
October	769,591	165,899
November	995,971	184,819
December	784,666	98,840
Jan–Dec 1995	12,637,054	
Change vs 1994	+1.4%	

Source: CBOT

Ten-year US Treasury Note Futures, 1995

Table 10.6

1995	Monthly volume	Month-end open interest
July	1,588,852	326,866
August	2,028,743	296,199
September	1,859,001	267,903
October	1,459,737	277,949
November	1,730,793	246,696
December	1,487,646	237,047
Jan–Dec 1995	22,448,356	
Change vs 1994	–6.8%	

Source: CBOT

US Treasury Bond Futures, 1995

Table 10.7

1995	Monthly volume	Month-end open interest
July	5,790,181	454,733
August	7,083,654	348,587
September	7,317,138	341,105
October	6,927,156	430,108
November	6,626,284	460,146
December	5,232,105	394,770
Jan–Dec 1995	86,375,916	
Change vs 1994	–13.6%	

Source: CBOT

Table 10.8

Options on Two-year US Treasury Note Futures, 1995

1995	Monthly volume	Month-end open interest
July	320	4,720
August	429	279
September	540	25
October	220	0
November	320	200
December	500	500
Jan–Dec 1995	13,189	
Change vs 1994	+2.5%	

Source: CBOT

Table 10.9

Options on Five-year US Treasury Note Futures, 1995

1995	Monthly volume	Month-end open interest
July	365,942	300,296
August	313,191	132,511
September	212,695	158,052
October	286,711	151,617
November	246,343	76,904
December	183,840	98,840
Jan–Dec 1995	3,619,462	
Change vs 1994	+35.3%	

Source: CBOT

Options on Ten-year US Treasury Note Futures, 1995

Table 10.10

1995	Monthly volume	Month-end open interest
July	665,057	444,896
August	562,856	266,907
September	456,205	334,744
October	577,289	391,932
November	627,053	323,651
December	587,430	432,036
Jan–Dec 1995	6,887,102	
Change vs 1994	+7.0%	

Source: CBOT

Options on US Treasury Bond Futures, 1995

Table 10.11

1995	Monthly volume	Month-end open interest
July	1,999,376	655,729
August	2,068,987	482,416
September	1,887,499	569,898
October	2,299,006	700,605
November	1,947,535	507,661
December	1,582,910	611,103
Jan–Dec 1995	25,639,950	
Change vs 1994	–8.9%	

Source: CBOT

ISSUANCE

The Treasury conducts more than 150 regular auctions each year using the sealed-bid multiple price method.

All government securities brokers and dealers registered with the SEC are allowed to submit bids at the auctions on behalf of customers.

To avoid the possibility that one trader might come to control an issue the Federal Reserve engages in spot-checks of customer bids to ensure that they are authentic and awards of over US$500 million at auction are required to be individually verified by the bidder to the FRBNY by 10.00 on the business day following the auction. The Treasury has the ability to reopen issues of which there is an acute, protracted shortage in the market. This possibility reduces the likelihood of short squeezes.

Treasury bills

Treasury bills are usually issued on Thursdays. Thirteen and twenty-six week bills are issued each week. fifty-two-week bills are issued every four weeks. Non-competitive bidders are allowed to submit bids for US$1 million and receive the weighted-average yield of accepted competitive tenders.

Treasury notes and bonds

Competitive auctions are held according to a schedule:

Maturity	Frequency
2-year	Monthly, every month
3-year	Quarterly in February, May, August, November
5-year	Monthly, every month
10-year	Quarterly in February, May, August, November
30-year	Semi-annually in February and August

An announcement of the maturity and size of issue usually occurs six to ten days before the auction. The issue is traded on a "when-issued" basis in yield terms until the auction. Bids expressed in terms of yield to two decimal places must be submitted before 1.00 pm on the day of the auction and results are announced about one hour later.

Non-competitive bids are accepted up to US$5 million but may not be submitted with competitive bids by the same bidder. A non-competitive bidder is not permitted to have a position in the security being auctioned in the when-issued, futures or forward markets. "When-issued" trading is not permitted in securities awarded to non-competitive bidders.

The 35 percent rule limits the amount that the Treasury will accept as bid at a single yield by a single bidder to 35 percent of the public offering amount and limits awards to a single bidder to 35 percent of the public offering amount. This is the rule which Salomon broke in 1991.

Volume of issuance

The fact to note is that the amount of new money being borrowed each year is not much different to the sums being borrowed ten years ago. What has changed is the refinancing need each year which now exceeds US$2,000 billion.

The volume and its growth can be summarized as shown in Table 10.12.

Volume and growth, 1980–95 (US$ bn)

Table 10.12

(US$ bn)	Maturing debt	Net cash raised	Total issuance
1980	497.8	94.4	592.1
1981	606.5	98.9	705.4
1982	675.5	164.7	840.1
1983	818.4	178.3	996.7
1984	895.7	189.6	1,085.3
1985	1,017.8	176.6	1,194.4
1986	1,066.8	181.0	1,247.9
1987	1,089.8	105.8	1,195.6
1988	1,068.0	115.1	1,183.1
1989	1,154.7	123.6	1,278.3
1990	1,293.3	232.3	1,530.6
1991	1,423.8	275.9	1,699.7
1992	1,708.0	282.5	1,990.5
1993	1,830.7	235.4	2,066.1
1994	1,948.3	163.3	2,111.6
1995	2,157.7	173.6	2,331.3

Source: Federal Reserve Bank of New York

SETTLEMENT AND DELIVERY

Auctions settle between three and seven days after the auction date.

Secondary market settlement typically occurs on T+1 via the commercial book-entry system maintained by the Federal Reserve or via the Government Securities Clearing Corporation (GSCC). The GSCC is a clearing agency registered with the SEC under the Exchange Act. One of its key functions is to net trades for each member and reduce the amount of trades (and the accompanying risk) which are cleared through the commercial book-entry system.

GSCC accepts trade data until 22.00 and makes available netting reports to members at about 02.30 on the morning of the settlement date.

Table 10.13

Net Sales or purchases of Marketable US Treasury Bonds and Notes for foreign investors

US$ billions	1995 Jan–Nov	1994	1993	1992
Europe	51.1	38.5	−2.4	19.6
Belgium & Luxembourg	0.4	1.1	1.2	2.0
Germany	5.7	5.7	−10.0	2.1
Netherlands	1.5	1.3	−0.5	−3.0
Sweden	0.6	0.8	1.4	−0.8
Switzerland	0.2	0.5	−1.5	0.5
United Kingdom	39.2	23.4	6.2	24.2
Other & former USSR	3.5	5.8	0.8	−5.3
Canada	0	3.5	10.3	0.6
Latin America & Caribbean	44.8	−10.4	−4.6	−3.2
Asia	44.2	47.3	20.6	23.5
Japan	22.6	29.8	17.1	9.8
Africa	1.2	0.2	1.2	1.1
Other	1.2	−0.6	−1.7	−3.6
Nonmonetary intnl. organisations	0.9	0.2	0.2	1.4
Total Foreign Countries	142.6	78.6	23.4	37.9

Source: Federal Reserve Bulletin

INVESTORS

One of the notable trends in 1995 was the increase in foreign investment in US Treasuries to almost US$850 billion or 28 percent of all private investors in the market. Net foreign purchases and sales of US Treasury securities are published by the Federal Reserve. The history of recent years may be summarised as in Table 10.13:

The analysis of investors over time is shown in Table 10.14. Much of the government account holdings are accounted for by Social Security and Federal retirement trust fund investments. The Federal Reserve acquires Treasuries as part of its execution of monetary policy.

> "One of the notable trends in 1995 was the increase in foreign investment in US Treasuries to almost US$850 billion or 28 percent of all private investors in the market."

Analysis of investors, 1991–5 (US$ bn)

Table 10.14

Amounts in US$ billions at year-end	1995	1994	1993	1992	1991
Total Federal Securities outstanding	4,950.6	4,689.5	4,408.6	4,061.8	3,662.8
Held by:					
US Treasury and other federal agencies	1,320.8	1,211.7	1,113.5	1,010.8	919.6
Federal Reserve Banks	374.1	355.1	325.7	296.4	264.7
Private Investors	3,279.5	3,168.0	3,047.4	2,839.9	2,563.2
Commercial banks	295.0	290.6	322.2	294.4	232.5
Money market funds	64.2	67.6	80.8	79.7	80.0
Insurance companies	255.0	242.8	234.5	197.5	181.8
Other companies	224.1	226.5	213.0	192.5	150.8
State and local treasuries	370.0	440.8	508.9	476.7	485.1
Individuals					
Savings bonds	183.5	180.5	171.9	157.3	138.1
Other securities	162.4	150.7	137.9	131.9	125.8
Foreign, etc.	847.8	688.6	623.0	549.7	491.7
Other investors	877.5	879.9	755.1	760.2	677.4

Source: US Treasury Department
Note: Data for 1995 as at 30 September 1995.

QUOTATIONS, INTEREST AND YIELD CALCULATIONS

Quotations are on a price basis clean. Interest is semi-annual on an actual/actual basis. Interest accrues from the previous coupon date

> **"The repo market is very large with daily financing by US government security dealers running at perhaps US$800 billion in repos and reverse repos including government, agency and agency-backed securities."**

> **"Repo is an important part of the Fed's open market business which operates through the open market desk of the New York Fed. "**

(inclusive) to the settlement date (exclusive). Yields are compounded on a semi-annual basis and, according to the Street method, over partial coupon periods. The Treasury method used at auctions does not compound over partial coupon periods.

REPOS AND SECURITIES LENDING

The repo market is very large with daily financing by US government security dealers running at perhaps US$800 billion in repos and reverse repos including government, agency and agency-backed securities.

The primary dealers reported to the Federal Reserve Bank of New York the following monthly average positions in US$ billions (Table 10.15).

Repo is an important part of the Fed's open market business which operates through the open market desk of the New York Fed. If there is a shortage in the market it will undertake repos to add cash and when there is a surplus or it wants to drain cash it will undertake matched sale/purchases which equate to reverse repos. These operations are carefully watched as indicators of the Fed's policy.

Table 10.15

US Government Securities Dealers Finances, transactions

Reverse repos		1995	
	Sept	Oct	Nov
Overnight and continuing	219.0	228.2	249.0
Term	420.2	420.5	404.2
Repos			
Overnight and continuing	496.3	509.7	522.5
Term	356.1	356.7	370.9
Securities Borrowed			
Overnight and continuing	164.6	162.9	152.8
Term	64.8	65.5	64.6

Source: Federal Reserve Bulletin

SOURCES OF FURTHER INFORMATION

Internet

CBOT   www.cbot.com
Public Securities Association   www.psa.com
US Treasury   www.ustreas.gov

Screen pages

	Reuters
New York trading	MMKT-X
London trading	LGVT
Tokyo trading	GOVC

	Telerate
Brokers screen	8
Auction results	63/4
Commentary	4041

Addresses

Chicago Board of Trade
LaSalle at Jackson
Chicago, Illinois 60604
Tel: 312 435 3558
Fax: 312 341 3027

Chicago Board of Trade
European Office
52–54 Gracechurch Street
London EC3V 0EH
Tel: 44 171 929 0021
Fax: 44 171 929 0558

Department of the Treasury
Bureau of the Public Debt
999 E Street, NW
Washington, DC 20239
Tel: 1 202 219 3302
Fax: 1 202 219 3391

Federal Reserve System
20th St and Constitution Ave, NW
Washington, DC 20551
Tel: 1 202 452 3462
Fax: 1 202 452 3819

New York Stock Exchange
11 Wall Street
New York, NY 10005
Tel: 1 212 656 3000
Fax: 1 212 656 5557

■ ■ ■

"In 1996, with the government deficit likely to be 4.5% of GDP, the total borrowing requirement was expected to be about ¥21,000 billion."

Japan

INTRODUCTION

The Japanese government bond market is the second largest in the world after the US market. The market expanded quickly in the 1980s with the introduction of reforms and derivatives. The market has some unusual characteristics. For example, much of the trading in the secondary market is concentrated in a single issue.

LEGAL FRAMEWORK

Japanese Government Bonds (JGBs) are of three different legal origins.

In the beginning JGBs were issued for "construction" purposes and were mostly placed with banks. Such bonds, known as Construction Bonds, are still issued under Article 4 of the Public Finance Law.

After the first "oil shock" of 1975 larger government deficits required "deficit financing bonds" to be issued with the specific approval of the Diet (Parliament). Deficit Financing Bonds are issued under a specific law for each fiscal year where there is a deficit that cannot be financed with Construction Bonds.

There are also Refinancing Bonds which are issued under Article 5 of the Law Concerning Special Account of Government Bonds Consolidation Fund.

JGBs are a charge on the National Debt Consolidation Fund Special Account which is run by the Ministry of Finance (MOF).

Form

JGBs may be in registered or in bearer form. Compulsory registration in the name of the beneficial owner occurs on every interest payment date. This registration is required to take place before the seven business day suspension period which preceeds each interest payment date.

Regulation of the market

The Ministry of Finance acts through the Finance Bureau to manage new issues for the government and through the Securities Bureau to regulate the securities market.

The Banking Bureau, the Tax Bureau and the International Finance Bureau are also concerned in the operation of the market. The Bank of Japan has a supervisory function.

All ten- and twenty-year JGBs are listed on the Tokyo Stock Exchange.

> "Bonds which are in tax-exempt accounts are described as 'clean' and those which are in non-tax-exempt accounts are described as 'dirty'."

TAXATION

There is an 18 percent withholding tax which is reduced to 10 percent for investors in countries with a bilateral tax treaty. There is a 16 percent tax on the original issue discount for bonds.

Withholding tax is deducted at source by the MoF on all interest payments except in the case of securities registered as being held in a tax-exempt account. Tax exemption is available to most central banks, registered Japanese financial institutions and some charities. Withholding tax is deducted from all coupon payments on bearer bonds.

Bonds which are in tax-exempt accounts are described as "clean" and those which are in non-tax-exempt accounts are described as "dirty". Trading prices are always quoted for clean registered bonds.

Non-tax-exempt investors may keep their bonds "clean" by keeping them in the name of the financial institution which acts as their custodian in the period between coupon dates. At the coupon date the MoF restricts this practise. Non-tax-exempt investors must then either sell and switch to another security not paying a coupon or "wash" the bonds by effectively repoing them to a tax-exempt counterparty over the coupon period (about two weeks). This procedure can be expensive.

Transaction taxes

Transactions on the Tokyo Stock Exchange between non-residents are exempt from the 0.03 percent transfer tax (0.01 percent for registered financial institutions). If a nonresident investor sells to a resident dealer the latter pays a 0.01 percent transfer tax.

PROFILE OF THE DEBT

Table 11.1

Debt outstanding ¥ billions

	Total	Bonds over 10 years	Bonds 6–10 years	Discount bonds	Bonds 2–4 years	Treasury Bills
1993	184,867	19,286	148,666	1,654	4,236	10,990
1994	201,459	20,820	159,391	1,457	8,457	11,298
1995 Oct	215,578	22,490	166,023	1,392	12,637	12,999

Source: Bank of Japan Quarterly Bulletin, November 1995

INSTRUMENTS AND DERIVATIVES

- Refinancing Bonds
- Construction Bonds
- Deficit Financing Bonds

The market in publicly issued bonds may be divided into four sectors:

- Super long-term bonds (20 year)
- Long-term bonds (10 year, much the largest part of the market)
- Medium-term bonds (2, 3, 4 and 6 year)
- Discount bonds (zero coupon, 5 year).

All the fixed rate issues are semi-annual coupon bonds. JGBs have bullet maturities.

Treasury Bills

These have been issued in discount form since 1986. The Bank of Japan uses them for open market operations.

Financing Bills

These are 60-day maturities issued by the government mostly to the Bank of Japan and then sold on to financial institutions when needed to manage market liquidity. There is no secondary market.

There are derivatives traded on the Tokyo Stock Exchange (TSE) and on LIFFE in London. The LIFFE futures contract is virtually homogeneous with the TSE JGB contract. LIFFE positions may be rolled into TSE contracts with no price risk.

TSE 10-year JGB Future

Key features

Ticker symbol	BT.
Underlying	Notional 10-year JGB with 6% coupon.
Unit of trading	¥100 million of JGB.
Contract month	March, June, September, December cycle. Five contract months are always traded.
Delivery date	20th of the contract month.
Last trading day	9th business day prior.
Minimum price movement	0.01 equal to ¥10,000.
Daily price limit	2 points up or down (¥2 m per contract).
Trading hours	09.00–11.00 am and 12.30–15.00 pm.
Deliverable	Listed JGBs with a remaining life of 7–11 years.

Option on 10-year JGB Future

Key features

Unit of trading	1 TSE 10-year JGB future.
Contract maturities	Two closest months of March, June, September, December cycle.

Exercise	On any business day prior to expiration.
Exercise prices	Seven exercise prices are listed initially, straddling the futures at ¥1 intervals. More strike prices are added as the future moves.
Expiration date	Last business day of the month prior to the delivery month of the underlying future.
Last trading day	Expiration day.
Minimum price movement	0.01 equal to ¥10,000.
Daily price limit	2 points up or down (¥2 m per contract).
Trading hours	09.00–11.00 am and 12.30–15.00 pm.

LIFFE 10-year JGB Future

The LIFFE JGB contract is traded on LIFFE's Automated Pit Trading (APT) system.

Underlying	Notional 10–year JGB with 6% coupon.
Unit of trading	¥100 million of JGB.
Contract month	March, June, September, December cycle. Five contract months are always traded.
Delivery date	Next business day. Open positions at the close of a business day are closed out automatically at the first subsequent opening price on the Tokyo Stock Exchange for the same delivery month and cash settlement made accordingly through variation margin. In the absence of a TSE price the price established at the end of APT trading is used to generate interim variation margin.
Last trading day	16.00 one business day prior to Tokyo Stock Exchange last trading day.

Minimum price movement	0.01 equal to ¥10,000.
Daily price limit	¥1.00 from Tokyo Stock Exchange closing price. If limit is hit, price limits are removed one hour later for the remainder of the day. There is no limit in the last hour of trading on each day.
Trading hours	07.00–16.00 on APT (on TSE holidays trading opens at 08.00).

Note the TSE opening price is determined by the "Itayose" trading system whereby all orders to buy or sell at market are transacted at a single price.

MARKET-MAKING SYSTEM

All ten- and twenty-year JGBs are listed on the TSE. However, most trading takes place on the OTC market, particularly through the Tokyo Broker to Broker screen market. Trading hours are on weekdays as follows:

Tokyo Stock Exchange 09.00–11.00 and 12.30–15.00
Broker to Broker market 08.40–11.15 and 12.25–17.00

No market making obligation exists.

Commission rates

Futures
Commission in % of par value traded
Up to ¥500 million	0.015%
From ¥500 million to ¥1 billion	0.01% + ¥25,000
From ¥1 billion to ¥5 billion	0.005% + ¥75,000
Over ¥5 billion	0.0025% + ¥200,000

Source: Tokyo Stock Exchange Fact Book, 1995

> "Some three-quarters of trading is concentrated in the benchmark 10-year JGB. So great is the interest in this issue that it regularly trades at a yield well below the rest of the curve."

Options

Contract value

Up to ¥5 million	1.30%
From ¥5 million to ¥10 million	0.85% + ¥22,500
From ¥10 million to ¥50 million	0.45% + ¥62,500
Over ¥50 million	0.25% + ¥162,500

Note these are for opening or settling a position. When a position is settled by exercise the commission applied is the futures commission.

Source: Tokyo Stock Exchange Fact Book, 1995

TRADING

Secondary market trading can be dated from June 1984 when banks were permitted to trade seasoned public bonds including JGBs in short-term trading accounts. The JGB future was introduced in October 1985.

Some three-quarters of trading is concentrated in the benchmark 10-year JGB. So great is the interest in this issue that it regularly trades at a yield well below the rest of the curve.

There are four considerations which influence the market choice of the benchmark bond. First, it must have adequate liquidity which implies an issue size of ¥2 trillion or more, probably issued in two or more tranches. Second, the coupon should be close to ten-year market yield levels. Third, the maturity should be close to ten years when the bond becomes a benchmark. Fourth, there must be a market consensus and there can be some confusion at changeover time if there are two or more possible new benchmark bonds.

Most trading in Tokyo is through the Broker's Broker market. Bids and offers are entered in a centralized matching system with all market participants being shown all the existing orders. Trading is also possible on the Tokyo Stock Exchange (TSE) which publishes closing yields for all listed JGBs each day. The Broker's Broker market continues after the TSE close until trading in London begins.

The bid/offer spread in a benchmark issue can be as little as 0.5 basis points. For less liquid bonds the spread may be 5 basis points. Minimum transaction size on the Broker to Broker market is ¥500 million.

Government Bonds

The majority of trading in Government bonds is off the Stock Exchange. The trading volume of listed bonds expressed in par value terms in recent years was as shown in Table 11.2.

Trading volume of listed bonds (¥ bn)

Table 11.2

Amounts in ¥ bn	Off-market[1]	Exchange[2]	Total
1993[3]	3,242,242	4,781	3,247,023
1994	3,341,128	3,372	3,344,500
1995 (H1)[4]	2,112,758	2,255	2,115,013

Source: Bank of Japan Quarterly Bulletin, November 1995
Notes:
[1] Double counted, data from Japan Securities Dealers Association
[2] Single counted, data from the Tokyo Stock Exchange
[3] Year from April
[4] Six months April to September 1995

Futures

TSE trading may be summarized as shown in Table 11.3. The overwhelming majority of trades are in the 10-year future.

Futures trade, TSE

Table 11.3

	Total	Daily average
1992	11,872,099	48,065
1993	15,165,265	61,647
1994	13,002,892	52,643
1995[1]	14,213,134	57,117

Source: Tokyo Stock Exchange Monthly Statistics Report
[1] Annualized from 11 months data

Trading in Government Bond Options may be summarized as shown in Table 11.4.

Table 11.4

Trade in Government Bond Options (¥ bn)

	Total volume	Daily average	Total value ¥ bn	Daily average
1992	1,140,541	4,618	532.6	2.2
1993	1,506,836	6,125	699.5	2.8
1994	1,691,834	6,850	836.7	3.4
1995[1]	2,071,041	8,334	1,030.0	3.9

Source: Tokyo Stock Exchange Monthly Statistics Report

[1]. Annualized from 11 months data

> "It is an unusual feature that there are no variation margin requirements in the JGB future on LIFFE because there is no open interest."

JGB Futures trading on LIFFE

The LIFFE contract is not interchangeable with the TSE contract though both are based on the same underlying. Open interest in the LIFFE contract is automatically closed out at the end of each session at the opening price of the next trading day in Tokyo for the respective delivery month of the TSE's JGB future. Therefore a trader can place a buy or sell order at the opening price in Tokyo and be guaranteed no price risk on rolling into the TSE. This is because the opening price is determined as that price at which all orders at the opening price may be satisfied. It is an unusual feature that there are no variation margin requirements in the JGB future on LIFFE because there is no open interest. The only exception is when the TSE does not trade before the next LIFFE trading session.

Trading volumes

Trading volumes in the JGB future on LIFFE during 1995 were as shown in Table 11.5 opposite.

Trade in JGB Future, LIFFE 1995

Table 11.5

Month	Volume
January	46,785
February	69,821
March	68,824
April	70,187
May	81,359
June	74,045
July	67,306
August	119,577
September	63,660
October	65,293
November	81,013
December	37,459
Total for 1995	845,329
Change vs 1994	+38.37%

Source: LIFFE

ISSUANCE

In 1996, with the government deficit likely to be 4.5% of GDP, the total borrowing requirement was expected to be about ¥21, billion. Recent volumes of issues can be summarized as shown in Table 11.6.

Volume of issues

Table 11.6

	Total	Bonds over 10 years	Bonds 6–10 years	Discount bonds	Bonds 2–4 years	Treasury Bills
1993	51,314	1,346	19,937	266	2,707	27,058
1994	55,855	1,534	21,441	265	5,751	26,865
1995						
Apr	5,004	337	1,738		230	2,699
May	5,400		1,220	52	728	3,399
June	6,056	399	2,964		193	2,500
July	5,418		2,112	50	755	2,500
Aug	5,756	335	2,136		185	3,100
Sep	5,790		1,527	51	1,313	2,900
Oct	4,825	299	1,832		209	2,500

Source: Bank of Japan Quarterly Bulletin, November 1995

Table 11.7

Distribution MJGBs

(Amounts in ¥ billions)	Frequency	Value per issue	% distributed by	
			Syndicate	Auction
			%	%
3–6 month T-bills	Twice a month	¥700–¥1,700	0	100
2–4 year Notes	Monthly	¥100–¥200	0	100
5–year Discount Bonds	Quarterly	¥50–¥75	100	0
10–year Bonds	Monthly	¥200–¥3,200	40	60
20–year Bonds	Bimonthly	¥300–¥400	0	100

JGBs are issued both through the fixed underwriting syndicate described below and also by auction. Auctions were introduced in April 1989. Initially 40 percent of each 10-year JGB was auctioned. This was subsequently increased in October 1990 to 60 percent. The remaining part of each issue continued to be distributed through the traditional syndicate. The MOF has indicated a long-term intention to increase this percentage to 100 percent. Medium-term notes, twenty-year JGBs and T-bills are all fully distributed by auction. All five-year discount bonds are distributed through the syndicate. The picture may be summarized as shown in Table 11.7.

Table 11.8

Syndicate members

Organisation	No. of members
City banks	11
Foreign banks	30
Long-term credit banks	3
Local banks	64
Trust banks	7
Member banks of second association of regional banks	66
Credit associations	441
Central Cooperative Bank for Commerce & Industry (Shokochukin)	1
Central Cooperative Bank for Agriculture and Forestry (Norinchukin)	1
Securities companies	124
Foreign securities companies	33
Life insurance companies	22
Property casualty insurance companies	23
Total	**826**

Japan

There are 826 members of the syndicate which is composed of banks, life insurance companies and securities firms. There are 63 foreign banks and securities firms in the syndicate. Underwriters receive a selling fee of 0.63 percent on bonds issued by auction or to the syndicate.

Government bonds are offered publicly and also placed directly with the Trust Fund Bureau, the Postal Savings Special Account and private savers through the Post Office.

> **"JGBs are not settled or delivered abroad. JGBs must be held by a custodian in Japan."**

Ten-year bonds, which account for a very large part of total government issuance, are issued every month.The coupon is set after consultation with the syndicate on the previous day so as to produce an auction price close to but not above par. The coupon and amount of each issue are announced at 08.30 on the same day as the auction by the Ministry of Finance (MOF). Of each issue 60 percent is sold by competitive auction to syndicate members. The remainder is allocated by a system of fixed percentages to members of the syndicate at a price determined by the average auction price.

Individual syndicate members may not bid for more than 18 percent of the total issue amount. Each underwriter of an issue, whether as a syndicate member, auction participant or both, receives a 0.63 percent selling fee.

Twenty-year bonds are issued, less frequently, by competitive auction with no part reserved for the syndicate. Two-year bonds and five-year zero coupon bonds are also auctioned. The zero-coupon bonds are auctioned every second month (January, March, May, July, September, and November).

Since 1987 bonds pay interest either in March and September or in June and December. Since bonds are issued monthly many issues have odd first coupons which may be shorter or longer than six months. Bonds with the same coupon and maturity date that are issued in the same budget year are fungible after the first coupon payment.

SETTLEMENT AND DELIVERY

JGBs are not settled or delivered abroad. JGBs must be held by a custodian in Japan. Settlement is through different accounts for bonds and cash.

Most domestic trading is OTC but JGBs are also traded to a lesser extent on the eight stock exchanges.

OTC trades

OTC trades settle on dates specified by the Ministry of Finance. Settlement is on fifth, tenth, fifteenth, twentieth, and twenty-fifth, or the last day of the month. These are adjusted on the modified succeeding day principle (ie if these days are not business days then the next business day is used unless it falls in the next month when the preceeding business day is used).

The rules relating to settlement date are that there must be at least seven business days between trade date and settlement date; if there are two valid dates within ten business days of the trade date then the latter is used. Settlement cannot take place within fourteen days of a coupon date and is postponed until the coupon date.

TSE trades

TSE trades settle on T+4. A transfer tax of 0.03 percent is payable, in principle, by the seller except on transactions between non-residents.

QUOTATIONS, INTEREST AND YIELD CALCULATIONS

JGBs

JGBs are quoted in prices calculated to 3 decimal places with no rounding up.

Simple yield

Bonds traditionally trade on a simple yield basis. This is defined as

Yield (%) = [Annual Coupon (%) + (100-price)/Years to maturity]/price × 100

Example A 5-year bond with an annual coupon rate of 4% trading at 95 would have a simple yield of

$$[4\% + (100–95)/5]/95 \times 100$$

which is a simple yield of 5.26316%. The alert reader will suspect that this formula tends to overstate the yield to maturity of bonds trading below par. In this case the conventional yield to maturity is 5.15999%.

Conversely in the case of bonds trading above par the simple yield formula will tend to understate the real yield to maturity. If this same bond was trading at 103 the simple yield calculation would be

$$[4\% + (100-103)/5]/103 \times 100$$

which is 3.30097%. The real yield to maturity is 3.33859%

Day basis

Interest is calculated on an actual/365 day basis. Semi-annual coupons are calculated on an actual/182.5 day basis. The extra day in a leap year is not counted.

Accrual

Interest accrues from the previous coupon date (inclusive) to the settlement date (exclusive). The dated day is one day prior to the issue date for new issues. Therefore first coupons have one extra day's interest.

Discount bonds

The yield on discount bonds with more than one year to maturity is calculated on an annual compound interest basis.

T-bills

Investors in T-bills must have a specific T-bill account with a custodian in Japan. Settlement is on T + 3.

T-bills are quoted on a money-market yield basis that takes account of the withholding tax payment due to the Bank of Japan. Prices are quoted to 4 decimal places and the withholding tax is calculated to 5 decimal places. The withholding tax (WHT) calculation is

$$WHT = (100\text{-Average Auction Price}) \times 0.18$$

This WHT is recredited by the Bank of Japan at maturity. Most central bank investors can obtain a refund on the purchase date and thus receive effectively a higher yield than normal holders.

The yield for non-central bank holders of T-bills is:

$$\text{Yield} = ((100 + WHT) - \text{price})/\text{price} \times (365/\text{days to maturity})$$

The yield for central bank holders of T-bills is:

$$\text{Yield} = (100 - (\text{price} - WHT))/(\text{price} - WHT) \times (365/\text{days to maturity})$$

REPOS AND SECURITIES LENDING

Bond borrowing and to a lesser extent Gensaki (a form of repo) are available. Gensaki are for one, two or three months and are subject to the securities transaction tax. It has been described as an "idiosyncratic non-collateralized market between professionals."

SOURCES OF FURTHER INFORMATION

Screen pages

	Reuters	*Telerate*
News	JMMS	
Market rates	MBSJ, NJEB	
Futures	TQOB	9752-3, 9137
Options	NJEJ, TQOB	27750
Auctions		3025

Addresses
Ministry of Finance
3-1-1 Kasumigaseki
Chiyoda-ku
Tokyo
Tel: 81 3 35 81 41 11
Fax: 81 3 35 93 74 94

Nippon Ginko (Bank of Japan)
2-1-1 Hongoku-cho
Nihonbashi
Chuo-ku
Tokyo 103
Tel: 81 3 32 79 11 11
Fax: 81 3 32 45 05 38

Tokyo Stock Exchange
2-1 Kabuto-cho
Nihonbashi
Chuo-ku
Tokyo 103
Tel: 81 3 36 66 01 41
Fax: 81 3 36 63 06 25

GLOSSARY

Above par A security whose market value is above its normal, or par, value.

Accrual rate The interest rate or coupon rate used to compute accrued interest.

Accrual interest Interest earned but not yet due and payable. The buyer of a bond pays the seller the price of the bond plus interest accrued from the last interest payment date up to and including the value date. In the case of bonds traded ex-dividend the interest is calculated from the value date to the next coupon date and is paid effectively by the seller to the buyer.

Active management Fund managers actively manage assets by changing portfolios to exploit opportunities relating to interest rate levels, the shape of the yield curve, or spreads between different markets. Contrast with indexation, dedication, immunization and passive management.

Actual Day count basis where the number of days used is the actual number of days elapsed. Differs from 365 in leap years, for example.

After-hours dealing Dealing after the end of mandatory trading hours on an exchange.

After-tax yield The return on a security net of income withholding tax and capital gains tax.

Algorithm A formula devised to solve a problem (eg the **Black–Scholes Model**).

All-or-Nothing Option An option where the holder is paid a fixed amount if the underlying reaches or exceeds the exercise or strike price.

Alligator Spread Another name for a **Butterfly Spread**.

Alternative Option An option where the holder has the choice of a payment based on two or more underlying instruments, indices, currencies or commodities.

American Option An option which may be exercised on any business day during the life of the option.

Amortization Either the reduction of a premium over a period of time, or the repayment of debt by a borrower in a series of instalments as in the retirement of debt by a purchase or sinking fund.

Annual equivalent The yield of a bond which does not pay interest at annual intervals expressed as an annual equivalent.

Annuity bond A security in which the principal and interest payments are combined in order to form a series of equal annual payments.

APT Automated Pit Trading – a screen-based, after-hours trading system at LIFFE.

Arbitrage The simultaneous sale and purchase of financial instruments with the intention of profiting from the expected change in price relationships or anomalies.

As, if and when issued Trading in an asset which is expected to be issued but which has not yet been issued.

Asian option An option where the payout is based on the difference between the exercise price and the average price of the underlying on a specified dates during the life of the option.

Asked price The price at which a security is offered for sale. In the UK it is referred to as the offer price, the opposite of the bid price.

Asset allocation Investment methodology, which specifies the proportion of funds to be invested in different asset classes.

Assignment Notice to the writer of an option that it has been exercised by the holder and also the process by which exercise notices are allocated among the writers of options.

At-the-Money An option with an exercise price at the current spot price of the underlying.

Automatic Exercise A rule of many derivative exchanges that options which are in-the-money are exercised without a specific instrument from the holder.

Average life The weighted average of the maturities of each cash flow arising from a particular security.

Average Rate Option See **Asian Option**.

Average Strike Option An option where the strike price is set as an average of the price of the underlying over the life of the option. The payoff is determined as the difference between this strike price and the price of the underlying at expiry.

Back month Expiry date of an exchange traded futures or option contract other than the next contact to expire.

Back office Settlement, accounting and management information processes.

Barrier Option A form of path-dependent option. When the strike is set another barrier price is set. If the underlying reaches or exceeds that barrier price the option is cancelled (in the case of a knockout option) or (in case of a knockin option) the option only exists once the underlying has reached the barrier price.

Barrier price The price which causes a barrier option to be triggered.

Basis The spot or cash price minus the forward or futures price, or the changing relationship between prices or rates in two markets.

Basis point 0.01 percent in yield.

Basis risk The possibility that prices in two related but not identical markets or instruments may vary.

Basis Trade A transaction which tries to profit from an expected change in the relative prices of two instruments or of a derivative and its underlying.

Bear Someone who believes a price will fall.

Bear Spread An option spread position which increases in value as the value of the underlying falls.

Bellweather bond Another name for a **Benchmark bond**.

Below par A security whose market value is below its nominal, or par, value.

Benchmark bond A large, liquid issue, the price of which is considered to be a good indicator for similar securities of a similar maturity or sometimes for the market as a whole.

Bermuda Option An option which may be exercised only on certain specified dates over its life.

Bid (price) The price the buyer will pay for a financial instrument, commodity or currency.

Bid to cover ratio The ratio between the number of bids made at an auction and the number of those which were successful. A high ratio indicates good demand and a successful auction.

Bid-asked spread The difference between the offer price and the bid price which is the dealers' spread.

Binomial Model A model put forward by Cox, Ross and Rubinstein based on the tendency of a binomial distribution to approach the normal distribution. The weighted present values of the outcomes are used to calculate option values.

Black–Scholes Model An elegant and relatively simple option pricing equation, which is consistent with the capital asset pricing model of portfolio theory but which makes quite restrictive assumptions. First published in the *Journal of Political Economy* in May 1973.

Board of Trade Clearing Corporation (BOTCC) The clearing house for the Chicago Board of Trade.

Bond Debt security, generally long-term and bearing interest. See also **Note**.

Bond basis Method used to calculate accrued interest on bonds. Differs from money market basis.

Bond equivalent yield Method used in the USA to calculate compound interest on a bill by assuming semi-annual coupons.

Bond Option Option where the underlying securities are bonds.

Bond washing The practice of selling securities cum interest in order to convert interest income into a capital gain. This has been legislated against in many countries.

Bons du Trésor à taux annuel et internêt annuel (BTANs) Fixed-rate French Treasury notes with a maturity of two and five years.

Bons du Trésor à taux fixe et internêt précompté (BTFs) Discounted French fixed-rate Treasury notes with maturities ranging from four to fifty-two weeks.

Book-entry system An ownership registation system under which securities do not have a physical existence. Ownership rights are represented by entries in a computerized register.

Boston Option A break-forward or cancellable option.

Bourse The French Stock Exchange.

Box Spread Offsetting synthetic long and short positions.

Broker An intermediary who introduces the two parties in a transaction to each other. Brokers do not in general take positions but inter-dealer brokers (IDBs) and other matched-book brokers act as principals to preserve the anonymity of their clients.

Brokerage The commission charged by brokers.

Bull Someone who believes a price will rise.

Bull Spread An option spread position which increases in value as the value of the underlying rises.

Bullet Maturity Bond A bond where the principal amount is only redeemed at maturity.

Bundesanleihen (Bunds) German Government bonds.

Bundesbankliquiditäts unverzinsliche schatzanwiesungen (BULIS) German Discounted Treasury certificates with maturities from one to two years.

Bundesobligationen (Bobls) German fixed-rate bonds with annual coupons, a five-year bullet maturity and no puts or calls.

Bundesschatzanweisungen (Schätze) German Federal Treasury notes. Fixed-rate bonds with annual coupons and a four-year maturity.

Bundesschatzbriefe Saving notes of the German Federal Government with maturities of six or seven years.

Buoni del Tesoro in ECU (BTE) Italian Treasury bills denominated in ECU. Short-term instruments having maturities of about twelve months.

Buoni del Tesoro poliennali (BTP) Italian fixed-rate Treasury bonds with maturities ranging from three to thirty years.

Buoni ordinari del Tesoro (BOT) Italian Treasury bills with maturities of three, six or twelve months.

Business day In most markets any day excluding Saturdays, Sundays and legal or statutory holidays on which business can be conducted.

Butterfly Spread A vertical Bear Spread and a vertical Bull Spread with all options having the same expiry date and with the short options having the same strike price.

Buy–Write Simultaneous purchase of the underlying and sale of a call to create a covered call position.

Calendar Roll Procedure whereby a position is closed in one contract month and reopened in a further contract month.

Calendar Spread A position where the option sold expires before the option bought. The amounts bought and sold are the same and the options have the same strike price.

Call The right, but not an obligation, of an issuer to redeem a bond before its specified maturity date.

Call-adjusted yield The yield of a callable bond calculated to the date of the first call and incorporating the price at which the call may be exercised rather than the par value.

Callable bond A bond which may be redeemed at the option of the issuer before its specified maturity date.

Call date The date on which, at the option of the issuer, a bond may be redeemed before its specified maturity date.

Call Option An option which gives the holder a right but not an obligation to buy a financial instrument, commodity or currency at a specified price on or before a specified date.

Call Spread An option position in different calls on the same underlying.

Candlestick chart Japanese charting technique similar to bar charts.

Capital Adequacy Directive (CAD) European Union legislations which determines the minimum level of capital required by financial institutions which became effective from 31 December, 1995.

Capital Asset Pricing Model (CAPM) A theoretical framework for structuring investment portfolios. The risk and reward characteristics of a portfolio are not equivalent to the aggregate of the individual components. Risk may be divided into systematic (or beta) and unsystematic (alpha) risk. The former depends on factors common to all investments, while the latter is security specific and may be reduced by diversification. The expected return on a specific asset equals the risk-free return plus a risk premium. The formula is expressed as:

$$E(R) = R_f \beta(R_m - R_f)$$
Where

$E(R)$ = Expected return
R_f = Risk free return
R_m = Return on the market
β = Beta, the measure of the sensitivity of the asset to the marketto

Capital gain A profit realized from buying a security at one price and subsequently selling it at a higher price.

Carrying cost The interest expense incurred when a position is established.

Cash-and-carry A combination of a long position in the underlying and a short position in a futures contract such that the net position is equivalent to a short-term money market security.

Cash market The market in an actual financial instrument, commodity or currency on which derivatives may be based.

Cash Settlement Settlement of a derivative contract not by delivery of the underlying but by a cash payment calculated as the difference between the strike or exercise price and the settlement or spot price of the underlying.

Central Gilts Office (CGO) A department of the Bank of England which operates the book-entry transfer system between CGO members by which ownership of gilts is registered.

Central Money Markets Office (CMO) Bank of England book-entry system which clears sterling money market instruments.

Centrale de Livraison de Valeurs Mobilières (CEDEL) A book-entry clearing facility (in Luxembourg) originally for euro-securities through which transactions in domestic securities may also be cleared.

Certificate of Accrual on Treasury Security (CATs)   Coupon-stripped US Treasury bonds. Trade name devised by Salomon Brothers. See also, for example, LYONs (Merrill Lynch).

Certificati del Tesoro in Ecu (CTE)   Italian Treasury 5-year certificates denominated in ECU.

Certificati del Tesoro zero-coupon (CTZ)   Italian government 2-year zero-coupon bonds.

Certificati di credito del Tesoro (a cedola variabile) (CCT)   Italian floating-rate Treasury certificates.

Chambre de Compensation des Instruments Financiers de Paris (CCIFP)   French financial futures and options clearing system.

Cheapest to deliver (CTD)   Bond futures are usually priced on the basis of notional bond while delivery requires actual bonds. Futures contract specifications include a range of actual bonds which can be used for settlement and a price factor which is applied to each bond. Futures sellers will try to find the cheapest to deliver.

Chooser Option   An option which allows the purchaser to choose at expiration whether the option is a put or a call. In either case the exercise price is the same.

Clean price   The price of a bond without accrued interest.

Clearing   The process of matching, registering and guaranteeing trades, often performed by a Clearing House.

Clearing house   Also known as a Clearing Corporation. Company which registers, monitors, matches, settles and often guarantees trades on a futures or options exchange.

Clearing House Automated Payment System (CHAPS)   An electronic system for settling payments between the banks in England.

Clearing house funds   Payments made through the New York Clearing House's computerized Clearing House Interbank payments System (CHIPS).

Clearing House Interbank Payments System (CHIPS)   New York electronic system through which most Eurodollar transactions are cleared. Depository institutions in New York are linked by computer. Participants' net positions are settled through the Federal Reserve's funds transfer system.

Clearing member   A member firm of a futures clearing house. Each clearing member must also be a member of an exchange, but not all members of an exchange are also members of a clearing house. The trades of a non-clearing member are settled through a clearing member.

Clearing system   A depository or transaction settlement system. Three international security clearing systems are Cedel, Euroclear and First Chicago Clearing Centre.

Cliquet Option   French term applied to ratchet options and/or knock-out options.

Close out A transaction which leaves the trader with a net nil position.

Combination   Any position involving put and call options which is not a straddle.

Commission des Opérations de Bourse (COB)   French Stock Exchange Commission.

Commodity Futures Trading Commission (CFTC)   The US regulatory agency which oversees the futures and options markets.

Compagnie des Agents de Change (CAC)   Former name of the French stockbrokers' association now the Société des Bourses Françaises (SBF).

Competitive auction   An auction for securities where participants buy securities at the price they bid if their bid is at or above the minimum price accepted. With variations, known as Dutch auction, American auction or English auction.

Compound interest   Interest accrued on interest not paid.

Compound Option   An option on an option.

Condor   A butterfly where the two short options have different strikes.

Confidence level   The probability of the price of a given security (or the value of a portfolio) staying within a specified range during a specified period of time, usually expressed as a percentage. Used with value at risk methodologies to estimate potential losses based on analysis of historical price data.

Conseil des Bourses de Valeurs   French Stock Market council.

Conseil du Marché à Terme   French body which supervises the MATIF under the Chambre de Compensation des Instruments Financiers de Paris (CCIFP).

Consol   Consolidated annuities. An English irredeemable gilt-edged security issued during the Napoleonic wars and still traded.

Constant Maturity Treasury (CMT)   The interpolated average of yields on US Treasury instruments of specified maturity expressed as the yield of a theatrical treasury of constant maturity.

Contingent Premium Option   An option where the buyer pays a premium only if the option has value at expiry.

Contract   Standard specification of the terms of futures or options traded on an exchange.

Contract expiration date The last date on which an option holder can exercise his right to buy or sell the underlying instrument or currency.

Contract month In a futures or options market, a future calendar month for which contracts may be traded. Also known as a delivery month.

Convergence The process whereby the prices of the underlying and derivatives converge towards one price as delivery approaches.

Conversion The purchase of the underlying and a put option together with the sale of a call. The whole is a low risk strategy designed to lock in a profit, or in the context of convertible securities, the exercise of the right to acquire a new security in exchange for an older security on previously specified terms.

Convertible A bond which, at the option of the holder, can be exchanged for another bond with different terms.

Convexity Sensitivity of duration to (large) changes in yield. If duration decreases as yield rises and increases as yield falls then the price of the bond in question will follow a curved path when plotted on a yield/price graph which would be attractive to an investor.

Corpus Treasury Receipt (corpus TR) A zero-coupon certificate issued in respect of the principal payment of a US Treasury security.

Coupon (CPN) The nominal rate of interest paid on a security, expressed as a percentage of the principal value. Also the certificate attached to a physical security which entitles the holder to a particular interest payment.

Coupon dates The date when a coupon is to be paid.

Coupon stripping The manufacture of a zero-coupon security from a conventional bond.

Coupon Treasury Receipt (coupon TR) A zero-coupon certificate issued in respect of an interest payment of a US treasury security.

Coupon washing Sale of a security before an interest payment date with a repurchase after the interest payment date intended to avoid tax

Covered Call Sale of a call option while being long the underlying.

Covered Straddle Sale of a straddle while being long the underlying.

Credit risk The risk that a counterparty to a financial transaction will fail to perform.

Currency overlay Currency exposures deliberately acquired separately from the acquisition of assets as part of an asset management strategy.

Current coupon A fixed-rate security with a coupon close to current yield levels for similar securities and therefore with a price close to par. Also, in the case of a floating-rate security, the rate of interest for the current interest period.

Current issue The most recently issued US Treasury bill or note.

Current maturity The remaining time to maturity of a security.

Current yield The interest rate of a security expressed as a percentage of the security's market price. Also called flat yield, income yield, interest yield or running yield.

Cusip number system A US alphanumeric system used for the identification of security issues. A nine-digit code is assigned to each issue and is printed on the face of the security. The first six digits identify the issuer in alphabetic sequence, the next two characters (alphabetic or numeric) identify the particular issue, and the ninth digit is a check digit.

Customer repurchase agreement A sale and repurchase agreement arranged by the US Federal Reserve for foreign central banks.

Daily price limit The maximum price change permitted by the rules of an exchange for a futures contract.

Day count bases Conventions employed to calculate interest. In each case the numerator shows the number of days between the dates and the denominator indicates how many days are assumed to be in a year (eg 365/360).

Daylight exposure The risk of counterpart default during the day on which a transaction is to be settled after funds or securities have been delivered but before the corresponding funds or securities have been received.

Dedication The structuring of a portfolio so that its cash flow matches specific future liabilities.

Deep discount bond See **Original Issue Discount (OID) bonds**.

Defeasance The use of a portfolio of riskless (usually government) bonds to provide for the service and repayment of other debt. In legal defeasance, the bond issuer puts the riskless bonds into an irrevocable trust for the benefit of the bondholders. The trust then becomes the primary obligor to the bond-holders.

Deferred Premium Option An option where the premium is paid at expiration.
Deferred Start Option An option which may be bought and sold before all of its terms are fixed.

Delivery Settlement of a contract by tender of a financial instrument or cash.

Deliverable In derivatives markets, a financial instrument which meets the contract specifications and which may therefore be delivered against it.

Delivery date The day, or days, during which delivery against a futures contract can be made.

Delivery factor With futures contracts which have a number of deliverable securities the delivery price of each is adjusted by a factor to determine the delivery amount of each security. Also known as the conversion factor.

Delivery notice A seller's notice of intention to make delivery against a short futures positions on a specified day.

Delta The ratio of the movement of the price of an option to the movement in the price of the underlying.

Delta Hedge A hedge where an option position is offset by a position in the underlying which will neutralize, within a narrow range of price movements, the price change of the option position.

Dematerialize The replacement of physical securities with electronic book-entry systems.

Designated broker scheme At LIFFE Designated brokers undertake to market actively a new contract prior and to provide a full-time broker in the pit for a specified period following the launch of the contract.

Designated Primary Market Maker (DPMM) A specialized floor member of the Chicago Board Options Exchange (CBOE).

Diagonal Spread The combination of a purchase of a longer term option with a sale of a shorter option with the longer option having a higher strike price.

Digital Option An option where the holder is paid a fixed amount if the underlying reaches or exceeds the exercise or strike price.

Dingo Zero-coupon Australian dollar security created by stripping an Australian government bond.

Dirty price The price of a security which includes accrued interest.

Discount The difference between the par value and the price of a security when such price is lower than par.

Discount securities Money market instruments which do not pay interest but which are issued at a discount and redeemed at maturity at face value.
Double Option An option to buy or sell but not to do both.

Double-dated A security which besides having a final date of redemption also has a date or period during which it may be redeemed early.

Double Taxation Agreement (DTA) An agreement or treaty between two countries intended to avoid double taxation of income.

Down-and-in-Call Option contract where the option becomes a standard call if the underlying falls to a predetermined (the instrike) price.

Down-and-out Call A call option which expires if the underlying falls to a predetermined (the outstrike) price.

Duration Duration is calculated as the average time to maturity of the cash-flows of a security, the time to maturity being weighted by the present value of each cashflow. For all except zero-coupon securities duration is less than the nominal maturity. Duration changes with substantial changes in yield.

Early Exercise Exercise of an option (American) before its expiry date.

Embedded Option An option which is part of another security and which cannot be separated from it.

European Option An option which may only be exercised on the expiry date.

Exercise To use the right granted under an option contract either to buy or to sell the underlying.

Exercise Price The price at which the underlying may be bought or sold under an option.

Expiry Date The last business day on which an option may be exercised.

Fair Value The worth of an option determined by a mathematical model. Not the same as the price.

Fast market A term used to denote hectic market conditions during which price information displayed on screens may not keep up with activity in the pit and must be treated as only indicative.

Federal funds (Fed funds) Funds on account with the US Federal Reserve to meet reserve requirements. Can be transferred to other banks in the Federal Reserve System over Fedwire at the Fed funds rate.

Federal Reserve Open Market Committee (FOMC) A committee of the US Federal Reserve which sets monetary policy and open market operations acting through the open market desk of the Federal Reserve Bank of New York.

Fedwire Book-entry transfer system run by the US Federal Reserve transfers Fed funds and US Treasury securities between banks.

Finanzierungsschätze German Treasury discounted financing bills with maturities from one to two years.

Floored broker A trader on an exchange floor who executes orders for those who do not have access to the trading area.

Floored Put An option contract where the maximum gain is limited.

Free of tax to residents abroad (FOTRA) stocks UK government securities (gilts) where interest may be paid gross to holders who can prove they are resident outside the UK. Less significant than formerly.

Front contract A futures or options contract that is the nearest to expiry of those on that underlying available on a given exchange. Also referred to as front month.

Front office The dealing room of a financial institution, contrasted with the **back office**.

Fungible Securities which are fungible may be exchanged for each other on identical terms.

Futures contract Exchange-traded contract to buy at a specified date in the future a unit of a commodity or financial instrument, standardized as to amount, date and place of delivery.

Gamma The rate of change in delta.

General Collateral (GC) In the repo market collateral which meets the general requirements.

Gilt-Edged Market Maker (GEMM) A market-maker in UK government bonds (gilts) with a direct dealing relationship with the Bank of England.

Gilt-edged security Domestic sterling-denominated security issued by the UK Treasury.

Government broker Formerly the agent of the Bank of England who acted in the gilt-edged market on behalf of the UK government and its departments.

Grantor The writer of an option.

Gross Domestic Product deflator (GDP deflator) A measure of inflation in an economy expressed as the percentage difference between real Gross Domestic Product (GDP) (ie GDP at constant prices) and nominal GDP (ie money GDP) or GDP at current prices.

Gross National Product (GNP) Gross domestic product (GDP) plus income earned from investment or work abroad.

Hedge A transaction intended to reduce or neutralize an existing risk.

Hedge ratio Proportion of the notional principle amount underlying a derivative which has to be bought or sold to offset exposure in the derivative for a unit change in the price of the underlying, or vice versa.

Historical Volatility The variation of the change in price of the underlying during a particular past period.

Holder The holder of an option has the right to exercise it.

Horizontal Spread A calendar spread.

Immunization An asset management strategy which matches the Macaulay duration of a bond portfolio to the duration of a specified set of future liabilities and the present value of the portfolio to the present value of the liabilities. The implicit assumption is that any changes in the yield curve will be parallel shifts.

Implied forward interest rate Future interest rate uimplied by the current term structure of interest rates (yield curve) which is in fact not an accurate predictor of future rates.

Implied repo rate The financing rate at which a long cash-short futures arbitrageur would neither gain nor lose on a transaction. The implied repo rate can also be thought of as the rate of return earned on the funds used to purchase the cash security in a cash and carry trade.

Implied Volatility The volatility assumption implied by an existing option price.

Implied yield A future yield derived from present yields and based on the assumption that the yield curve on one particular day is a reliable indication of its future shape.

Initial Margin The margin required by an exchange to secure a derivative position at inception.

In Option A type of option contract which is like an ordinary option only when the price of the underlying reaches an agreed barrier price before expiry.

Index-linked debt A debt instrument whose redemption value and/or interest yield is linked to a specified index.

Instrike The barrier price at which an in option becomes like an ordinary option.

Inter-dealer broker (IDB) Intermediary between market-makers. IDBs are matched-book or blind brokers since they act as principals but only between two matching counterparts, in order to provide anonymity to each side.

Interest coupon The coupon attached to a certificate which gives the holder the right to interest payments at specified dates.

Intermarket Clearing Corporation (ICC) A subsidary of the Chicago-based Options Clearing Corporation (OCC) which clears and settles futures contracts.

Internal rate of return (IRR) The interest rate that equates the present value of a future stream of payments to the price of the security (eg yield to maturity).

International Monetary Market (IMM) A division of the Chicago Mercantile Exchange (CME), specializing in currency and Eurodollar futures. The IMM was the first financial derivatives exchange in 1972. Many over-the-counter derivatives transactions are arranged to match IMM settlement dates.

International Security Identification Number (ISIN) Identification numbers which have replaced other security code numbers at Cedel and Euroclear. They are allocated by the International Organisation for Standardisation. The ISIN includes a country identification code, a base number allocated by the relevant numbering agency and one numerical check digit.

In-the-Money An option with intrinsic value is said to be in-the-money.

Intrinsic Value An option has intrinsic value if it could be exercised profitably. This value is equal to the difference between the strike price and the current market price of the underlying.

Investment Services Directive European union (EU) directive establishing common standards for investment services firms other than banks, effective from 31 December 1995.

Irredeemable A UK gilt-edged security which may be redeemable at the UK government's option but which need not be redeemed ever. The outstanding irredeemable gilts have low coupons and are unlikely to be redeemable in present circumstances.

Itayose A method employed to determine opening and closing prices on the Tokyo Stock Exchange so that for instance all orders to buy or sell at the market opening price are satisfied at one price.

Jump A price movement larger than a random process would generate.

Kappa The sensitivity of option prices to a change in implied volatility.

Knockin Option See **Barrier Option**.

Knockout Option See **Barrier Option**.

Kurtosis The extent to which changes in a variable (or the logarithm of the variable) differ from those of a variable with normal distribution. In particular, risk managers are concerned with leptokurtosis, or "fat-tailed" distributions (ie the risk of occasional large price moves).

Ladder Option An option contract which provides that when the price of the underlying reaches certain preset levels, the payout ratchets upwards.

Lambda The leverage factor (ie the percentage change in the price of an option divided by the percentage change in the price of the underlying).

Last notice day The final day on which notices of intent to deliver on futures contracts may be issued.

Last trading day The final day during which trading may take place in a particular contract.

Letras del tesoro Spanish Treasury bills with three, six, and twelve-month maturities.

Life-to-call The time remaining until a borrower's first option to call or redeem a security.

Life-to-put The time remaining until an investor's first option to put or have redeemed a security.

LIFFE London iInternational Financial Futures Exchange.

Limit up/down A price movement by a futures contract or option which is the maximum allowed under the rules of an exchange.

Liquidity risk The risk that a financial instrument cannot be sold quickly or close to its theoretical market value. Also the risk that a financial institution will not be able to raise funds when needed.

Listed Option An option which is traded on an exchange.

Listed security A security which has satisfied the requirements of an exchange to be listed on that exchange. This usually implies a minimum standard of financial information though not necessarily a minimum standard of value or credit worthiness. Such a security need not be actively traded on the exchange where it is listed. Certain institutions are allowed only to buy listed securities.

Local A dealer who trades for his own account on a futures exchange.

Lognormal Distribution A security is said to have a lognormal distribution if the logarithm of the price has a normal distribution. If such a distribution is plotted in price terms the curve will appear to be positively skewed in a manner similar to the observed price behavior of stocks.

London Code of Conduct Guidelines on the conduct of derivatives business published by the Bank of England.

London Traded Options Market (LTOM) Options market merged with LIFFE in 1992.

Long Owning a financial instrument, commodity or currency.

Long bond The on-the-run 30-year US Treasury bond.

Lookback Option An option which operates retroactively to give the holder the right to buy or sell the underlying at its minimum or maximum price in the lookback period.

Lookforward Option An option which gives the holder the right to the difference between the strike price set at the beginning of the period and the highest (or lowest) price during the period.

Maginot spread The difference between German bunds and French OATs (Obligation assimilable du Trésor) spreads.

Maintenance Margin The additional margin posted to reflect price changes and consequent increased exposure in securities or derivatives markets.

Mambo Combo An option position combining an in-the-money put and an in-the-money call where the holder is the long or short of both options.

Mandatory quote period On the London Stock Exchange, the period during which market-makers must make bid and offer prices available to the market.

Marché à Terme d'Instruments Financiers (MATIF) The French futures and options market for financial instruments and commodities.

Marché des Options Négociables de Paris (MONEP) The French stock options market.

Margin A deposit required to be placed with an exchange or clearing house to secure a derivatives position.

Margin call A demand by a futures exchange or by an individual broker for clients to increase their margin payments in response to a change in the value of their positions.

Mark-to-Market The process of adjusting the price of a security to reflect its market value, often done daily.

Matched repos Securities acquired through reverse repurchase agreements and matched with a repurchase (repo) agreement on the same security for the same period of time.

Mercato telematico delle opzioni su futures (MTO) Italian market for the options on government securities futures.

Mercato telematico dei Titoli di Stato (MTS) Italian primary bond dealers' screen-based market.

Middle office The risk control and valuation department in a financial institution.

Modified duration A measure of the percentage price sensitivity of a bond to changes in yield. Unmodified duration is used to immunize a portfolio. Modified duration is preferred when measuring a security's price volatility.

Money market basis The way to calculate interest on money market instruments (such as CDs, FRCDs, FRNs and sometimes short-dated bonds). The rate of interest is multiplied by the actual number of days elapsed and divided by the number of days in the accounting year (eg 360, many European markets, and 365, UK).

Mutual offset system A system of substitution between futures exchanges. A trade executed on one exchange may be use to offset or establish a position on another exchange. Also called inter-exchange transfers.

Naked Option An uncovered option position.

National debt The total outstanding value (usually expressed in nominal terms) of a central government's debt.

Net present value (NPV) The discounted value of all cash flows associated with an investment.

Non-callable A security which does not give the issuer the option to redeem the bonds before the specified maturity date.

Non-competitive auction That part of an auction where non-competitive bidders accept the average price bid by competitive bidders, usually with a maximum amount stipulated by the authorities.

Normal yield curve The yields of securities which when plotted on a graph of yield against maturity form a line which is slightly upward sloping to the right, reflecting the fact that interest rates for longer maturities are "normally" higher than for shorter maturities.

Notionnel The French government bond futures contract on the Matif, based on a "notional" bond of 7–10 years maturity and a 10 percent coupon.

Normal Distribution A probability distribution in which about two-thirds of total observations fall within one standard deviation on either side of the mean and about 95 percent of total observations fall within two standard deviations on either side of the mean.

Obligaciones del estado Ten- and fifteen-year fixed-rate Spanish Government bonds with an annual coupon.

Obligation assimilable du Trésor (OAT) French Treasury bond issued for maturities of seven to thirty years.

Obligation linéaire/Linéaire Obligations (OLO) Belgian government bonds issued for maturities of three to thirty years.

Off-the-run issues US Treasury issues which are not the most recently issued in each maturity range and therefore are less liquid.

Old Lady Short for 'Old Lady of Threadneedle Street', a slang name for the Bank of England.

Offer The price at which a seller is willing to sell.

Omega Either the currency risk when translating the value of a currency option position in another currency, or the third derivative of the option price related to the price of the underlying.

On-the-run issues US Treasury issues which are the most recently auctioned and therefore highly liquid.

Open Interest The sum of outstanding "long" and "short" positions in a given option or futures contract.

Open market operations Central bank operations in the markets intended to achieve objectives of monetary policy.

Open outcry Trading method on the floor of an exchange in which buyers and sellers call out their bids and offers face to face, often using hand signals because of the noise.

Open position A trader's risk position.

Open repurchase agreement (open repo) A repo transaction with no definite term continued from day to day by mutual agreement. Also known as a demand repo.

Option An option gives the holder the right, but not the obligation, to buy (in the case of a "call" option) or sell (a "put" option) a specified instrument, currency or commodity (the underlying) during or at the end of a given period at a specified price (the "strike" or "exercise" price). The option may be for physical delivery of the underlying or cash settlement. The option buyer pays the grantor a premium for this right.

Options Clearing Corporation The entity which guarantees listed security options in the USA.

Option series Options of the same type with the same strike price and expiration date.

Original Issue Discount (OID) bonds Securities issued at a discount to par with low or no coupons, also called deep discount bonds.

Out-of-the-Money An option without intrinsic value.

Out Option An option which has an expiry price as well as an expiry date.

Outperformance Option An option where the payout is determined by the amount by which the price of one underlying outperforms the price of a second underlying.

Outstrike The price at which the terms of a non-standard option change, or it expires.

Over-the-Counter (OTC) Lightly regulated trading separate from established exchanges. Contrasts so traded can be tailored to a counterparty's needs.

Overfunding Tactic sometimes used by the Bank of England to influence the money supply by selling more gilts than is at once necessary to fund the government's deficit.

Overnight limit Net position that a dealer is permitted to carry over into the next dealing day.

Overnight money Money placed in the money market for repayment the next day.

Overnight repo Repo which matures on the business day after its value date.

Par yield curve Yield curve established by estimating the coupon rates for bonds to be priced at par for each maturity.

Parallel shift A change in the level of interest rates across all maturities so that the shape of the yield curve does not change.

Partial Lookback Option A lookback option where the lookback period is shorter than the life of the option.

Participating Option One of a number of possible structures where the holder obtains only a percentage of any favorable price movement.

Partly paid A bond which requires the holder to pay only part of the face value at the time of issue with provisions for the balance to be paid in one or more parts on specified later dates.

Path-dependent Option An option where the value depends not just on the value on expiry but also on the price pattern or path which led to it. Asian (average rate), barrier and look-back options are path-dependent.

Pay Later Option See **Deferred Premium Option**.

Payoff The value of an option at expiry.

Pension livrée French securities sale and repurchase agreement.

Perpetual Bond which has no final maturity date but which may have call provisions.

Physical delivery Settlement of a futures contract by delivery of the underlying.

Pin Risk The risk of an at-the-money option just before expiry when it is difficult to know whether it will be exercised or not.

Pit Trading area on the floor of an exchange where a particular security is traded.

Pit broker Broker who executes orders for others on the trading floor of a futures exchange.

Plus (+) US government securities prices are usually quoted in 32nds. To quote in 64ths pluses are used. A bid of 3+ is "the handle" or big figure plus 3/32+ 1/64, which equals the handle plus 7/64.

Power Option An option where the payoff is determined by raising the value of the underlying to some power. For example the value of a power option at expiry might be calculated as $P^2 - E$ where P^2 was the square of the price of the underlying at expiry and E was the exercise price of the option.

Premium The price of an option. Premium can also mean the amount by which the price of an option exceeds its intrinsic value.

Present value (PV) The value of a payment or a series of payments discounted at a given interest rate.

Prêt de titres French securities lending mechanism.

Price value of a basis point (PVBP) A way of expressing the price sensitivity of a fixed-income security to a change in interest rates.

Primary dealer Recognized dealers in government securities usually with auction and market making responsibilities in exchange for privileged access to the monetary authorities.

Primary market The market in which new issues of securities are initially distributed.

Purchase fund Obligation set out in bond documentation on the issuer to attempt to repurchase a certain amount of the issue each year at any price up to par.

Put Option An option which gives the holder a right but an obligation to sell a financial instrument, commodity or currency at a specified price on or before a specified date.

Put Spread A combined long position and short position in puts on the same underlying.

Rainbow Option An option where the value at expiry is determined by reference to the highest price of two or more specified categories of underlying.

Range Forward Contract A contingent forward foreign exchange contract.

Ratchet Option A ratchet option has a resettable strike price. On specified dates the strike is reset to the then current price of the underlying and any intrinsic value is locked in at each reset.

Ratio Spread An option spread position where the numbers of contracts bought and sold are not the same.

Real interest rate Gross interest rate less the rate of inflation.

Recognized clearing house (RCH) Clearing house authorized to act as such by the Securities and Investments Board in the UK.

Reconstitution The process of recombing previously stripped coupons and principal into coupon securities.

Redemption The purchase and cancellation of outstanding securities through a cash payment to the holder. Securities called for redemption but not surrendered cease to earn interest after the redemption date.

Redemption price The price at which a security may be redeemed prior to its maturity date. This may vary with time or according to whether redemption is by exercise of a put or a call.

Registered security A security, the ownership of which is recorded in a register in the name of the holder.

Regular-way settlement In the US money and bond markets, delivery of securities purchased is made against payment in Federal Reserve System (Fed) funds on the day following the transaction.

Regulated Futures Contract (RFC) Futures contracts traded on or subject to the rules of an exchange designated by the Commodity Futures Trading Commission and which use the mark to market method of determining margin account requirements.

Reinvestment rate In the calculation of yield to maturity the rate assumed to be that at which interest received on a debt security can be reinvested over the life of that security.

Reinvestment risk The risk that an investor will find actual reinvestment rates to be lower than assumed.

Repurchase agreement (repo) Two simultaneous transactions: the purchase of securities (the collateral) against a commitment by the counterparty to repurchase the securities at the same price at an agreed future date and rate. A form of short-term secured borrowing or lending.

Retail Price Index (RPI) A measure of retail price changes in the UK which uses a basket of goods and services.

Reverse auction Method by which, for example, the Bank of England used to buy back gilt-edged securities.

Rho The price change of an option caused by a change in the risk-free interest rate.

Rolling down the curve The change in relative yield as a bond approaches maturity. Assuming a normal yield curve the yield of a bond will tend to fall as it approaches maturity.

Run The series of bid and asked quotes for different maturities exchanged by dealers.

Safekeeping repo Repo where the collateral is not physically delivered but is instead held by a depository in the name of the lender of cash.

Saitori Special members of the Tokyo Stock Exchange who act as intermediaries between the regulated members and match securities transactions but are not allowed to trade on their own account.

Sandwich Spread A Butterfly Spread.

Seagull A position where the holder buys an at- or near-the-money call and sells an out-of-the money put and an out-of-the money call.

Securities and Exchange Commission (SEC) Agency created by the US Securities Exchange Act of 1934 to administer securities legislation.

Securities and Futures Authority (SFA) UK self-regulatory organization formed from the merger in April 1991 of the Association of Futures Brokers and Dealers and the Securities Association.

Securities and Investments Board (SIB) UK regulatory body established by the Financial Services act 1986, responsible for overall supervision of the conduct of financial markets and services.

Separately Traded Registered Interest and Principal Security (STRIPS) Generic name for US Treasury securities from which the coupons have been detatched and for the detatched coupons themselves.

Short Selling a financial instrument, commodity or currency.

Shout Option A variation of the ratchet option. The reset occurs not on specified dates but at the request of the option holder.

Sigma The standard deviation or volatility of the underlying.

Sinking fund Money periodically set aside by a borrower to redeem all or part of a debt issue as provided for in the issue documentation.

Spécialistes en Valeurs du Trésor (SVT) Primary dealers and market-makers in the French government bond market.

Spécialisti in titoli di Stato Government securities specialists in Italy who have certain privileges relating to issues.

Spot Month The contract month closest to the current month.

Spot rate curve The zero-coupon yield curve in which every point represents the yield to maturity of a zero-coupon bond.

Spraddle A straddle but with different strike prices.

Spread Trade Simultaneous trades in two or more related contracts where risks are wholly or partly offset made with the intention of exploiting anticipated price changes.

Stack hedge A hedge executed in derivatives where the matching maturity is not available and so contracts in nearby months are used, in larger amounts than would be used for the exact maturity.

Standard deviation The square root of the mean of the squared deviations of members of a population from their mean.

Standard Portfolio Analysis of Risk (SPAN) A system of margining for options contacts. SPAN uses a portfolio approach to calculate the overall risk associated with a set of positions by evaluating the profit/loss in a number of scenarios. Development by the CME the methodology is also used by LIFFE.

Stock In the UK stock refers to fixed income Treasury debt securities among other things.

Straddle The simultaneous purchase or sale of both a call and a put option with the same strike price.

Strangle A straddle with unequal strike prices but the same expiration date.

Strap An option position, all either short or long, of two calls and one put.

Strike Premium The second premium paid under a compound option when the first option is exercised.

Strike Price See **Exercise Price**.

Stripped bond A coupon security which is traded separately from its coupons.

Surf and Turf A strangle.

Synthetic Call A position combining a long put and a long position in the underlying.

Synthetic Put A position combining a long call and a short positon in the underlying.

Synthetic Short A position combining a long put and a short call.

System repo A US Federal Reserve system (Fed) repurchasing agreement intended to influence short-term interest rates.

Tail The difference in government bond auctions between the yield at the average price and the yield at the stop-out price.

Tap A method of issuing securities on an as-required basis, often in irregular amounts.

Taplet In the context of the UK gilt-edged market, a small (£100m–£200m) further issue of an existing bond. Also called mini tap.

Tau The price change of an option caused by a change in the standard deviation or volatility of the underlying.

Term repurchase agreement (term repo) Repo for a period longer than overnight, up to one year or more.

Theta The price change of an option caused by a change in the time remaining – time decay.

Third-party repurchase agreement (third-party repo) Repo where collateral is held by an independent agent who transfers it only against payment of cash. Also called tri-party repo.

Tick size The minimum price movement of a futures or option contract.

Time decay The decline in value of an option as it approaches expiry.

Time value That part of the value of an option which reflects the time remaining until expiry.

Treasury bill (T-Bill) Non-interest-bearing discount security issued by governments. Typically issued for three, six, or twelve months.

Treasury bond Long-term government security. In the USA the term refers to a coupon security issued by the Treasury with a maturity of ten to thirty years.

Treasury note US Government fixed rate security issued with a maturity of up to ten years.

Treasury Receipt (TR) A zero-coupon certificate issued in respect of principal payments on specific US Treasury securities. It is a direct obligation of the USA.

Undated A security with no final maturity. It may be converted into a dated security by the holder subject to some penalty (eg a lower margin in floating rate notes, FRNs). See **Irredeemable**; cf. **Perpetual**.

Underlying The instrument upon which a derivative contract is base. It can be a security or any other financial instrument or asset.

Up-and-out Option   An option which pays off or expires if a preset price is reached.

Value at Risk (VAR)   There are two main modelling techniques which are referred to as VAR calculations.

(i) *Variance/covariance analysis*
This uses historic data on price volatilities and correlations within and between markets to estimate likely potential losses. Price changes are assumed to be normally distributed which allows a confidence level to be calculated.

   This confidence level is calculated by reference to the standard deviation of historic price changes (volatility) multiplied by a scaling factor. If returns are normally distributed, there is a 1 percent chance that the return will be greater than 2.326 deviations from the mean. Thus if we wanted to have a 99 percent confidence interval we would multiply the historic volatility observed by 2.326.

   The chief problem with this approach is that the assumption about distribution doess not accord with observations in many markets where "fat-tailed" distributions and skewed distributions are frequently seen. The approach implicitly assumes that a portfolio's value changes linearly with changes in the underlying, in other words it ignores the effect of gamma.

(ii) *Historical simulation*
Historical data are applied to a portfolio to calculate the changes in value of the portfolio which would have occurred if it had been in existence during that period. This allows the calculation of a 99 percent confidence interval without assuming a normal distribution by calculating the loss which would not have been exceeded on 99 percent of occasions. In this case the confidence interval is observed while before it was calculated statistically.

Value date   The date up to which accrued interest is calculated. The value date and the settlement date are usually the same.

Variation Margin   The amount of money paid after the payment of initial margin required to secure an option or futures position after it has been revalued by the exchange or clearing house. Often paid daily.

Vega   See **Tau**.

Vertical Spread   Option spread position where the same number of options bought and sold have the same expiry date but different strike prices. Using two calls or two puts, in a bear spread the option bought has a higher strike than the option sold. In a bull spread the option bought has a lower strike than the option sold.

Volatility   A statistical measure of price variance over time.

Warrant An option, sometimes of quite long maturity.

When Issued (WI) Trading in securities which have been announced but not yet issued. Such securities are said to trade on an "if, as and when-issued" basis. Also called the grey market.

Withholding tax Tax required to be deducted at source or withhold on share dividends, coupon payments or bank deposits.

Writer Party which sells an option and grants a right but not an obligation to the purchaser.

Yield basis Quotation of a security not in price terms but in yield terms. A bid yield and an offer yield may be quoted.

Yield to average life The yield of a security when the average life is substituted for the final maturity date.

Yield to call The yield of a security when the first call date and call price are substituted for the final maturity date and par redemption price.

Yield to maturity (YTM) The yield of a security calculated as an IRR. Assumes that any interest payments received over the life of the security are reinvested at the IRR.

Yield to put (YTP) The yield of a security when the first put date and put price are substituted for the final maturity date and par redemption price.

Zero-coupon bond Security issued at a discount to its nominal value and paying no interest. The return to the investor is the amount by which the redemption value exceeds the purchase price. The yield to maturity calculation for a zero-coupon bond does not involve any reinvestment rate assumptions. The duration of a zero-coupon bond is the same as its maturity.

Zero-coupon yield curve The yield curve formed by zero-coupon bonds of different maturities. It is more precise than a yield curve formed by coupon bonds where the maturity dates are plotted. A zero-coupon yield curve plots yields for duration.

Zero Strike Price Option A method of circumventing restrictions on the transfer of securities which gives the holder full participation in the price movement of the underlying.

INDEX

Pages containing a figure are shown in italics

Index

Index